Richard de Zoysa is Senior Lecturer in Politics at South Bank University, London. He has held academic appointments in Sweden and the USA, and has lectured at the Sorbonne in Paris. His work has been published in India, Sweden, the USA and Britain. He is also active in promoting international student-exchange programmes with American and Swedish universities.

THE AMERICAN DREAM IN THE INFORMATION AGE

Also by Otto Newman

GAMBLING: Hazard and Reward

THE CHALLENGE OF CORPORATISM

The American Dream in the Information Age

Otto Newman
Adjunct Professor of Sociology
San Diego State University
California

and

Richard de Zoysa
Senior Lecturer in Politics
South Bank University
London

First published in Great Britain 1999 by
MACMILLAN PRESS LTD
Houndmills, Basingstoke, Hampshire RG21 6XS and London
Companies and representatives throughout the world

A catalogue record for this book is available from the British Library.

ISBN 0-333-73379-7

 First published in the United States of America 1999 by
ST. MARTIN'S PRESS, INC.,
Scholarly and Reference Division,
175 Fifth Avenue, New York, N.Y. 10010

ISBN 0-312-22243-2

Library of Congress Cataloging-in-Publication Data
Newman, Otto.
The American dream in the information age / Otto Newman, Richard de Zoysa.
p. cm.
Includes bibliographical references and index.
ISBN 0-312-22243-2 (cloth)
1. United States—Social conditions—1980– 2. Information society—United States. 3. Social values—United States. I. De Zoysa, Richard, 1944– . II. Title.
HN59.2.N49   1999
306'.0973—dc21   98-53536
                                                              CIP

© Otto Newman and Richard de Zoysa 1999

All rights reserved. No reproduction, copy or transmission of this publication may be made without written permission.

No paragraph of this publication may be reproduced, copied or transmitted save with written permission or in accordance with the provisions of the Copyright, Designs and Patents Act 1988, or under the terms of any licence permitting limited copying issued by the Copyright Licensing Agency, 90 Tottenham Court Road, London W1P 9HE.

Any person who does any unauthorised act in relation to this publication may be liable to criminal prosecution and civil claims for damages.

The authors have asserted their rights to be identified as the authors of this work in accordance with the Copyright, Designs and Patents Act 1988.

This book is printed on paper suitable for recycling and made from fully managed and sustained forest sources.

10 9 8 7 6 5 4 3 2 1
08 07 06 05 04 03 02 01 00 99

Printed and bound in Great Britain by
Antony Rowe Ltd, Chippenham, Wiltshire

Contents

Acknowledgements vi
Introduction vii

Part I: Changing Values 1
1 America First 3
2 The Melting Pot 31
3 Good Governance 60
4 The Underclass and Joblessness 87

Part II: New Times 111
5 Globalization 113
6 Civic Society 141
7 Learning Curves 167
8 New Visions 190

Conclusion 215
Select Bibliography 218
Index 227

Acknowledgements

In the course of a long and happy academic career one is bound to owe thanks and appreciation to a great many colleagues, students and other friends. We both wish to extend grateful acknowledgement to South Bank University, London, the London School of Economics, and San Diego State University, California.

Richard de Zoysa would like to record his appreciation for help given to him, especially by Robert Keating, a graduate student of UEA, George Pappas of New York for hours of challenging conversation and David Hayes of Exeter College. Richard de Zoysa's friend and neighbor Miriam Smith provided a calming influence and technical advice on one memorable afternoon when his computer seemed to develop a mind of its own. Further thanks go to Jane Decker of the University of Washington, Seattle, for commenting on some of the earlier chapters. Above all Richard de Zoysa would like to express his gratitude to a supportive family – to both Tom and Eleanor and to his wife Alison de Zoysa. The authors would like to express their appreciation for the highly professional support and advice of Sunder Katwala and Jo North at Macmillan.

Otto Newman would like to dedicate the book to the immense and continuing support of his wife June, and gratefully acknowledges the ever supportive contribution of Vikky and David Pickett.

Introduction

> Most important of all, information has become global and has become king of the economy. In earlier history, wealth was measured in land, in gold, in oil, in machines. Today, the principal measure of our wealth is information: it is quality, it is quantity, and the speed with which we acquire it and adapt it....'
> President Clinton, speech at the American University,
> 26 February 1993
> (Reported in the *New York Times*, 27 February 1993, p. 4)

Having emerged from the 1980s recession, the United States has in this century's final decade once again enjoyed economic growth coupled with low inflation. It has, at the same time, conquered the European bane of mass unemployment and has generated new job opportunities as never before. US information technology companies – the engines of growth of the twenty-first century – dominate the global economy while erstwhile rivals are either sunk in crisis (Pacific Rim) or just emerging from their own prolonged recession (the European Union). In political, cultural, economic and military matters, where the US leads others follow. There is indeed much for Americans to celebrate as the twentieth century draws to an end. Yet a note of caution is appropriate at the same time. Millions of workers are located in the fast-growing contingent labor force without benefit of full-time salaries, security, or the prospect of a career, while the global market, if anything, adds to their worries. Criticism of the role of government and of the standards by which it operates have generated derision, apathy and disbelief that anything will ever change for the better, and this despite a president whose approval ratings remain exceedingly high despite the damaging evidence of the Starr Report. Domestic inequalities of wealth and income rise remorselessly, with much of their excess legitimated and celebrated via the normative standards of the media culture that now pervades. Meanwhile, the struggle for minority rights and opportunities appears stalled with many locked out of participation in the wider society, so that for many the 'American dream' remains an elusive chimera.

Abroad, the world wonders at the might and technological sophistication of the US military now acting as the undisputed world sheriff, a role that politicians find both flattering and oddly limiting in view of the UN's necessary seal of approval. This role is ambiguous for the sole remaining superpower, encountering both domestic political criticism for its perceived lack of decisiveness, and hostility when it fails to consult adequately with its allies. Not infrequently suspicion is rife that US diplomacy is more concerned with the self-promotion of business interests and satisfying domestic constituencies than in the defense of more profound human values. Yet again overseas, American culture is similarly admired and despised in equal measure, representing as it does a source of democratic enlightenment and hope, but also at the same time, the lowest values of commercialism and self-seeking excess. Generalization, it must be admitted, never comes easy with such a profoundly complex and at times contradictory culture. The values which served it so well in its formation and growth, though still valid in many ways, are in some aspects in need of rethinking, especially with the emergence of a world more integrated than ever before. This text will offer suggestions as to how this might be achieved.

We have advisedly stayed clear of both futurology, with its tendency to unwarranted speculative excursions, as well as the Orwellian pessimism that often accompanies future concerns. We are no better qualified than anyone else to foresee the future – always a hazardous enterprise when events have a habit of 'taking the wrong turn'. Instead we will argue for an alternative way to reconfigure American values in the decades ahead. The text extrapolates a number of current options that the USA alone and uniquely, as the world's leading power, could initiate especially given that it is unlikely to face any major rivals for some time ahead. Undertaking such a necessary adjustment to values and structures would help resolve some of the constraints that stand in the way of the full realization of the 'American dream'.

The text is organized in the following way: Part I, 'Changing Values', sets out in the first chapter the historical context to American development, outlining the economic and political forces that propelled her to dominance, beginning with the values of the early settlers and ending the narrative with the much-criticized and now redundant thesis of national decline. Chapter 2 explores the basis of 'American exceptionalism', the distinctiveness of the values that made up American society and especially the lack of a major socialist tradition. The chapter examines the 'open frontier', demographics, immigration, multiculturalism and affirmative action, offering both detailed analysis and consideration of the limitations of current policies. Chapter 3 looks at some of the domestic political problems besetting the US at both federal and local level, and also externally with the rise of new powerful global regulatory bodies which are having a pronounced impact on the sovereignty of the nation-state. Chapter 4 gives a detailed exposition and critique of the twin social problems of the underclass and joblessness (the latter transmuted into contingent labor practice in the USA), and points to a prospective way out of the dilemma.

In Part II, 'New Times', our focus moves to the possibilities inherent within the current situation. Chapter 5 analyzes the economic, cultural and military components of US society and examines how this affects and is being affected by the new emergent global age. A critique of the limits of US policy is offered with some suggestions as to a future prognosis. Chapter 6 offers an examination and criticism of communitarianism, arising due to concerns over community fragmentation as a result of resurgent market forces. Its theoretical replacement(s) offer a more complex definition of civic society, based on a variety of approaches stretching across the political spectrum, in many cases incorporating a demand for structural change. Chapter 7 points to the new social structure now emerging within the US which incorporates once again a revitalized conception of social class, and also addresses the opportunities and limits afforded by the informatics revolution. The final chapter gives a detailed exposition of how the United States could modify its values towards greater social inclusiveness. We also set out a new model of social existence appropriate to the decades ahead, together with a consideration of potential constraints.

In exploring the many ramifications of contemporary American society, the text has been designed to interest both the specialist and also the informed general reader. What happens to the US vitally affects the whole world. We hope that, however challenging our conclusions, they will be of appreciable lasting value to our readership.

Part I Changing Values

1 America First

1. INTRODUCTION

In this introductory chapter our discussion will examine the extraordinary rise of the former British colony to its becoming, at the close of the twentieth century, the reigning and undisputed global superpower, although one facing internal uncertainty as it learns to respond to the new information age which it pioneered. Americans have traditionally displayed little interest in their own history although they are proud of their achievements, but without a firm grasp of quite why this should be so. By contrast, the British are accused of not letting go of their past. One variant of American historical consciousness has been a belief in American 'exceptionalism' – that America, through its status as a nation of immigrants drawn from a diversity of cultures, formed a 'new world' different from all others. The resultant 'American creed' was indeed unique in a nation that set out to make itself anew. On a more cautionary note, the national self-confidence which accrued so rapidly with success often slipped into hubris and even jingoism. Recent controversy over the 500-year centenary of Columbus's arrival and the 50th anniversary of the dropping of the bomb on Hiroshima illustrate the dangers of opening up the historical record, and of showing a more negative side to those events when it goes against conventional wisdom. For many years the Anglo-Saxon, Protestant and Republican basis of American identity rested on the social exclusion of many different groups: Roman Catholics, Jews, the Chinese, native and hyphenated-Americans and above all the black community. In time those excluded became full citizens – some with relative ease, others through mass political mobilization leaving, in some cases, a residue of bitterness which has lasted until the present.

Yet there is much in American history that suggests the people's response to earlier challenges, and arguably greater ones than today, gives them reasonable grounds for future optimism and renewed opportunity. All historical periods are times of change but in our own era technological advancement has been accompanied by a marked shift in society's mores. Older industries and ways of doing things and habits of mind are fast becoming redundant as they give way to the new knowledge-based economy. This will have profound implications for all societal arrangements, not just in the USA, but globally as the world economy is now so interdependent. The pace of change and the political focus of concern often demand quick resolution as public anxiety, fanned by an ever-present media, confronts opinion leaders and politicians. In the late 1980s worries over the twin deficits – governmental budgetary deficit (and growing national debt), and a negative trade imbalance – plus concern over competitiveness in the face of a globalizing market led some to speak of American decline. In 1998, with a longstanding recovery in place, public finances generating a surplus quicker than previously thought possible, and unemployment at a 28-year low, any pessimism seems out of place, but there are some real and enduring problems which later chapters will examine. For the moment our concern is with those factors that propelled the US from its early days to becoming the pre-eminent economic and military power it is today. Certain themes emerge: the confidence associated with being the first new nation; adapting to changing values as the nation shifts from a rural to an urban-based economy; the dislike of government yet dependency on it; the preference for business and success; the unresolved question of race; the rise from isolationism to global power and the problem of sustaining hegemony. Trying not to anticipate too far ahead, what is immediately striking is how much of the past, its conflicts and triumphs, is reflected in contemporary concerns. A knowledge of the magnitude of the taming of this vast continent coupled with some understanding of the political, social and economic framework will provide a context for much that follows later. It will demonstrate the boundless self-belief Americans expressed in their desire to quickly rule themselves and become economically self-sufficient, and why for so many the American dream was not an empty promise.

2. EARLY DAYS: SETTLER COMMUNITIES

The global power and preeminence of the United States today is in marked contrast to its early origins, subservient as it was to the British crown. But, even early in their history, Americans developed a sense of their independence and a belief in progress (both moral and material) which was a characteristic feature of their mental outlook. From the first English colonization in 1607 to the beginnings of the revolutionary wars of independence in the 1760s, the economic and political development of what was to become the thirteen colonies was impressive, with a ready-made market for their exports, mostly of raw materials, in an industrializing Britain.

The first English colony at Jamestown was quickly followed by others although it was a struggle against, at times, hostile native tribes and the elements. The scattered Indians were relatively quickly neutralized either through conquest, death or through contracting European diseases, or internal migration to that elusive and constantly shifting 'permanent Indian frontier' (D. Brown, 1991). The new settlers' primary motive was both opportunity and freedom of religious belief. These adventurous souls – an apt and operative word – had a spiritual ardor which led them to risk the hardship and dangers of crossing a vast and dangerous ocean in order to create a godly society away from the religious turbulence and civil war of mid-seventeenth-century England. Many who left carried with them a sense of grievance against an oppressive Anglican order. Religious dissent and the desire to realize virtue informed the Quakers in Pennsylvania, the Catholics in Maryland, but perhaps most significantly of all, the Puritans in Massachusetts and New England. They embarked on a 'journey of the elect', a chosen people seeking a new predetermined destiny (Schlesinger, 1986). The hardheaded Virginians, on the other hand, sought land and wealth; as Greenfeld remarks: 'if the removal of the Virginians began as a business trip, the Puritans went into voluntary exile' (Greenfeld, 1992: 405). John Winthrop, governor of Massachusetts throughout much of the 1630s and 1640s, was instrumental in establishing the transformation of a joint-stock trading company into what was in effect a republic under the British crown. Unbeknown at least initially to his imperial host in London, the new colony granted annual elections rather than hereditary rule as the basis of governance, and gave itself a wide discretion in law-making – much of which was of doubtful legality with respect to the crown. This was, furthermore, coupled with the right to establish independent churches and sects replacing the formal hierarchical structure of the Anglican establishment back in the motherland (Dunn and Yeandle, 1997). This was a benchmark and an early example of self-confidence and independence of spirit. Another significant factor which parallels the struggle for self-government was the creation in 1636 of Harvard College and the widespread support for elementary public education.

The Bible had to be read, as the covenant with God's chosen was not mediated through the unquestioned authority of the priest as in Catholicism, but directly between the individual and his maker. Protestantism was a word not an image culture. One by-product, as Robert Hughes notes, was that later American art was to be molded by the Puritan distaste of decoration, of vanity and hence portraiture (too much associated with European aristocratic taste) and of the nude figure. Landscape and naturalism were to dominate American artistic fashion for many years (Hughes, 1997).

An early pattern which was true of all the colonies was that 'labor was scarcer than land', permitting even indentured labor the possibility of rapid upward mobility (Degler, 1985: 2). Small individual land-holdings became the norm, and the feudal social structure of Europe became impossible to sustain, despite some notable early attempts such as the great estates of the Dutch patroons which were later broken up. Of course in New England there could never be a reproduction of European social conditions. The colonies had sought new solutions to land-holding and early communal property arrangements soon became individualized. Crucially, as Degler notes, 'the absence of a feudal past in America has meant that there are no classes which have a vested interest in the social forms of an earlier age' (Degler, 1985: 5). This thesis of 'American exceptionalism', to be examined in more detail in the following chapter, has had profound consequences for subsequent development. To list a few well-known characteristics: the absence of primogeniture and concentrated land-holding; the more vaunted status of women; the absence of a ruling military caste; the easy acceptance of a capitalistic business ethic; and the intrinsic relationship noted long ago by Weber of the Puritan ethic and its compatibility with money-making, perhaps reaching its apogee in the US.

In the Southern colonies a different pattern became established. In Virginia large plantations along the Tidewater devoted to tobacco cultivation, with a county form of local government under the jurisdiction of a justice of the peace, were in marked contrast to the small nucleated towns and villages of New England which were organized around the meeting house. One available supply of labor were black slaves. First imported into Jamestown in 1619 they formed 5 percent of the population in Virginia in 1671, rising to 40 percent by 1756, and so helped establish the role of the squirearchy and great planter. The slaves' demeaning status was one of chattel property, and its institutionalization by the late 1600s and relative efficiency meant that across the Southern colonies the plantation became firmly established. The cash crops dependent on this form of labor were – in addition to tobacco – rice, indigo, sugar and, above all, cotton. With the Industrial Revolution in Britain and the development of new technologies cotton became a most sought-after staple commodity. Slavery had been considered a dying institution, incompatible with the founding ideals of free labor and equality expressed in the Constitution. The banning of the slave trade in 1808 was offset by the huge export potential of cotton coupled with rising demand from Northern factories, thereby ending the possibility that slave labor would simply disappear.

By the mid-eighteenth century the colonies had a growing population of nearly two million people of majority English descent, though with some diversification as Scots, Scots-Irish, and some Germans settled. A plethora of religious sects, with some reacting to the earlier austerity of the Puritans, led to a more emotional religious release in the Great Awakening of the 1740s, but in general as time went by the once-dogmatic forms of religious compliance became more secularized, and much energy became diverted into business activity. The heritage of Calvinistic Puritanism was of a positive orientation towards hard work, saving and a strong desire to succeed on one's own merit signifying a mark of divine favor. Achievement, literacy and self-restraint were positive values which fed into the egalitarian ethos of the revolution which swept aside many old-world values. Economically, most people were engaged in agricultural activities as there was little indigenous manufacturing. Along the seaboard significant cities developed (notably the Quaker city of Philadelphia, founded by William Penn in 1682), which traded with England and so helped in developing a merchant and commercial class. Indeed the general picture appears to be one of orderly growth and relative prosperity. Internally the need to integrate and supply the scattered property-holding population across the vast distances of the colonies led to both trade and road improvements. Though wealth was unequally distributed the open class structure and land availability led to a more egalitarian society than anything existing in Europe. What, then, led to the rupture with Britain and what were its consequences?

3. INDEPENDENCE, CONSTITUTIONALISM AND POLITICAL SETTLEMENT: UNDERLYING PRINCIPLES

What sort of society emerged after the war of independence and who were the beneficiaries of the conflict? What did they believe in and what sort of political and economic arrangements did they arrive at? Such questions need to be briefly addressed as the political framework established after the Philadelphia Convention provided both the stability and legitimacy without which economic activity cannot flourish.

The revolutionary war and the final Declaration of Independence were arrived at after many resolutions had been proposed by local communities and colonies, at least ninety according to Maier, between April and July of 1776 (Maier, 1997). At the basis of the colonists' calls for independence, despite protestations almost to the very end that they did not seek a break and wished to remain loyal to the crown, lay the accusation of the king's betrayal of the implied contract between himself and his American subjects, and their right to self-preservation. From 1765, when they had first opposed the Stamp Act, the crisis escalated. Central to the dispute was the right of the British parliament to impose taxes (light as they were) without American representation, although the colonists did concede for the moment the right of parliament to regulate their trade. By 1773–74 it had become a choice of rejecting parliament's authority and accepting the crown only. The second Continental Congress, later the first government of the United States, met in May 1775. Just over a year later and with the war in progress, the Declaration emerged with Jefferson responsible for its first draft, though it was revised by Congress. Maier notes that the document was not seen at the time as being particularly original since it drew its sources from other contemporary documents. The famous endorsement 'that all men are created equal' and the right to happiness (property had been substituted), were expressive merely of conventional opinion.

The American constitution, written in 1787 in Philadelphia, provided a solution to the problems engendered by the success of their own revolution. Religion was to be at the core of the new nation, 'one nation under God', with a borrowing of Roman stoicism – a belief in honesty and fidelity, to guide the new rulers. The thirteen colonies, each of which was almost sovereign with only loose ties binding them together, lacked proper central direction and control under the earlier Articles of Confederation (formulated in 1776 and designed to last thirteen years). Once peace with Britain had been secured the national unity forged in that struggle was in danger of being quickly dissipated, and there was a risk that each former colony would go its own way. Of much concern to all were the inflationary consequences of the war, debt payments, and the fear sparked by internal dissension. Shays' rebellion of angry Massachusetts farmers in 1786 protesting the Boston legislature's decision to raise the property qualification for voting, and approval of the seizure of debtor lands, had led to rioting and was only put down with difficulty. The ruling strata looked on these developments with understandable misgivings, powerfully suggesting to them the need for a coherent central authority. The convention delegates who drafted the new constitution in Philadelphia 'did not believe in men but they did believe in the power of a good political constitution to control him', and the compromise reached was a 'masterpiece of practical statecraft' (Hofstadter, 1961: 3 and 15), which 'conserved the past rather than repudiated it' (Degler, 1985: 79). In effect the new constitution checked the worst excesses of democracy yet carefully aggregated and balanced the governing institutions of the new republic by neutralizing the danger of recreating a new potential tyranny, a new George III. Precedence was given to the legislature and also to the states and localities at the expense of executive federal power.

Of the men who drafted the documents most, according to the eminent historian Charles Beard, were lawyers who propagated the work of 'consolidated economic groups' representing personal property interests including money, public securities, manufacturers, trade and shipping. The defense of property remained paramount and was not to be subject to majority popular control. Indeed their support extended into the state legislatures which were vital to the ratification of the constitutional proposals (it would need nine out of the thirteen to ratify), although there was a divergence of interest at state level between major property-holders who favored commercial wealth and the small farmers and debtors who did not (Beard, 1935). Later historians have argued that the central role given to the defense of property was reasonable given its widespread distribution. Those without property were anxious to acquire it and the property-based franchise qualification was so low that even 'mechanics' in the cities could vote. However, psychology is as important at times as economic self-interest, and as Brown argues: 'men are motivated by what they believe as well as by what they have' and more rhetorically asks: 'were the common people trying to eliminate the Washingtons, Adamses, Hamiltons and Pinckneys or were they trying to join them?' (R. E. Brown, 1956: 200). Furthermore, many of the rich opposed ratification and Hamilton, a close ally of Washington, did not achieve the strong chief executive he had desired. To gain support a series of newspaper articles – later known as the Federalist Papers – were published to debate the implications of the Convention. Fairfield notes their duality – Madison interested in balancing power, Hamilton in its concentration – and these articles were a practical response to real problems – both present and future – and how the constitution might resolve them. For Fairfield they were 'urbane, rational, optimistic and progressive' and represented 'a synthesis of empiricism and rationalism' (Fairfield, 1961: xxvii, xxi).

Another potential danger according to Wood was that: 'the most pronounced social effect of the revolution was not harmony or stability but the sudden appearance of new men everywhere in politics and business' (Wood, 1972: 476). The 'new men' were nouveaux riches, petit bourgeois, crypto-capitalist, social climbers, and some even without property or education. The traditional elite were mortified by their lack of virtue and supposed they had somehow duped the people in the elections to the state legislatures, now reformed and based on a more extensive franchise. So one priority was to save the republic and the people from themselves, so that 'only the respectable and worthy hold power', and to protect in that most felicitous of phrases 'the worthy against the licentious' (Wood, 1972: 510, 475). The filter to too much popular control was to be the separation of powers and balanced government (which itself was limited because individuals were granted rights against it in what were to become the first ten amendments to the constitution – the Bill of Rights in 1791). Wood comments wryly that: 'if the revolution had been a transfer of power from the few to the many, then the federal constitution clearly represented an abnegation of the revolution ... a transfer of power from the many to the few' (Wood, 1972: 516). The president was to be elected through an electoral college, and so Jefferson's fear of an 'elective despotism', of an unbridled majority overruling minority interest was curtailed. It is not for nothing that Hofstadter calls Jefferson 'the aristocrat as democrat'. Southern, rural opposition to these proposals, seen as betraying the principles of 1776, would later crystallize into the anti-federal party.

Though the people were sovereign their power was diffused – some to the House of Representatives at the federal level (and by delegation to the Senate), some to the states and local communities. The situation became pluralistic, with broad horizontal class groupings based on interest difficult to sustain, as each individual's vote was atomized. Federalism was born along with the split ticket. It was, however, a form of government which was subject to the sweeping powers given and later assumed by the Supreme Court, including the right of judicial review. The court had the legal right to annul state or federal law, and to arbitrate conflicts between the presidency and Congress, and for both of them in dispute with the states as well. What constitutes the limits of judicial review has remained controversial down to our own times, with periods of judicial activism followed by a narrower and more restrained interpretation of the court's role. The court is but one element, and often a controversial one in the tripartite separation of powers, and as such never became the final arbiter in determining what the constitution was trying to realize all those years ago (Griffin, 1997).

In economic and social terms the constitution was a compromise uniting Southern slave-holders with Northern moneyed interests into a growing commercial market. What initially emerged was a 'middling society' enjoying widespread support because of the deepening of those rights guaranteed by law inherited from the former colonial power (Boorstin, 1953). But the exclusion of the black community, and the moral and economic threat this posed to free labor and the values of the republic would poison debate and destroy consensus in Congress. Resolution only came with Northern success in the civil war in 1865.

4. FORGING NATIONAL IDENTITY AND DISTINCTIVE AMERICAN VALUES

By 1800, the population was nearly four million dispersed over a vast territory on a north–south axis, but with some gradual extension westwards. Settlement was blocked by France until Jefferson's opportunistic 'Louisiana purchase' doubled the size of the country in 1803, thereby affording unparalleled opportunities for further land acquisition and economic exploitation. The earlier seizure of Tory lands (many had moved to Canada or returned to the home country), and division of their large estates had resulted in sales to small farmers. Former crown land, now under the control of state legislatures, was also made available for settlement. With the removal of this socially conservative group the last remaining feudal elements associated with English rule, such as entail, were abolished, and the Anglican Church disestablished. The small but growing class of 'mechanics', mostly self-employed and comprising an embryonic future industrial class, were promised a protective tariff against cheaper British industrial imports, finally realized in 1816.

Externally the US remained largely free of foreign entanglements after the war with the British ended in 1814 concentrating, as might be expected, on the consolidation of her territories in the years ahead. There was a brief conflict with Mexico in 1846 which lost two-fifths of her territory to the US, which acquired above all the prize of California. A year earlier Texas (wrested from Mexico by Sam Houston in 1836) was formally annexed. One of the last major acquisitions, Alaska, was labeled 'Seward's folly', as the Secretary of State had paid the Russians over $7 million for a territory perceived at the time as being of doubtful economic utility.

Aside from economic motivation, a new sense of national identity partially transcended the more self-interested support for the new republic. Zinn argues that early signs were detectable in the camaraderie of the militia, in the collective experience of the Continental Army recruited from the 'lower orders' which held the line at Valley Forge until victory was finally secured, and helped create that feeling of being a 'people' (Zinn, 1980). An extensive property-based franchise meant that well over half of all white males could vote if they wished (women, blacks and native Indians were excluded), and given their earlier opposition to what they saw as the arbitrary taxing powers of the British some radicalization of consciousness emerged. Bonwick comments that: 'the people had become the only source of legitimacy and democracy was rapidly acquiring prescriptive authority' (Bonwick, 1986: 373). Political mobilization helped in creating a distinctive and self-confident emerging republic. Bailyn emphasizes both the highly politicized nature of the former culture of the colonies prior to the war and the intellectual ferment of ideas which molded an independent identity (Bailyn, 1967). For example, Paine's *Common Sense* of 1776 sold in the hundreds of thousands, with its refutation of the 'divine right of kings' including the specific claims of the English throne. Opposition defined that sense of being an American, and that peculiar understanding of virtue so prized by many although, as noted earlier, few were totally prepared until the outbreak of war itself to break decisively with the crown. The perceived superior cosmopolitan and aristocratic culture of Europe was now considered sadly lacking in moral worth. The leaders of the new republic were viewed as 'the servants of the people'. Merit counted more than birth or wealth and everyone championed the freedoms so eloquently expressed in the constitution. Equality extending beyond the simply legal included a recognition of individual dignity, accorded to all, in a new kind of social equivalence and respect, with free competition and a contempt for inherited privilege paramount, and notably remarked upon by De Tocqueville in his *Democracy in America* in 1830. America became, as Greenfeld writes, 'the ideal nation'. In co-opting English values based on a belief in reason, equality and freedom, their adoptive English identity was more perfectly realized and transformed within the community on the strength of active citizen participation. They were, Greenfeld argues, 'more English than the English', as only they could actualize and give real meaning to what these abstract principles meant, and which were to constitute the basis for a new, individualistic, civic nationalism resting on common-sense assumptions understandable to ordinary farmers (Greenfeld, 1992).

On the other hand, the position of the elite was now more exposed, as it lacked the former imperial prop and so was forced to admit others into political rule. However, one individual held in high regard by Americans, both then and today, was to play a pivotal role. As Lipset remarks: 'The early American Republic, like many new nations, was legitimized by charisma' (Lipset, 1964: 18). George Washington, America's first president, whose immense prestige as victor over the British enabled him to play a vital role in maintaining national unity, was an example for others to follow with his commitment to the new constitution. His implicit acceptance of factions within his own cabinet would anticipate future party organization and division, and so facilitate the voluntary transfer of power when his term of office ended. After 1797, Jefferson and Madison led in effect rival national parties with differing visions of what direction the US should follow. The Republican-Democratic party of Jefferson sought states' rights and was more populist, while the party of Hamilton, the Federalist, argued for greater national and centralized governmental power. The defeat of the Federalists in the 1800 election and the peaceful transfer of power expressed an underlying acceptance of the 'rules of the game'. The Virginia ascendancy was to last, with some minor interruptions, for twenty-four years until

1829 and the inauguration of Andrew Jackson, when those ruder elements, 'the licentious', were to rule under a revitalized two-party system (Democrats versus Whigs). Furthermore, the property qualification was soon to be removed by the late 1830s, as manhood became the sole criterion for voting and one which extended in some states to electing members of the judiciary as well.

By mid-century the 'Great Experiment' was well under way, with the expanding western frontier, rich in land, acting as a psychological safety valve. Corporations (granted a legal status in 1837) and trade unions (freed from being a restraint on trade in 1842) were also developing, and these reforms rested on the consent of the 'common man' now extolled by all politicians anxious for his vote. However, Pessen's data illustrates that wide inequality existed: thus 1 percent of the people owned 50 percent of the wealth and 50 percent held no wealth for taxable purposes. Wages of laborers actually fell in the Jacksonian era as the upper class consolidated its position through residential exclusivity and social endogamy. He writes: 'the age may have been named after the common man but it did not belong to him' (Pessen, 1985: 100). Despite this, it is evident that political legitimacy reinforced by economic effectiveness was linked to a sense of national purpose. However, before a proper national identity could emerge, slavery had to be abolished.

The development of the American economy in the nineteenth century is almost a tale of two countries: a more rural Southern plantation system dependent on slave labor providing cotton for the industrial revolution, and a rapidly industrializing North beginning to invest heavily in new labor-saving techniques epitomized by factory organization and technological development (for example, Whitney's cotton gin of 1794). In the 1790 census there was a recorded total of just under 700 000 slaves. Mostly by natural increase this had risen to 3 953 760 by the 1860 census. Peter Kolchin notes that 10–12 million slaves were transported to the Americas, with the vast majority working on the Caribbean sugar fields or Brazilian plantations. Of that number some 600 000 to 700 000 went to the colonies mostly in the South (Kolchin, 1995). In fact there were virtually no slaves in the North after 1820, although this did not stop a marked increase in racism and segregation there.

Politically, but not economically, the South had dominated the union till 1860, providing more leaders than the North in Congress and the presidency. With the expunging of the Southern vision through defeat in the civil war, a new sense of nationhood was rekindled, one resting on a vigorous capitalistic outlook with the triumph of economic freedom (albeit with a protective external tariff) and free labor. By 1870, the export of industrial goods to Europe, by far America's largest market, was greater than that of agricultural commodities. Industrialism not only fed the desire for material gain, it dramatically changed the environment – both physically and socially. In 1890 the census announced the closing of the frontier, suggesting that open land was no longer available for settlement, so that in less than 300 years a continent had been physically possessed with easy rail communication linking east and west. Between 1865 and 1914, the huge industrial expansion meant that 'America emerged from that period the arsenal of two world wars and the prime industrial power of the planet' (Degler, 1985: 258). However, despite the hopes of the reconstructionists in the South after 1865, the position of the ex-slaves was not to be materially improved as they exchanged their former servitude for cash cropping. Property and literacy tests denied them the vote and Jim Crow legislation by the end of the century segregated them into differing communities and opportunities.

5. STATE-SPONSORED PRIVATE ENTERPRISE, THE DEVELOPMENT OF INDUSTRY AND 'MODERNITY'

The American economy's growth in the nineteenth century was assisted by capital investment from England in particular (backed by the US government), and also from borrowing many of its manufacturing techniques, so that by 1830 it was up with the best. Early on, Jefferson, although an admirer of the self-made virtues of the independent farmer, was also mindful of the manufacturing needs of the growing republic. Labor shortages meant that investment in technology and labor-saving methods was imperative. Both parties accepted the vital need to develop public works especially in transport, and much sponsorship of new canals and roads was led by public investments at state and local level with the assistance of the federal government. Attempts at wider national planning were always beset by states' rights advocates. A complicated pattern emerged of government regulation and inspection, of direct government investment in companies with joint private–public banks, turnpikes and canals, the so-called 'mixed enterprise'. The financing by New York through the sale of state bonds in the Erie canal (of

1825) proved a spectacular success. There was also direct public ownership, as in Pennsylvania which built the first mainline railway, which quickly supplanted the canal as the favored means of transport. Railways both reduced the cost of transporting goods and people, and were instrumental in binding the newly opened west – the corn and pork regions – into the Northern interest in the decade prior to the civil war. Southern investors also built railways, but cotton was a more attractive investment and by 1860 over two-thirds of the 30 000-mile network was in the North. As Lipset comments: 'The doctrine of "laissez faire" became dominant only after the growth of large corporations and private investment funds reduced the pressure for public funds' (Lipset, 1964: 52). The need for 'internal improvements' to boost economic growth and physically integrate the country meant that public officials often acted in the place of absent individual private enterprise. A heady combination of a supportive ideological framework of hard work, initiative and love of the 'good life' mixed well with available capital and a reasonable chance of success, as the economy expanded producing a national mood of confidence and material success.

There was a down side as well. Rapid growth fueled by rising immigration throughout the century often meant that urban life deteriorated. In crude terms the urban population grew from 7.25 percent of the population in 1820 to 40 percent of the population by 1890, this at a time when the population itself increased by one-third every decade between 1810 and 1860. Till 1860, a third of the urban population lived in only two cities – New York and Philadelphia (Glaab and Brown, 1967). Thus in Philadelphia public initiatives fell victim to what Bass Warner terms 'the cult of privatism' (1979), with a failure of planning, adequate zoning and building regulation, of urban parks and any public amelioration of widespread poverty until the Progressive remedies at the turn of the century. Population growth created its own peculiar urban problems, compounded not just by rural migration into the cities, but also immigration (from Ireland and Germany) of a mostly Catholic population – poor, unskilled, and socially conservative, and demanding their own parochial schools. The 'Know Nothing' Nativist party saw the Catholics as a threat to a sober Protestant nation, being both difficult to assimilate and a deterrent to proper reform. They feared too their voting power (it only took between three and five years to gain the right to vote in most states for new immigrants), as they were quickly co-opted by the Democrat machine.

A parallel development to the expansion of urban factory and office work was the organization of leisure and consumption in the latter part of the century. Hays notes that: 'in this domain of leisure and recreation that protecting the older, traditional ways of life was undermined most thoroughly by the attractiveness of the new' (Hays, 1995: 45). A distinctively urban 'mass culture' was emerging based around the ball park, theaters, amusement parks and a mass press. Opportunities for leisure had once been relatively limited, but rising incomes and a gradual shortening of the working day and more public holidays meant more spare time needed to be filled. Earlier attempts in the 1840s–1850s (a time of serious rioting and social disorder in many large cities) at controlling behavior were undertaken by the voluntary sector – churches, mutual aid societies, Bible societies and others in a 'nationwide network of voluntary moral control societies'. They sought, as Boyer notes, 'to revive the moral authority of a communal order that for many Americans was no more than a memory' (Boyer, 1978: 15, 33). The Protestant churches simply lacked the resources and could not cope with the pace of change. Their voice, invoking 'the power of shame', was seen as irrelevant by many workers (many of whom were Catholic), and so their quest proved fruitless. By mid-century a more professionalized, secular and targeted approach developed through such practical agencies as the YMCA. The moral panic of those times is eerily reminiscent of our own worries regarding an underclass divorced from the mainstream. Then it was liquor rendering people incapable of employment and responsibility. Now it is drugs. By the end of the century and into the new one many of these earlier worries had receded. The influence of Wesleyanism with its more liberal and personal ideas was symptomatic of the changes. The idea of personal conversion and action coupled with an evangelical drive in the cities based on the 'social gospel' linked social reform to Christian practice.

Following the civil war the attitude of the government to the inventor, entrepreneur and business in general was one of sympathy and material help. Huge government assistance poured towards railroad construction with land grants, cash loans, tax exemptions and stock purchase coupled with a militantly hostile attitude to trade union activities. As the old oligarchy was swept away, a new revitalized central government opened the door to the new emerging captains of industry. The power of money spoke volumes, and the new 'gospel of wealth' espoused by the steel baron Andrew

Carnegie was to erode the older values in the sanctity of labor. The depression of the 1870s and 1880s led to the rise of the business corporation followed shortly by the emergence of trusts attempting monopoly control of the market. The US Steel Corporation brought and fused together over 158 companies controlling 60 percent of production in the iron and steel industry – and was financed by another trust, J. P. Morgan's investment banking house. In 1901 it was the first billion-dollar corporation. Such moves were met by government regulation (Sherman, Pujo, Clayton and others), with their aim of thwarting monopoly and protecting the consumer. The fast pace of expansion and its inevitable human cost led to the Progressive reform movement comprising the respectable middle class. This movement achieved some amelioration of the corruption evident in business practices (with consumer and factory laws), and some reform of politics especially at state and local level (for example, the appointment of city managers and other professionals to prevent the city bosses and their political machines from getting out of hand). They also reinstated the federal income tax. In the process, Progressivism defused the more radical strivings of the nascent Socialist party. Much trade-union activity was designed to accommodate itself to the prevailing capitalist ethos with more radical elements suffering state repression. Gompers, a practical realist, who led the skilled craft workers of the AFL, sought higher wages and viewed the unions as 'business organizations of the wage earners'. Businessman were honored while the corporation was distrusted: exemplars of those quintessential American values of hard work and individual achievement, enemies of privilege and national champions. It was not surprising that socialism and the earlier Populists (a farmers' party founded in 1892, opposed to the 'money power' of banks and corporations who controlled their credit supply) had struggled to gain a foothold with such a weak prevailing sense of class consciousness. Both were doomed third-party challengers to the system. Eugene Debs, the leader of the Socialist party, at the height of his success achieved only 6 percent of the vote in the presidential election of 1912, soon to be eclipsed by party decline.

Rapid growth, rising and generally high standards of living (still beset by labor shortages despite a renewed burst of immigration from southern and central Europe), and a more specialized division of labor marked by the separation of management and labor functions, characterized the economy at century's end. The population in 1900 was over 76 million, adding another 30 million over the next twenty years. Industry, through the standardization and interchangeability of parts, could produce cheaply and in quantity not just for its own domestic market, by now the single largest, but also worldwide. There was a wider availability of choice, including lifestyles, jobs and status. Women's earlier home-centered existence had been expanded through work and increasing involvement in civic affairs. In 1920 the nineteenth amendment finally provided the vote for women. The demand for better public elementary education continued unabated. Harvard introduced 'liberal arts' in 1885 based on a wider syllabus, and the new universities of the Midwest expanded secular education further. More settled cities with distinctive suburbs catering for the different classes, plus the new forms of mass entertainment, offered a powerful antidote to earlier disorder. The society that was emerging was 'not only an "industrial" society marked by new forms of production, but a "modern" society marked by new values and ways of life' (Hays, 1995: 229). Finally, and as a harbinger of later developments, the growing power of the US was exhibited to the outside world. American intervention in the short-lived war with Spain in 1898 led to the acquisition of Cuba, Puerto Rico, Guam and the Philippines, thereby becoming a quasi-colonial power.

6. WARS, BOOM, ECONOMIC DEPRESSION AND RENEWAL

After the First World War the US assumed world leadership but did not exercise it, retreating from involvement in European affairs, although it did appropriate the former British mantle of being the world's source of credit. War had forced many European states to liquidate their American assets to help fund the conflict. In the process, they became debtor nations to the US and had to admit her to some of their former protected colonial markets. For Americans, the war meant a fully employed economy which had seen real wages increasing by 50 percent. The only doubt on the horizon was the 'red scare' of 1917, but this was in a faraway country although restrictions on radicals and activists, despite the remoteness of their threat, increased. Paradoxically, given the greater personal freedom enjoyed by the public following the war, the passing of prohibition in 1919 banning the sale of alcohol was perhaps the last gasp of a fundamentalist morality associated with earlier times (though a politicized Christian fundamentalism re-emerged in the 1970s, but with different targets). The war had strengthened the executive branch of government and the dominance of business groups over it. In the 1920s boom, economic protectionism still ruled, extending even to strict immigration controls in 1924. The huge consumer market epitomized by the success of the automobile industry based on classic 'Fordist' principles, and the growth of retailing and servicing left most people unprepared for what was to follow. With unemployment averaging only 5 percent across the decade it masked a declining agricultural sector (employing in 1920 some 29 percent of the working population, but comprising only 15 percent of GNP), which constantly ran up surpluses which could not be sold, depressing farm prices and incomes (Kemp, 1992: 51). This, coupled with endemic banking weaknesses and a speculative stock market frenzy, meant that when the crash came in 1929, 'the blow to the American dream was so sudden and severe that the reaction of many was one of severe disbelief and passivity rather than of anger' (Kemp, 1992: 64).

'The primal force of the Great Depression' (Galbraith, 1987: 193) witnessed unemployment rising to nearly 25 percent in 1933 (from 3.2 percent in 1929), with falling capital investment, industrial production and demand. Steel output collapsed from a peak of 56 million tons in 1929 to one of only 13.68 million in 1932. Roosevelt succeeded Hoover to the presidency in 1932 at the height of the crisis. His first priority was to stabilize and reconstruct the financial system. Adopting a policy of pragmatic experimental adjustment known as the New Deal, designed 'not to end private profit making but to harmonize its pursuit with the public good', he developed a range of practical state-sponsored proposals which were to intervene in the former sanctity of the market (Kemp, 1992: 77). This was not Keynesian demand management (such an increase in demand did not emerge till 1937), but a practical attempt to raise purchasing power in an economy marked, according to conventional wisdom, by under-consumption and a lack of confidence. Although public opinion was mobilized, only some of his efforts worked, while others ran into problems not least from the Supreme Court which barred them as unconstitutional. The net effect was a shift in the role of the state (marked by the growing autonomous power of the presidency, symbolically recorded with the creation of the Executive Office of the President in 1939), which became a major influence on the market with a doubling of federal spending (as a proportion of GDP) between 1929 and 1939.

Roosevelt was to acknowledge the needs of labor with the Wagner Act of 1935 (which gave workers a legal right to organize and be recognized, and was especially vital for the new mass-based industrial unions organized through the CIO), and through the social security and housing acts. The latter, tackling the slum tenements through clearance and replacement with public housing, was to be the first breach in the 'cult of privatism'. Furthermore, direct public works schemes, such as the Tennessee Valley Authority, providing both flood control and cheap electricity, made some contribution to cutting the dole queues. These proposals helped cement that political link with labor, the working class and black community which formed part of the Democratic coalition that lasted until Nixon's presidential victory in 1968. However, on the eve of the Second World War, unemployment still stood at 14.6 percent of the labor force and deep anxiety remained as to future prospects. Government spending as a percentage of GDP in 1937 was still only 8.6 percent. The war was to re-equilibrate the economy, and propel America into a position of global power, prosperity and success.

By war's end a much enlarged economy had been subjected to further state regulation, price controls and central organization in allocating scarce supplies, all in the interests of national security. The military-industrial complex was born. Large corporations were favored for government contracts and were guaranteed future profitability. Full employment was quickly restored with resulting labor shortages which meant, for example, that southern black cash croppers and women were given unprecedented opportunities, so that one-third of women were employed by 1945. A third of the workforce became unionized and the guarantee of higher wages was met by no-strike pledges. To finance the war, government borrowing (the national debt had multiplied fivefold) and taxes were raised. New industries of the future were established, such as civilian aircraft. Furthermore, fears of a postwar slump went unfounded. Pent-up consumer demand fueled by demobilization (plus a population upsurge and housing boom), and the needs of a war-ravaged Europe for reconstruction assistance, meant the demand for American goods was total. One inescapable indicator of confidence in the future was the promise to returning GIs to provide them with low mortgages and a free university education, if desired. The US could not retreat into prewar isolationism. The need to assist Europe, both materially and militarily (Marshall Aid and Nato), plus the necessity of protecting overseas economic interests and supplies (such as oil from the Middle East), ensured a role for the US as the free world's policeman. This was given a flourish by locating New York as the site of the new UN headquarters.

7. FROM GLOBAL DOMINANCE TO FEARS OF ECONOMIC DECLINE

The immediate postwar decades were, with a few minor interruptions, marked by ever-rising prosperity as personal income and GDP rose relentlessly. The Korean war of the early 1950s was soon shaken off. Nothing seemed to stand in the way of American success as American culture, exported on the back of Hollywood, influenced millions across the globe (with New York replacing Paris as the world's cultural capital). The world turned to America for leadership in the Cold War, for credit and for inspiration. Domestically, the political culture of the 1960s, marked as it was by egalitarian liberalism, was in stark contrast to the conservative 1950s' paranoid fears of communism, exploited by Senator McCarthy in his witch-hunts against alleged subversives in all walks of life. The 1960s saw marked confrontation with established authority, and at last major civil rights legislation bringing to the black community, after a prolonged struggle, the legal and political rights associated with full citizenship. This was followed by affirmative action which used legal and moral means to offer disadvantaged groups easier access to jobs, education and contracts, although the major beneficiaries were in fact white women rather than blacks and other minorities. The struggle against the war in Vietnam (and the draft) on many American university campuses in the late 1960s, and the mobilization of an activist Students for a Democratic Society resulted in one of the largest protest groups ever witnessed in the US. This later splintered, but in the process spawned new forms of protest such as the campaign for homosexual rights, feminism and later multiculturalism. President Johnson's 'Great Society' program introduced a plethora of social reforms including the Job Corps, War on Poverty, Medicare (healthcare for the elderly), Medicaid (healthcare for the poor), new housing and neighborhood schemes, and an economic stimulus initiative which sought higher growth and help for those in need. This was to be the highwater mark of liberalism followed by a slow but steady retreat irrespective of which party was in government. Government spending, which had reached 27 percent of GDP in 1960, was to continue rising, but more slowly, so that by 1996 it consumed just over a third of GDP, a figure still low by the standards of other advanced industrial nations (Crook, 1997).

The US became the focus of the world's attention. Marking a line since the 'fall' of China in 1949 with what it saw as a further threat of communism in southeast Asia resulted in over half a million troops committed to the defense of South Vietnam by late 1967. Their role was not just to contain, but to 'rollback' the forces of the north Vietnamese threatening the south. Domestically, the introduction of social legislation seemed to bring the country closer to the social democratic, welfare frameworks of Europe. In both instances judgments were to be confounded. Welfarism was to be drastically scaled back from the 1980s, with critics suggesting it promoted state 'dependency', thereby undermining individual initiative, responsibility and respect for family values. The war in Vietnam became the first major reversal ever suffered by the US when it was forced to leave Saigon finally in April 1975, an event symbolically measured by the ending of dollar convertibility (1971) and a wave of successive devaluations. But perhaps more important was the revelation that the public had been misinformed by their own government, both as regards American involvement (the doubtful legality of the Gulf of Tonkin Resolution and Cambodian destabilization), and also the conduct of the war, with widespread manipulation of Congress and the news media producing a mistrust of the political executive and system which has yet to be healed. The Watergate crisis which led to the forced resignation of President Nixon due to his concealment of a felony undertaken on behalf of his re-election campaign was merely confirmation that all was not well, and was in marked contrast to the seemingly heroic mold in which Kennedy had assumed the presidency in 1960 (McQuaid, 1989).

Finally, the era of cheap oil was coming to an end with the OPEC cartel's challenge to the West in 1974–75 (quadrupling its price), and later in 1979, thereby compounding incipient inflation – a growing problem stimulated by the costs of the Vietnam war. The net result was stagflation – high inflation and low or non-existent growth – producing recession and a lowering of expectations that income and opportunity would for ever follow an upward trajectory. The Keynesian panacea appeared redundant as the government began the painful process of redressing spending levels, although the Reagan era in retrospect seems almost anomalous with its tax-cutting supply-side budgets and huge increased expenditures on military procurements to offset the 'evil empire' of the Soviet Union. The need to borrow massively with spiraling national debt coupled to a deteriorating balance of payments, led many critics in the late 1980s to argue for a reassessment of America's role in the world, and for measures to revive an industrial performance and productivity record seen as inferior to strong German and Japanese competition. This prompted a speculative debate as to whether the US was in decline.

8. THE DECLINIST THESIS

> Everything falling apart, airplanes, bridges, eight years under Reagan of nobody minding the store, making money out of nothing, running up debt, trusting in God.
>
> Harry Angstrom (John Updike, *Rabbit at Rest*)

The ongoing debate of whether or not the US is in decline is not just a complex one, but is marred by ideological distortion and differential interpretation of the same sets of statistics. The decline is understood not just in economic terms, but has a moral dimension too. It is well to remember at the outset that the US has by far the world's largest economy, enjoying since 1991 uninterrupted growth, and prompting the head of the Federal Reserve in 1988 to wonder at 'America's miracle economy'. Its major competitors have suffered either a financial and property collapse leading to recession, as in Japan, or high structural unemployment, as in Germany. The US is the sole remaining military superpower, but one which usually prefers to act multilaterally and in consultation with its allies. This means taking the lead in discussions and action, as in the decision to extend Nato eastwards in 1997 to incorporate some of the former members of the Warsaw Pact and, after much hesitation following the seeming paralysis of the European Union, to broker the Bosnian peace accord. Many argue there has been relative, but not absolute economic decline, mirrored in growing import penetration in key industries such as consumer electronics. The poignancy with which this is viewed is that in so many of these markets in which American-produced goods had been dominant for so long – including the domestic automobile industry – are now prey to the imports of America's enemies of fifty years earlier – Germany and Japan. The rapid run-down of the old industrial base from the late 1970s has been replaced by the growth of 'weightless' services, so that financial, entertainment (and civil aircraft) vie for the lead in export earnings. What complicates the analysis is that the decline dates to a period of industrial supremacy which by its very nature could only be short-lived. The immediate years after the Second World War were aberrant. Old rivals were neutralized and exhausted by war. The US became the world's source of goods and credit, and the extraordinary hegemony of those years could not last as other nations, often with American help, rebuilt and sought a market share of a rapidly expanding world economy. Furthermore, the domestic bliss of those years when American women returned to the home to bring up their children in a safe suburban environment, and the male breadwinner enjoyed rapidly rising wages in what was described as 'the affluent society', were unusual and unique times, but they act as a moral benchmark to criticize the present.

Conservatives argue that since the 1960s the country has spiraled into moral decline. Excessive 'liberalism' based on radical egalitarianism and individualism has distorted the judiciary, education, religious values and popular culture. A leading critic, Robert Bork, actually entitling one of his books *Slouching Towards Gomorrah*, writes: 'it seems highly unlikely that a vigorous economy can be sustained in an enfeebled, hedonistic culture, particularly when the culture distorts incentives by increasingly rejecting personal achievement as the criterion for the distribution of rewards' (Bork, 1996: 2). A further response to the purported decline has been for some politicians across the political spectrum to press for economic protectionism. By only the narrowest of margins President Clinton successfully gained Congressional approval for the North American Free Trade Agreement (NAFTA) and for further liberalization of trade through the WTO, but it was a close-run thing and suggests how narrowly balanced is the commitment to free trade.

The decline, or since we do not share the tenets of this thesis, the changes wrought to the economy need some explication. Paul Kennedy was one of the first to outline what could be the future fate of the US, echoing what befell the British earlier, with his concerns over 'imperial overstretch' (Kennedy, 1989: 665). Excessive levels of military spending skew research and development into esoteric armaments and technologies, away from useful consumer labor-saving devices which promote a greater market and provide more employment. It can also damage public finances and crowd out the non-military sectors. America's major competitors spent far less on defense, enjoying the protection of the 'nuclear umbrella' during the Cold War. The resulting opportunity cost meant that their investments in world-beating consumer goods industries enjoyed far higher rates of return. One problem for Kennedy is that his thesis was published prior to the collapse of the USSR and since then military spending has been halved. Furthermore, the US has become more astute in burden sharing with her allies during times of war, as was demonstrated during the Gulf conflict of 1991. The question of public finance has also been successfully addressed, at least in the medium term. The 1988 budget is now forecast to be in surplus well ahead of earlier projections. The national debt at 65 percent of GDP is significant but beginning to fall. After social security and defense spending, the third item of federal spending are interest payments on financing this debt. However, this is unexceptional compared to the European Union where levels of taxation and state spending are well above US levels.

One area where the statistics do seem to have a vital impact is that of productivity. Productivity is rising but at a rate well below that of America's rivals. This is partly to do with their catching up, but a level of increase of around 1 percent per annum since 1973 has punctured confidence in the 'American dream' as incomes have just barely kept pace with inflation since then (from 1948–73 the rate was 2.5 percent) (Peterson, 1994: 43). Thurow points out that in the decade of the 1980s all of the earnings gains went to the top 20 percent, and 64 percent went to the top 1 percent, a situation that breeds resentment and a search for easily available scapegoats, such as single welfare mothers or immigrants (Thurow, 1996). US productivity overall is still by far the world's highest, and arguably the qualitative gains from the new computer-based industries with vast investments made in the late 1980s are inadequately reflected in national statistics. At the time of writing unemployment is below 5 percent (1998) with literally millions of new jobs created in the past few decades, and not just low-wage unskilled ones. President Clinton boasted over 14 million since 1992, a record unmatched anywhere and a dismal reflection on Europe's incapacity to generate employment where, even in the engine house of the European Union – Germany – current unemployment levels are around 10.6 percent (December 1998).

In terms of trade, the 1950s were insignificant for the US, as imports and exports accounted for only 5 percent of GDP in what was almost an autarkic economy. The 1996 annual report of the IMF put the US share of world trade at 19.6 percent, fractionally below that of the European Union. The rise of the global market has seen America's exports expand significantly, though with constant nagging trade deficits, currently running at $150 billion annually. Its share of world output at just above 24 percent in 1996 is markedly lower than the 48 percent it recorded in the late 1960s, and per capita wealth has dropped down the world league tables to thirteenth now. Concern is expressed that too much of America's efforts are in support of the powerful transnational corporations which seek out highly profitable export markets and locate branch plants overseas to the detriment of the domestic economy. A contradiction looms between an expanding economic overseas empire supported by tax breaks and Wall Street at the expense of a decaying republic subject to periodic bouts of downsizing (Petras and Morley, 1995: 64–5). Domestically, critics of the US have a stronger platform but in the global marketplace of the twenty-first century the US seems ideally placed. In 1990 services accounted for 36.1 percent of world trade and are growing twice as fast as the trade in merchandise (McRae, 1995). The US enjoys the highest share of service exports of any major economy and often those with a high value-added content of which the new knowledge and information-based industries enjoy unrivaled ascendancy. No other nation remotely compares in terms of its exports of intellectual capital. The economy has only 16 percent (and falling) of the labor force engaged in manufacturing as the new future industries pioneered in the US take root. Yet the downside to this equation is that too many citizens are still operating on the margins, and the unresolved social questions – exclusion, drugs, family breakdown and racial discord – are the Achilles heel that punctures confidence in the future. Other nations suffer similar problems, but they are perhaps more intense within America. This is as much a testimony to the values that people subscribe to and understand America to represent, and which naturally creates profound disillusionment when incapable of being realized. Subsequent chapters will examine some of the underlying structural problems that are only partly economic in origin. The evident lack of sufficient political will and the necessary means of resolution may carry seeds of bitterness from one generation to another.

The individualism which underpinned the success of the US and its associated values needs modification in these new times. In removing the mystique of the elite the media have made them more accountable and accessible, thereby exalting a form of populist democracy within the nation. Though critics scornfully contend that self-reliance has given way to a culture of victimization this greatly overstates the case. The vastly changed role of women and their concern with the personal and 'culture of intimacy' fosters a new self-confidence in their political role as citizens. On the other hand, widening inequality, the declared erosion of support for many public institutions, and the exalting of the private market have nurtured insecurity in a society with a less anchored and changing set of values. A more inclusive vision is necessary, one that unites all but builds in restraints in the interests of the wider community. That this is possible is demonstrated by the incorporation today of the booming Southern economy into the mainstream and by the success of many minority groups. After examining some of the difficulties currently besetting the US, this book will argue for a necessary value modification so that everyone benefits from the glittering prospects being opened up by the information age.

At the beginning of our narrative the US was overwhelmingly agricultural; now less than 3 percent are employed on the land. Manufacturing and blue-collar employment is currently downsizing, but new jobs are being created which rely less on physical labor and more on intellectual accomplishment, so potentially offering more rewarding careers. Individualism and intellectual freedom promote a creative culture, but the obvious danger is that they can also lead to excessive and self-destructive values both for the individual and civic society. The pursuit of happiness defined by each and every one of us in our own confused ways can, for example, promote rewarding alternative lifestyles, or extremist notions of individualism as exemplified by the Militias or crazy religious cults, or more prosaically, a strong sense of duty to established norms. Government, as trustee of the nation's divergent interests, must define not just its own moral imperatives, but has to accommodate them to the dictates of what this national interest consists of, and in the process redefine its own priorities within wider societal values.

REFERENCES

Bailyn, B., *The Ideological Origins of the American Revolution* (Cambridge, Mass.: Harvard University Press, 1967).
Bass Warner, S., *The Private City: Philadelphia in Three Periods of its Growth* (Philadelphia: University of Pennsylvania Press, 1979).
Beard, C. A., *An Economic Interpretation of the Constitution of the United States* (New York: Macmillan, 1935).
Boorstin, D. J., *The Genius of American Politics* (Chicago: University of Chicago Press, 1953).
Bonwick, C., 'The American Revolution as a Social Movement', *Journal of American Studies*, Vol. 20 (1986), 373.
Bork, R., *Slouching Towards Gomorrah: Modern Liberalism and American Decline* (New York: Regan Books, 1996).
Boyer, P., *Urban Masses and Moral Order in America 1820–1920* (Cambridge, Mass.: Harvard University Press, 1978).
Brown, D., *Bury My Heart at Wounded Knee: an Indian History of the American West* (London: Vintage, 1991).
Brown, R. E., *Charles Beard and the Constitution* (Princeton: Princeton University Press, 1956).
Crook, C., 'A Survey of the World Economy: the Future of the State', *The Economist* (London: 20 September 1997), 1–56.
Degler, C. N., *Out of our Past: the Forces that Shaped Modern America*, third edn (New York: Harper Torchbooks, 1985).
Dunn, R. S. and Yeandle, L. (eds.), *The Journal of John Winthrop: 1630–1649*, abridged edition (Cambridge, Mass.: Belknap Press/Harvard University Press, 1997).
Fairfield, R. P. (ed.), *The Federalist Papers* (New York: Doubleday Anchor, 1961).
Galbraith, J. K., *A History of Economics* (London: Penguin Books, 1987).
Glaab, C. N. and Brown, A. T., *A History of Urban America* (New York: Macmillan, 1967).
Greenfeld, L., *Nationalism. Five Roads to Modernity* (Cambridge, Mass.: Harvard University Press, 1992).
Griffin, S., *American Constitutionalism* (Princeton: Princeton University Press, 1997).
Hays, S. P., *The Response to Industrialism 1885–1914*, second edition (Chicago: University of Chicago Press, 1995).
Hofstadter, R., *The American Political Tradition* (New York: Vintage Books, 1961).
Hughes, R., *American Visions: the Epic History of Art in America* (London: Harvill, 1997).
Kemp, T., *The Climax of Capitalism. The US Economy in the Twentieth Century* (Harlow: Longman, 1992).
Kennedy, P., *The Rise and Fall of the Great Powers: Economic Change and Military Conflict from 1500 to 2000* (London: Fontana, 1989).
Kolchin, P., *American Slavery 1619–1877* (London: Penguin Books, 1995).
Lipset, S. M., *The First New Nation* (London: Heinemann, 1964).

Maier, T., *American Scripture: Making the Declaration of Independence* (New York: Knopf, 1997).
McQuaid, K., *The Anxious Years. America in the Vietnam-Watergate Era* (New York: Basic Books, 1989).
McRae, H., *The World in 2020. Power, Culture and Prosperity: a Vision of the Future* (London: Harper Collins, 1995).
Pessen, E., *Jacksonian America: Society, Personality and Politics* (Chicago: University of Illinois Press, 1985).
Peterson, W. C., *Silent Depression – the Fate of the American Dream* (New York: W. W. Norton, 1994).
Petras, J. and Morley, M., *Empire or Republic? American Global Power and Domestic Decay* (London: Routledge, 1995).
Schlesinger, A. M. Jr., *The Cycles of American History* (New York: Houghton Mifflin, 1986).
Thurow, L., *The Future of Capitalism: How Today's Economic Forces Shape Tomorrow's World* (New York: William Morrow, 1996).
Updike, J., *Rabbit at Rest* (London: Penguin Books, 1991).
Wood, G. S., *The Creation of the American Republic 1776–1787* (New York: W. W. Norton, 1972).
Zinn, H., *A People's History of the United States* (London: Longman, 1980).

2 The Melting Pot

1. THE IMPORTANCE OF VALUES

Values are deeply embedded beliefs that hold societies together. The more voluntaristic and universal, the greater their impact and combined effect. Traditions matter a great deal. Common experience, historic consciousness, a sense of shared triumphs and tribulations surmounted, engenders togetherness, joint identification, a spirit of loyalty, plus expectations of future success. Yet adaptability is also important. History does not stand still. Internal conditions undergo change, the world outside presents new exigencies, and new challenges arise. What had seemed timeless and immanent might well turn obsolete. If it does, it poses a hindrance to progress, produces confusion and drives people apart. Demographic factors, material change and new inventions, often in concert, transform the scenario. They invoke novel insight as well as a response, demand adaptability, plus a readiness to modify values which are no longer functional. At such crucial times, responsible guidance on the part of those who hold power, is critical. The adherence to redundant and obsolete values, the resistance to making way for imminent change, indecisiveness, prevarication and lack of leadership can turn order into chaos and unity into discord.

Signals are always there and at the very least dimly apparent. Critical junctures call for critical evaluation. Yet critique is not always welcome. Habits are hard to break, new ways are often unwelcome and strange. Yet when new situations arise and a critical point of departure is reached the reappraisal of values cannot be shirked.

Evidently, as the century draws to an end, the United States stands at the crossroads. Some of its values, once functional and rightfully deeply entrenched are now volatile and need to be reappraised. In particular we refer to the values of, firstly, the open frontier, secondly, the melting pot, and thirdly, the notion of American exceptionalism that categorically sets the nation aside from all others. All are centrally placed and vital to the nation's sense of well-being and identity. The open frontier vision, we consider, is no longer appropriate and has ceased to serve America well. The melting-pot notion, more recently set aside in favor of a multiculturalist version, has gone astray and needs to be readdressed. Finally, the presumption of American exceptionalism, in the past no doubt valid, now no longer applies. We will examine each in turn and then move to a synthesis that, within the context of the 'melting pot', suggests new approaches to the challenge ahead.

2. AMERICAN EXCEPTIONALISM

We will consider American exceptionalism first. It is the essence of patriotism that all nations, new and old, big and small, consider themselves unique. At the very least, they conceive of themselves as exhibiting certain characteristics that others lack. Be it a question of firm, far-sighted leadership, of valor in battle, of prominence in science, literature or the arts, or of a special set of fundamental beliefs – be they religious or secular – it will be a quality that sets them apart. Real or imagined, past glories and current events, or more likely still, the shining vision of future prospects, will instill a sense of national pride amongst the citizenry. Adherence to collective values can become so integral to personality that when it comes to the ultimate test, the majority will willingly lay down their lives.

In this sense American exceptionalism is not something special. From the vantage-point of each and every nation, its particular identity will seem exceptional. Yet, the American experience, for its protagonists, has a unique quality that, for all their past glory and splendor, other societies lack (Lipset, 1996; Walzer, 1992). The claim is that America started as a new nation, *tabula rasa*, at a time when others were already historic (Lipset, 1979). The past histories of older nations reaching back many centuries had formative implications for the United States, the exemplary first nation. America consciously and deliberately set out to make itself anew. A small group of settlers in a vast, open, new territory began with a wish to turn over an entirely new leaf. There was no monarch to indulge in fancies or lord it over his serfs, no standing army to live off the fat of the land, no edicts peremptorily handed down from the invisible powers above. Crucially, there was no enforcement of taxation without representation. Minimal government, popular will, restraint from foreign entanglement, and above all the luxury of personal freedom – of speech, of assembly, and of private faith – constitutionally inscribed, became the essence of the new nation.

Everyone stood as equal, all were free to strive and succeed, while none was held down and oppressed. In this simple form the thesis seems self-evident. It is taught in schools, attested in literature and history books, universally internalized and forms part of American lore.

Michael Lind makes the point that, as a settler nation, the United States was by no means unique (1995). Canada, Australia, New Zealand were similar virgin territory. Equally, the entire South American continent experienced colonization, closely parallel to the US. Valid as these reservations appear to be, they are not really significant. Exceptionalism and uniqueness are qualitatively not one and the same. For all the parallels, the United States remains exceptional at least in regard to the scale of the change, the early assertion of sovereignty, the huge demographic expansion, and above all the leading role that, for all its late entry, the country has from its early days played in global affairs. The exceptional nature of the American creed, in regard to its commitment to the values of liberty, egalitarianism, individualism and *laissez-faire* are, as Lipset argues, unique (Lipset, 1996: 19).

Interesting as these considerations might be, in the wider context they are no more than secondary. The focal issue lies elsewhere. It relates to the critical question: 'why has there been no socialism in the United States?', first posed by the German sociologist Werner Sombart as far back as 1906 (Sombart, 1976). The matter is crucial. In one way or another, with the sole exception of the United States, all the modern industrial states have been drastically transformed by the experience of socialism. Only America remained immune. Yet, on all the valid criteria, the United States ought to have been in the forefront of socialist development. In terms of Marxist analysis, industrialization and class formation go hand in hand: the more advanced the process of industrialization, the more extensive will be the character of working-class organization, and the more intensive will be proletarian consciousness (Marx and Engels, 1960: 123). Well before the start of the twentieth century, the United States had already gained the status of the most industrially advanced state. Advanced mechanization, diversified finance, time and motion techniques, plus mass production had begun to leave rivals behind. Concurrently, exploitation, immiseration together with alienation – the ineluctable hallmarks of dialectical materialist analysis – had gone as far, if not further, than in other societies. Countless descriptions of every kind, from diaries and literary accounts to scholarly texts and public data, attest to the fact that for the broad mass of the less skilled, life in Hobbesian terms was 'nasty, brutish and short'. They were subject to ill-health and inadequate housing with insecure, unsafe and badly paid employment, even extending to child labor. The incessant fear of losing one's job, plus the employers' implacable hostility towards working-class organization, were just the more obvious manifestations of their miserable fate.

In all other industrialized countries, the response was collective. In one country after another, from the last decade of the nineteenth century, socialist parties committed to ending the capitalist system were starting to sprout. Characteristically linked to the burgeoning trade union movement, and increasingly supported by the industrial working class, their voices were clamoring to be heard. Particularly after the 1917 Russian Bolshevik revolution, the transformational impact of the socialist movement was making itself felt. A parliamentary presence linked to socialist media of every kind, coupled with solidaristic trade unions were actively promoting dramatic change. That, plus the privileged classes' fear of uprising and expropriation, led to substantial concessions.

Uniquely, America stood aside from this historical pattern: no socialist party of any realistic account with merely the most sporadic tentacles of working-class organization and, above all, only the merest glimmer of proletarian consciousness. Even today, trade union membership is only 16 percent of the labor force. American exceptionalism, in this context, is more than a concept. It is a fundamental collective experience without which the US would be substantially divergent in many ways.

The question of 'why has there been no socialism in the United States?', is therefore of critical significance. A number of explanations for the phenomenon have been advanced. The principal presumed causes are:

- 'Americanism' as a rival ideology;
- the absence of feudalism;
- working-class emancipation;
- the effect of mass immigration;
- economic well-being.

Antonio Gramsci, a leading communist voice in the interwar years, was the first to introduce the concept of 'Americanism' into the exceptionalism debate. 'Rationalization' ('pragmatism' would seem the better translation), 'regardless of class', is claimed to motivate Americans, humble or privileged, to 'emphasize the virtues of hard work by all, of the need to exploit nature rather than people' (Gramsci, 1992: 21–2). In consequence, proletarian self-identification, solidarity, an aspiration towards 'collective ownership of the means of production', let alone any inclination towards manning the barricades, are alien notions. Conceivably, they could perhaps have been the obsessions of coteries of recent newcomers, but were altogether at odds with the 'American dream'.

The 'no feudalism, no socialism' formula has a great many adherents. The feudal legacy of hierarchical social division predetermines a 'them versus us' schism of class struggle within the industrial stage. Now classes, rather than status groups, stand opposed in incessant combat where social relations cannot be cooperative, but turn into a zero sum game. Not so in America, where the motto 'from the log cabin to the White House', despite its doubtful empirical authenticity, makes relations more fluid. Internalized values of an open society, equal opportunity and personal responsibility, enhanced a social climate in which socialism did not easily take root.

In these circumstances, political and social emancipation was freely awarded. The United States was spared the struggle over political enfranchisement that, for many years sundered the Old World apart. Working people, including recent immigrants, were readily assimilated into the mainstream. Local political wards with their capacity for providing bounty in housing, welfare and jobs, widely served as instruments of acculturation. Significantly, while a majority of Americans, for generations past, have readily identified themselves as 'middle class', almost one-half of all Europeans questioned rank themselves within the 'working class'.

Mass immigration has similarly acted as a damper to class formation. Fresh waves of newcomers eagerly offered themselves for the lowest paid jobs, enabling the previous occupants to move upwards on the occupational scale. The socialist orientation that many immigrant groups frequently carried with them, from the shtetles and slums of Europe into the New World, generally rendered that ideology emphatically *déclassé* in indigenous eyes. The newcomers' readiness to act as scabs in industrial disputes was to further weaken the prospect of working-class solidarity. 'Divide and rule' strategies on the part of employers ensured that industrial organization remained chronically weak.

In the final analysis, the issue may well boil down to the wistful conclusion that Werner Sombart attained at the end of his early twentieth-century American tour. 'All Socialist utopias', he averred, 'came to nothing on roast beef and apple pie' (Sombart, 1976: 106). Particularly in regard to consumption, the average American has, for generations, enjoyed a quality of life that is the envy of the world. Good living, in terms of Sombart's conclusion, has been the prerogative not just of a tiny elite, but of the broad popular mass. Security and comfort are emphatically a strong disincentive towards radicalization. The great majority of Americans, in all walks of life, are generally satisfied with things as they are. Extremists and agitators arguing for revolutionary change attract meager support.

Whatever the principal cause, for the past hundred years the absence of socialism – both as a political movement as well as a belief system – has been the distinguishing mark of a remarkable differentiation. American exceptionalism has been a meaningful feature of US life, retaining a significance to this day. However, since the fall of the Soviet Empire and the end of the Cold War, matters have changed. Marxism, communism and socialism have been discredited to such an extent the world over, that political parties have been abjuring their basic creed. Voters have deserted the cause in droves, whilst manifestoes have been shorn of their radical content and political agendas moved to the right.

Americanism, as Gramsci predicted in terms of its free-market philosophy, has conquered the world (Gramsci, 1992). The American media, its consumer products, plus social habits are spreading to such an extent that, globally, many national cultures feel they are being submerged. Yet debate continues. With the market triumphant, as the subtitle of Lipset's latest critique implies, American exceptionalism has turned into a 'double-edged sword' (Lipset, 1996). In the midst of its triumph, from both inside and out, the American 'way of life' is under attack. European brusqueness, rampant 'Asian values', plus multiple variants of sectarian fundamentalism, excoriate Americanism for its crass amorality, avaricious materialism and destruction of civic life. Individualism and achievement orientation, as Lipset, a staunchly consistent champion of American values observes, clearly 'foster a sense of personal responsibility, independent initiative and voluntarism' that has immunized the nation from the crises erupting elsewhere, yet it 'also encourages self-serving behavior, atomism, and disregard for the common good' (Lipset, 1996: 268).

In what used to be considered the land of milk and honey, a crisis mentality has established itself to an extent where three-quarters of those questioned assert 'that the country is in a moral decline' (Zuckerman, 1994: 88). The crime rate is three times higher than in other comparable countries (Shelley, 1985), while in states like California more money is spent on the means and maintenance of incarceration than is being devoted to higher education, with other states poised to follow suit (Madrick, 1997: 41). Criminality, violence, drug abuse, illegitimacy and decline in family life, allied to a contemptuous cynicism in regard to the ruling classes' proneness to scandals, deceit and corruption are disturbingly rife.

Yet, at the same time, 81 percent of Americans subscribe to the statement that 'I am optimistic about my personal future', and 64 percent declare themselves 'optimistic about the American future' (Hudson Institute, 1994). There is obviously something seriously remiss with a value system where such disparate values coexist: at one level a deep-seated crisis mentality, while on the other, a bright view of the prospect ahead. American exceptionalism has in the past positively contributed to national consciousness. Revised and reevaluated, it will do so again. We will explore possible contingencies in the sections below.

3. THE OPEN FRONTIER

The open frontier notion is a similarly moot point. Essentially, infinite open space philosophy is as old as the country itself. As much as it is a truism that America is an immigrant country, it needs repeating again. The settlers came to a near-empty continent. Then successive immigrant waves peopled the open spaces. The first Anglo-Saxon inflow was numerically modest. A few intermittent shiploads of pioneers were drawn to the New World by their Protestant republican affirmation of freedom of government and security of religious belief. Hardy, upstanding settlers, although often decimated by sickness, warfare and shortage of food, were emboldened by their founding father fortitude to hew out the nature of the American state (Tagaki, 1993: 161–4). Within the nineteenth century, mass immigration started to develop in a significant way. Between 1815 and 1860 five million Europeans, almost one-half in the final decade alone, were to enter the country. Outnumbering the entire population preceding their entry, the United States' demographic character was starting to change. In addition to British, but now with a strong contingent of Irish, the bulk of the newcomers originated from the north European territories. From a modest 3 929 214 inhabitants in 1790, the population by 1860 had risen to 31 443 321 (Jones, 1992: 255). Nativist 'Know-Nothings' might cavil at the 'papist' Catholic inflow, or at the increasingly evident poverty of those who embarked, but on the whole the inflow was widely welcomed. It represented new skills and initiatives, new hands to the plough, progenitors of the next generation and producers as well consumers. Thomas Paine spoke for the nation when he declared that 'we claim brotherhood with every European Christian and triumph in the generosity of the sentiment' (Paine, 1986: 246).

Uneasiness set in with subsequent migration. In the following thirty years, immigration rates more than doubled. Between 1860 and 1890, ten million new settlers entered the US, still almost entirely coming from Europe. Then, in the twenty-four years from 1890 until 1914 and the outbreak of the First World War, a further fifteen million made their way across the Atlantic as immigrants. Dramatically, during that period the ethnic composition had significantly changed. Though still European, their origins were now overwhelmingly from eastern and southern regions rather than the Anglo-Saxon communities. Italians, Russians, Austro-Hungarians and Greeks, with a great many Jews from all parts of the east, arrived in their quest for the 'American dream' (Jones, 1992: 153–4). Asiatics, Chinese and Japanese, although admitted as indentured laborers, were still debarred from permanent settlement.

During the war, there was a standstill. By that time, public opinion had considerably hardened. All kinds of pressure were making themselves felt. One such scare was 'reds under the beds', following in the wake of the Russian revolution which made many chary of admitting subversives and firebrands, while the fears of the 'yellow peril' maintained the barriers against the Far East. Increasingly, settlers, now typically industrial workers and city dwellers, proved reluctant to try their luck as pioneers in the wide open spaces. Instead they veered towards their ethnic beachheads in the burgeoning inner cities. Their conditions were pitifully overcrowded and unsanitary, with their social character and environment becoming sullied and chaotic. Premonitions of urban disorder and conflict were evident in the festering slums. Fear of epidemics, crime and incipient revolt were ever present in the minds of settled inhabitants. Though the settlers were still overwhelmingly European, but now with Latins, Slavs and Hebrews in the forefront, there arose a fear of genetic dilution. Darwinist concerns over the loss of genetic quality found expression in many ways. Observers' warnings of escalating depravity, degeneracy and godlessness caused alarm. Job competition, with the newcomers persistently outbidding the indigenous labor force for lower paid jobs, aroused opposition among the working class. Then, with the advent of the Great Depression, and with more than 25 percent of the labor force unemployed, demands for a total embargo found an echo in numerous quarters.

Prior to this, however, numerical controls had been imposed. The 1921 quota system overtly directed the inflow towards the original stock. Legislated on the basis of proportionate ratios to established national origin settlers, it openly favored the initial Anglo-Saxon heritage – though in the interwar years British immigration reached a virtual standstill and some time later the German quota came to be preempted by German Jews. Amended legislation in 1924 reduced the annual quotas by one-third, ensuring that 'the slots for southern and eastern Europeans virtually disappeared' (Isbister, 1996: 54). Uniquely, during the first interwar decade, the net outflow exceeded the number of immigrants. Then, from 1950–70, the annual rate, with white Europeans predominant, was around a modest quarter of a million. All seemed smooth sailing, until from that point on immigration started rising rapidly again.

Immigration during the 1970–80 decade was three times that of the earlier postwar years, and then rose to fourfold in the 1980–90 decade, when close to ten million, disregarding illegals, came to settle in the United States (Isbister, 1996: 37). A further 2.81 million illegal immigrants were later given the benefit of naturalization (Hohm, 1995: 149).

Under the terms of the new law in 1965, the barriers were unintentionally opened. Family reunification, plus the lesser category of rare occupational skills, became the ruling criteria. Though intended to reduce numbers, while favoring white immigration, the effects were the very reverse. With more non-Europeans – Latinos and Asiatics – claiming family affiliation, the numbers multiplied. The annual Latin American inflow, mostly from Mexico, now exceeds half a million. Add to that the uncountable number of illegals, purportedly amounting to three million per year, according to the more alarmist sources (Fair, 1994: 2), and the case in favor of making the 'open frontier' considerably less inviting than now appears overwhelming. Significantly, according to a recent survey, not only 74 percent of 'anglos' call for tighter controls, but between 66 percent to 75 percent of Hispanics agree with their view (Grant, 1993: 3). Peter Brimelow, a prominent critic, warns that continued immigrant arrival from the developing world will in all likelihood create public health hazards, increase welfare costs, worsen the conditions of Afro-Americans, disrupt the natural environment, negatively affect educational institutions, and perhaps most seriously of all, deharmonize the prevailing self-concept of the American nation (Brimelow, 1995: 113–20). Much as these categories demand consideration, Brimelow notably disregards other criteria of even greater magnitude. Manifestly, the current admission criteria are dysfunctional and severely flawed. They neither achieve the desired objective of reducing numbers, nor do they provide America with the type of new settler the country most needs. Family reunification has proved an invidious category, while with the informatics revolution now underway the immigrant 'ideal type' has been reversed. Instead of 'the drawers of water and the hewers of wood' of old, the national need today is for skilled, qualified, educated contributors to the workforce. Advanced technology, research, plus the human skills of teaching, caring and lifestyle promotion, are the capacities the nation requires. Maintain an open frontier, but alter its framework appears to be the major consideration as the century nears its end.

The most pertinent issues appear to be:

- demographic projection;
- immigration costs and benefits;
- multiculturalism;
- affirmative action.

The first two rightfully belong to the present section. The latter two will be reserved for consideration within the 'Melting Pot' section below.

The 'open frontier' notion has deservedly been a cherished part of the American value system. A great deal of fortitude, endurance as well as tolerance are related to the presumption of wide open, near infinite space. These have fostered a spirit of enterprise, independence and inventiveness that has helped to forge a great nation. They have been instrumental in making men and women of all classes and of all social groups endure hardship and tribulation. The values have stimulated effort and enterprise not only in the interest of self-enrichment, but also in serving the cause of

The Melting Pot

public good. And finally, due to the need for mutual accommodation, they have helped in generating a spirit of tolerance recognizing that should situations become excessively irksome there is always a way out. The open frontier notion dictates compassion to strangers and newcomers, a willingness to live and let live, plus a vivid curiosity towards modes and manners beyond one's own personal experience. It has made America a unique forward-looking society, while at the same time never forgetting its past.

Virtues enough, one might think, to legitimate the 'open frontier' value once and for all. Yet within changed current contingencies, and more so for the future ahead, reservations cannot be ignored. Though vast areas of the continent are still barren and vacant, the 'open space' value assumption is no longer realistic. Overwhelmingly, today's immigrants are urban dwellers who settle in inner cities where problems of overcrowding are already evident. Lack of low-income housing, chronic congestion, job shortages, budget constraints and infrastructural decay already proliferate. Add to that the more advertised problems of street violence, gangs, drugs and ethnic tension and the case for reform appears axiomatic. Family reunification, to all intents and purposes, means what it says: newcomers live, settle and earn their living close to their kin. Developing world newcomers (though Asiatics are swiftly finding their way up the ladder and increasingly refuse to conform to the model), congregate within the confines of urban slums. That is where – one must never disregard the prior presence of African-Americans – the ethnic enclaves proliferate. Within the white middle-class majority now settling in suburbs, gated communities and edge cities, cultural and social resegregation, the very antithesis of the Civil Rights legislation, is a developing trend. What makes the situation more dire is the mounting evidence that it is the newcomers who come to preempt inner-city employment opportunities at the expense of the black community, thereby further condemning the community's descent into joblessness, poverty and marginalization. With a staggering 'one third of all African American teenage males ... negatively involved with the justice system' (Mosley and Capaldi, 1996: 83), the pressure of newcomers helps to consolidate the blacks as the core of the underclass, critically considered as rapidly sinking into the sloth of third-world conditions in terms of housing conditions, homelessness, schooling and public hygiene (Luttwark, 1993). This is a regrettably long distance from the cherished 'open frontier' ideal.

Questions of optimal population or of carrying capacity are notoriously fraught with uncertainties. On the one hand, the Negative Population Growth Association contends the optimal US population to be in the region of 100 to 150 million, less than one-half of today. Nothing else, in their view, can restore air quality, ease of transport, or the quality of American life with regard to interaction or access to open space (Grant, 1997). Opposing demographic viewpoints, on the other hand, perceive volume as analogous to prestige and power ('there is safety in numbers'), population expansion as a stimulant to growth and initiative, and new blood as essential to revitalize settled communities. Immigration, they remind us, serves as a safety-valve to excess elsewhere, while with no domestic food shortage anywhere on the horizon, ease of access stands as a moral debt owed by the rich to the poor (Sen and Germani, 1994). Demographically, for the near future, the stage is already set. The mothers and fathers of the next generation, with their predictable reproductive behavior, are already born. Under conditions of immigration continuing at anything like current levels, by 2050 the US population 'will be 392 million. That's 65 percent more than there are today, and 92 million more than the Census Bureau projected a few years ago' (*New Republic*, 3 January 1994: 13). Immigrants now account for 39 percent of national population growth as against 11 percent in 1970. Further, in the next thirty years, the white population will grow by some 25 percent, while the Hispanic component will rise by 187 percent (Lind, 1995: 133). President Clinton proudly declares that 'half a century from now there will be no majority race in America'. Can Americans truly find comfort in this assurance in the face of such ongoing trends?

Were this to come about there is no reason to assume that the nation would not adapt and accommodate. However, such expectation ought not to blind one to the evident problems ahead. Added numbers mean added pollution as well as congestion with additional major resources deflected to schools, housing, medical services and public provision of all kinds, and an intensified struggle for lower skilled jobs, and last but not least, sharpened crises of acculturation. As much as one-half of the best estimate of annual growth will be swallowed up by population increase. The impact of immigration, with newcomers typically accustomed to higher birth rates, is bound to be a significant factor in the equation.

The population growth question has become closely interlinked with the equally vital cost–benefit computation. It is no less contentious, while at the more popular level it is characterized by similarly partial and conflicting claims. Donald Huddle, an economics professor, puts forward the staggering claim of an annual immigration cost of some $44.18 billion, with 2.3 billion falling on California alone (Hohm, 1995: 147–54). At the opposite end of the spectrum, Fix and Passel, astonishingly on the basis of identical data, arrive at a net surplus total of $25 billion (Hohm, 1995: 155–61). For more plausible data one needs recourse to sources with no axe to grind. While making reference to a recent American National Academy of Science report putting forward an annual benefit of some $10 billion, *The Economist*, taking all factors into account, arrives at the conclusion that, within the immigrant states, inhabitants suffer an annual 'penalty' of $1000 for each indigenous household and that immigration has lowered domestic wages by as much as 5 percent in the past fifteen years (*The Economist*, 19 July 1997: 25–6). In an extended debate in the pages of the *Atlantic Monthly*, David Kennedy notes that in the Census Bureau report of 1994, foreign-born people represented 8.7 percent of the population, a figure a little more than half of the proportion recorded in the 1910 Census. He argues that, absolutely, immigration benefits the host country but relatively, this time round, the low-level skills of newcomers are less valuable. In a more critical stance Borjas notes that the economic impact of immigration produces winners and losers in its distributional consequences. It is a debate about 'how the economic pie is sliced up'. Immigration, he writes: 'redistributes wealth from unskilled workers, whose wages are lowered by immigrants, to skilled workers and owners of companies that buy immigrant services, and from the taxpayers who bear the burden of paying for the social services used by immigrants to consumers who use the goods and services produced by immigrants' (Borjas, 1996: 80).

Understandably, such considerable communal outlays have added fuel to the debate. Mutual charges of 'racism' are commonplace. Undeniably, even some thirty-odd years after the Civil Rights legislation, racism is still a fact of American life, affecting not only the Afro-American community but also newcomers from the developing world. The protracted hold-up of California's proposition 187, designed to deal with immigration in a more rigorous way, demonstrates the intricacies of the value dysfunction. Specifically, penalizing the children of illegals by refusing them access to education may well create more trouble on the streets. More generally there is the hallowed belief in American uniqueness as an open door country, with help and compassion to all, but this is now confronted by the realities of the late twentieth century's potential for ubiquitous mass migration. Journeys previously confined to a limited range of pioneer spirits who were willing to uproot themselves from traditional ties, and undertake hazardous journeys of some weeks' duration, are today a matter of just a few hours. The easy availability of air travel with ethnic community ties in the host country, plus networks of smuggling rings, have opened the vista to millions. In such a climate tensions are chronic, and when they erupt a source of deep fission.

Margaret Talbot describes a telling recent incident in a small Nebraska community. It concerns an Iraqi Islamic family of recent settlers, who have fallen foul of American laws. Motivated by his two young daughters' (then aged 13 and 14) increasingly troubling exposure to American teenage values, and fearful of their chastity, the father hurriedly married them off to two young co-national immigrants, who understandably insisted on their conjugal rights. The younger daughter, making her escape to the home of a school friend, exposed the illegal set up, and the two girls were rescued by social services while both the parents as well as the bridegrooms now find themselves in jail faced with serious charges of child abuse (Talbot, 1997: 18–22). The accused, still not speaking much English, through their lawyers plead ignorance of the law. Their defense is one of recourse to indigenous traditions where, in the interest of young women's moral protection plus reproduction, child marriage is commonplace. Within a community, previously friendly and hospitable, opinions have hardened. Not merely lawyers but equally a broad citizen consensus resists the notion of one strict law for Americans, and another for diverse newcomers whose pleas, sincere or not, defy the standards of equality before the law. Defense groups, on the other hand, with some justice assert rabid ethnocentrism, insisting that had there not been public interference, matters would have sorted themselves out. Why not leave the newcomers alone to settle the matter within their own cultural codes, as used to be the case in the past? Turn a discreet blind-eye to non-serious infractions for just a short while, and then await the next generation when assimilation would have bridged the cultural divide.

Cases like that have tended to throw into prominence entire subcultures where customs alien and antithetical to American values persist. 'Cultural divergence' pleas, claiming allowance for divergent behavior and the social experience on the part of ethnic minorities, are becoming a thriving new legal industry. Marriage customs, female circumcision, wife-beating and, as the O. J. Simpson defense displayed to a spellbound world, even capital charges when refracted through a 'multicultural lens' can be deconstructed to acquire an aura of ordinariness and innocence. Instead of there being one law for the rich and one for the poor, there is now the potential for the emergence of a cluster of notional systems of law where, on the part of ethnic minorities, deviations could be pleaded away under the rubric of cultural diversity. Mutual charges of racism are common currency within the immigration debate. All too easily advocates of reform are liable to be branded as ethnocentric and racist when voicing concern. Indifference and inaction, however, are themselves likely to stir up a racist backlash on the part of ordinary citizens – the proverbial 'man in the street' – disturbed by norms undermined, reverse discrimination and values decried. A backlash against the deleterious effects of the current immigration policy, as the California vote on proposition 187 demonstrates, is by no means confined to fanatics and hotheads. It is especially the illegals who, for all their dire domestic misfortunes invade the host country's integrity from the moment of entry, have emerged as a matter of major concern. Several measures appear almost self-evident. We consider the principal reforms call for the following:

(i) the principle of the 'open frontier' needs to be reassessed. America is an immigrant country, and for moral as well as pragmatic purposes, controlled migration should be upheld. It needs recognizing, however, that current levels of population growth are likely to harm the national interest and that therefore immigration levels need to be curtailed.
(ii) the distinction between legal and illegal immigrants needs to be strengthened. Legal immigrants will be welcomed according to statute. Illegal immigration, possessing neither legal or moral status, must be stopped.
(iii) the criteria for admission should be confined to the following three categories: immediate close relatives; possessors of rare, needed skills; political refugees. A total annual immigrant level of initially 500 000 reducing to 250 000 within one decade, should be upheld.
(iv) sponsors of immigrants must demonstrate adequate resources and will assume full liability for any undeclared costs of their protégés plus dependants for given periods.

Two parallel innovations appear appropriate:

(a) a new category of 'sojourners' (guest-workers), admitted to the country for limited periods and issued with work permits for specified tasks.
(b) reinforcement of regulations covering illegals' employment by means of the issue of forgery-proof security cards, and rigorous fines on offending employers.

While, within the affected states, the public at large has for some time supported restrictive legislation, it has been the business community who covertly have championed the maintenance of the status quo. The new sojourner provision should pacify employers' desire for casual low-paid workers and thus induce fewer breaches, both on their part as well as that of the illegal entrants. It will mitigate the scandals of illegal cargoes, sweatshops and other abuses now rampant. Changed legislation, successful in stemming the flow, will also permit more generous policies with regard to refugees, now sadly remiss.

4. MULTICULTURALISM

The 'melting pot' figure of speech was adopted by Americans after 1908, following a play of that title on the New York stage written by the English-Jewish author Israel Zangwill. Depicting the embracing of 'the American dream' by European ethnic immigrant groups, and their rapid acculturation, it proved an instant success. It put into dramatic terms what, since the early days, had already existed, namely, the easy-going conjunction between incoming settler groups, only too keen to shed the ways of 'the Old Country', and the settled communities, many of recent origin and eager to welcome new faces within their midst. Given favorable preconditions, plus the amazing strides America was making in development, employment and affluence, what occurred seemed easy and natural. Within one mere generation, the newcomers had turned into Yankees. Not that this meant altogether discarding their heritage in regard to language, culture or folkways. On the contrary, subcultures thrived in regard to newspapers, theaters, clubs and associations. By not hampering acculturation but promoting instead a cultural process blending the old with the new, the 'American dream' above all – that unique blend of democracy, individualism, enterprise and togetherness – served as the common cement. Rapidly, class barriers dissolved while clothing, demeanor, speech and aspirations were 'Americanized'. The way to the top appeared open to all.

Demonstrably, one single social group was left aside. The black community through time had found itself distanced from the 'American dream', though sharing many of its assumptions. Even when freed from slavery, formally enfranchised and awarded civil rights, their access to the melting pot was still debarred. Traditionalism, with ingrained racism defined in genetic or cultural terms, plus ongoing discrimination nurtured a deep cultural chasm which, coupled with their ubiquitous poverty, stood in the way. Within liberal circles, and the black community gaining strength over time, the call for Civil Rights legislation was issued as the one and only pathway to emancipation and to end the indignity of Jim Crow law. The struggles that accompanied the movement, fascinating as they are, cannot detain us here. Suffice it to say that the movement came to triumph in the 1960s and the legislation that followed assured all that barriers to full integration had been removed. The melting pot finally seemed available to everyone.

That this has not happened is only too readily apparent. The *e pluribus unum* presumption that had always stood as a cornerstone of the American dream, has reversed into the *e unum pluribus* direction (Schlesinger, 1991). At first the American blacks – 'African-American' in their current self-appellation – and then all other kinds of 'minority' groups – women, gays, the disabled plus a range of ethnic minorities – latched onto the benefits that the legislation had originally designated for the black community. Regenerating, as many claim, an 'imaginary identity' and self-consciousness long left behind, special treatment claims started to multiply. According to Nathan Glazer's recent new book *We Are All Multiculturalists Now*, as he states on his cover page: 'The melting pot no longer defines us. Where not long ago we had sought assimilation, we now pursue multiculturalism' (1997). Multiculturalism, we suggest, has taken a wrong direction. Affirmative action regrettably follows closely behind. Both, as events have turned out, are subverting the aspirations of the melting pot, and even the updated metaphor of the 'salad bowl' or even 'ethnic mosaic' to describe the situation, divides more than it unites.

With regard to the black community, the hopes of the Civil Rights legislation have tragically remained unfulfilled. Though the middle class has perceptibly multiplied and though the achievement of leadership positions in all walks of life has become commonplace, for a large minority of blacks conditions have hardened. For various reasons (more closely explored in Chapter 4), a high proportion have consolidated within an inner-city underclass which is fragmented, cut off from the mainstream, leaderless and, all too frequently, appears economically redundant and affixed to the bottom of the social structure even more firmly than in the past. Their plight is dramatic enough to invoke *The Economist* – a journal not customarily given to apocalyptic prognostication – to comment in reference to the American black underclass that it had already 'passed the point of no return' (*The Economist*, 15 April 1995: 13).

Glazer attributes multiculturalism's shortcomings to good intentions gone awry. The goal of original preference legislation in the 1960s was directed to bringing the black community into the mainstream (Glazer, 1997). Acts such as school busing and desegregation, however, have proved ineffective in closing the gap. Indeed in some cases whites have been prompted to establish their own private schools implicitly segregated by income. Additional measures in the way of employment quotas and educational preferred admission, built into the system, were confidently expected to be fully effective. These efforts have proved to be in vain. What has happened instead is that women and then a succession of minority groups have preempted the scene. Thanks to superior access and skills, women in particular (but with others not far behind) have availed themselves of the legislation and have disproportionately benefited.

Objectively many blacks are still where they were, if not further behind. Structurally they are in a cleft stick. Neither Martin Luther King's hallowed strategies of peaceable reconciliation, nor the far more militant rumblings of Louis Farrakhan, effectively close the gap. Admittedly, in the wake of reforms, there has grown a substantive black middle class (albeit still socially and residentially isolated), but for the inner-city underclass this has been a mixed blessing. With their former role models and leadership departed to more salubrious environments, their destiny seems to be one of despair and frustration. Overtaken by hostility and radical norm rejection, they have found themselves taking refuge in a fantasy ideology that hives them off even more deeply from the mainstream. Benjamin Disraeli's dictum, coined in nineteenth-century England in regard to the mounting schism between the poor and the rich, referring to 'two nations, between whom there is no intercourse and no sympathy... ignorant of each other's habits... and ordered by different manners' (Glazer, 1997: 149), aptly describes the increasingly separate, hostile and unequal conditions between white and black.

Meanwhile, as Gitlin observes, the multiculturalist profusion threatens to get out of hand. 'American culture', he states, 'in the late twentieth century is a very stew pot of separate identities. Not only blacks and feminists and gays declare that their dignity rests on their distinct identity but so in various ways do white Southern Baptists, Florida Jews, Oregon skinheads, Louisiana Cajuns, Brooklyn Lubavitchers, California Sikhs, Wyoming ranchers' (Gitlin,1995: 227). In place of the projected assimilation, American society has witnessed fragmentation, polarization, the rise of identity politics, plus an intensifying crisis between whites and blacks. While other ethnic minorities are upwardly socially mobile, more than ever many blacks are consigned to the normative wilderness.

What this has done to the melting pot ideal, let alone the 'American dream', is a matter of serious concern. As the fate of the Soviet Union and Yugoslavia, and the no less incendiary situation in Canada prove, even well-established nations cannot consider themselves immune from ultimate break-up. America, quite evidently, is far removed from such a risk, but the trends that multiculturalism implies are clearly disturbing.

According to Himmelfarb, America has stood on the slippery slope for some time. Where in the past virtues had reigned, since early this century, values have taken their place (Himmelfarb, 1995). Virtues, morally based as they were, assured stability plus mutuality where melting pot conditions were likely to flourish. Victorian society fostered piety, thrift, a spirit of permanence and integration. Values, the product of industrial society, promoted moral relativism and self-seeking pursuits that opened the door to communal disruption. Multiculturalism moves the progression one step beyond. Now identity politics, multiculturalism's *alter ego*, dominates the normative scene. The victim is mutuality and national unity. Schlesinger perceives America as increasingly composed of polarized ethnic groups. The historic ideal of one nation comprising free individuals making their own choices has been abandoned. The *e pluribus unum* motto has been dissected. While *pluribus* has been discarded, the *unum* is glorified to an extent where the center may ultimately no longer hold. He asks: 'Will the center hold? Or will the melting pot yield to the tower of Babel?' (Schlesinger, 1991: 18).

Multiculturalists aver that Eurocentrism has in the past colonized the national agenda. European history, the English language, curricula composed of the panoply of the Western world's 'great and the good', plus the occidental Judaeo-Christian religion despising all else, have dictated values and norms. Undoubtedly such assumptions are not without truth. Yet, as frequently happens, in this instance the ailment may turn out less bad than the cure. In Geyer's perception, today's multiculturalism 'has become a kind of shorthand for wanting to change the unity of this country, wanting to dilute citizenship into group (and often foreign group) rights, and wanting this in essence to transform the country... if we continue the civic permissiveness and sentimental indulgence... America will have changed irreparably' (Geyer, 1997: B6).

Piore regards today's identity politics as tantamount to a minussum game: each ethnic, social or cultural group pursuing its own self-centered ends irrespective of others' rights, and even less so the national interest, so that the various handouts invariably exceed available resources. The outcome inevitably leads to inflation, dissension and disregard for the civic good (Piore, 1995). The more benefits identity groups carve out for themselves through sectarian agitation, the greater becomes their appetite. Conversely, the less successful their efforts, the more abundant will be their claims for compensatory awards. Politicians have not lagged behind in seizing on the advantages that identity group prominence brings to their particular cause: another example for 'public choice' theorists to mull over.

Ever mindful of their potential voting support, politicians have imperceptibly redrawn the electoral map to reflect minority identity interests. Initially, the effect was to ensure color matched black representation. Soon after, the scheme was extended to include Hispanics as well. Since the Supreme Court interpretation of Section 5 of the 1965 Voting Rights Act as mandating 'the reconstruction of state and local districts and electoral mechanisms to ensure that racial minorities will elect candidates of their own race, in the interest of ethnically based proportionate representation', black majority congressional districts have grown from 17 to 32, and the black caucus from 26 to 39, with Hispanic districts similarly expanding from 9 to 20 (Lind, 1995: 174–5). Following the 1990 census, de-districting according to racial lines will be further undertaken. Not without warrant, Hollinger refers to a 'quintuple melting pot', made up of whites, blacks, Hispanics, Asiatics and American Indians as the communal future ahead (Hollinger, 1992: 850) – five mutually antagonistic, racial melting pots, instead of the previous one. For many this appears predetermined to perpetuate tension and sectarian strife.

The various privileges conceded to non-white minorities – specifically the right of admission to schools and higher education with dramatically lower performance criteria than the bypassed white applicants, plus the preferential treatment in respect of public housing, employment and communal contracts – have not gone unnoticed amongst the mainstream community. Backlash, customarily a harsh term to denote reactionary obstructionism, is an understandable widespread response. The tug-of-war cycle, once underway, is hard to break up. While the majority are inhibited from reversing the momentum by their reluctance to appear racist, the diverse minority groups, feeling their weight for the time being at least, seem rightly content.

However, little of this is benefiting the black underclass, though this has not deterred the leadership from pressing sectarian claims to the full. The prevailing mood has remarkably shifted from Luther King's compromise stance to Farrakhan's espousal of militant separatism. Black studies, in the hands of scholars dedicated to Afrocentrist analysis, has engendered a spirit of self-confidence in which collective myths of achievement and power are displacing stigmatic presumption. The black leadership, within the context of the multicultural trend, has been sensitive to the groundswell of interest. Employing imaginary history to mobilize collective action has been a well-established and much-used global device. Extreme as some of the claims appear – for example, of black Egyptian civilization prefiguring by millennia the technological advances of the West, or of blacks having 'encountered' the American continent centuries prior to Columbus, or of Aids being an invidious ruling-class plot to decimate blacks – they have the potential for regenerating a spirit of collective consciousness that could induce change. The most imminent threat to American stability may well lie in a descent to 'Brazilianization', implying a deep total fissure where race and class destructively interact. In neglecting to address the problematic of multiculturalism together with those of affirmative action could have deleterious consequences.

5. AFFIRMATIVE ACTION

Affirmative action and multiculturalism essentially have a great deal in common. Both refer to policies instituted for the best possible motives but which, in implementation, have gone badly astray. While multiculturalism has so far stayed out of the limelight, affirmative action has been the focus of public attention. Race, in the 1990s, has once again emerged as a major issue and is nowadays as good as synonymous with the workings of affirmative action. And, overwhelmingly, the repair of race relations is analogous with affirmative action reform. The National Commission on Race, invoked by President Clinton in his July 1997 San Diego address, centers almost entirely on the remaking of affirmative action. Regrettably, however, the early portend gives little promise of progressive reform. The White House mantra of 'just mend it, don't end it', does not sound as a clarion call for determined reform. Nor does the President's ascription of the allegedly still extant discrimination merely to Americans' 'blindness' as to what does occur, bode well for a policy of searching inquiry.

That affirmative action has comprehensively turned into a nightmare of snowballing claims and bureaucratic confusion, seems apparent. Even as many as 49.8 percent of blacks – the programs' putative primary beneficiaries – disapprove of 'preferential treatment' and endorse the call for rigorous reform. When the program first began in the early 1970s it rested on widespread support. It seemed evident that the removal of overt and covert barriers alone would not bring an end to racial discrimination. Inequality of access to education, housing, employment and business enterprise would not be bridged by market forces alone. Federal action was needed to equalize life chances, taking into account past historic circumstances plus the continuing residue of segregationist traditions. Distributive justice, as Mosley argues, is the essence of affirmative action. The aims set out are: compensation for the harm that racism causes; promotion of suppressed talent so that it can rise to the top; empowering the powerless to exert their rightful autonomous skills; and the provision of indigenous leadership for the black community (Mosley and Capaldi, 1996: 23–38).

Capaldi's assertion that 'affirmative action is illegal' seems excessive (1996: 68). The act has been tested in numerous court actions and reaffirmed in voting preferences (for example, the city of Houston's anti-preferences initiative was rejected by voters in

November 1997), and a great deal of good has been done in its name. One most readily thinks of the socioeconomic advancement of women, of the burgeoning black middle class, as well as the pathways open to the lesser qualified in a number of new directions. These achievements, significant as they are, must not, however, be allowed to disguise the problems that have now arisen. We identify three principal concerns. They are: diversity; quotas; and the black underclass.

In the name of distributive justice, the affirmative action program soon came to be opened up to all kinds of groups, from Hispanics, Asiatics and Native Americans, to a number of white ethnic groups, gays and lesbians, the disabled and, above all, women. As of now, preference covers some two-thirds of Americans, with the remaining third, mainly white males, destined to shoulder the entire burden (*The Economist*, 15 April 1995: 13). Moreover, administration has become absurdly complex, with a total of 160 federal agencies involved in ensuring that justice is done (Rosen, 1995: 22); little wonder that many protest at the expanded level of eligibility, at the bureaucratic confusion, at the droves of lawyers and lobbyists who thrive on the pickings, with indications of widespread incompetence as well as corruption. A huge slice of the budget is consumed by the process of administration alone, monitoring has virtually run aground, and while the most vociferous have established their bridgeheads, the most needy are left out in the cold.

'Resembling America' has emerged as a dominant theme. Attention has moved from the criterion of need to diversity to such an extent that Loury declares: 'The tendency to conflate these two distinct issues ... the increase in American diversity and the plight of the black Americans is mischievous ... It is the pariah status of the Negro in America ... that has given the phenomenon of race its peculiar power in our political and cultural imaginations' (Loury, 1997: 23). In setting out to transform the US into a color blind society, affirmative action has paradoxically turned it into the very reverse. Under the guise of 'diversity', it has been instrumental in institutionalizing racial identity, while reinforcing internal division. Absurdities, such as the first Clinton cabinet's claim 'to reflect America' while being made up of predominantly multimillionaire lawyers of diverse hues, have gone almost unremarked. While it is only proper for institutions to reflect the rapid growth of the Latino and Asian communities, some of the undercurrents cannot be ignored. The view that past minority settlement is a poor model of what happens now is gaining acceptance well beyond the political fringe. Many would endorse Massey's opinion that the 'new immigration' as 'part of an overflow that can be expected to be sustained indefinitely, (is) making the United States a country of perpetual immigration... (that) will create complex ethnic groups fragmented along the lines of generation, class, ancestry, and, ultimately identity' (Massey, 1995: 648) is a forecast of the future ahead.

It is well to be reminded of Karl Popper, one of the century's leading social philosophers, who offered a definition of an *open society*. The 'open society', Popper declares, 'is an association of free individuals respecting each other's rights within the framework of mutual protection supplied by the state, and achieving, through the making of responsible, rational decisions, a growing measure of humane enlightened life' (quoted in Magee, 1973). Both the emphasis on diversity, as well as the officially disclaimed existence of quotas, are at odds with the philosophy implicit in the concept of an open society. The official formula that all individuals, irrespective of origin, are given the same chance, persists in the practice of quotas in a number of fields. Increasingly, within the ambit of government contracts, the implementation of 'goals and timetables' reflecting the racial composition at large determines the fate of a tender. As Zelnick points out; 'The use of selection or promotion tools, such as ability testing or requiring a high school diploma which had a "disparate impact" upon black employees' (Zelnick, 1996: 57), can not only make or break the fate of a government contract, but can actually bring on an adverse costly judgment of discrimination. Within the educational sphere, disguised quota intrusion is even more prominent. For years a silent assault on standardized tests has been rife. As Zelnick puts it: 'Standardized tests that measure intelligence or academic potential are frequently attacked, not for lack of fairness, but rather because blacks and Hispanics do less well than whites and Asians' (Zelnick, 1996: 25).

The Berkeley undergraduate admissions department, known for its liberal leanings, has estimated 'that strict reliance on academic criteria... would reduce the percentage of freshman blacks from 6.4% to between 0.5% to 1.9% and Hispanics from 15.3% to between 3.0% and 6.3%'. Whites and Asians, 'at present excluded, would correspondingly benefit from the change' (Zelnick, 1996: 186). The widely deplored 'dumbing down' is only one aspect taken into account. Choices, once made, tend to be perpetuated in the face of divergent results. For the sake of appearance alone, grades will be adjusted to avert failure, jobs will be simplified, and contracts delayed or poorly performed will be sanctioned nevertheless. Frum estimates that the various rule-rigging practices depreciate the national annual budget by as much as 4 percent, not an insignificant total in the face of tightening global competitiveness. In addition there is the apparent falling behind of American students in academic achievement (Frum, 1994).

The most grievous concern in the final analysis is that the most deprived sector, made up of the black underclass, is virtually left out of account. In the past thirty years, the black community has undergone dramatic change. From a homogeneous, largely undifferentiated group, it has evolved into a tripartite structure that, at an appreciatively lower level, mirrors divisions within the mainstream. The two upper tiers, made up of the qualified black middle class, together with the employed working class, are fairly well able to look out for themselves. However, the third tier – part of which incorporates the 'underclass' – is in a category all of its own. 'Composed of unemployed or under employed people who subsist on occasional work at the minimum wage, public welfare, private charity, or illegal activities, ranging from petty welfare chiseling to drug dealing and violent crime' (Fredrickson, 1995: 10), they represent a phenomenon that post-industrial societies have barely started to appreciate. By all accounts they still comprise a small minority, but the impact of unwed mothers, drug users or vendors, the muggers, rapists and casual killers are extensive enough to move *The Economist* to conclude, in regard to this strata, that American society had already 'passed the point of no return' (15 April 1995: 13). Whether their dire condition is due to their social and moral shortcomings (D'Souza, 1995); whether it is caused by the absence of leadership (Rosen, 1995); or whether it reflects the natural reaction to white Americans' indifference to the fact of black suffering (Henderson, 1997): these are issues that need not detain us here (they will be examined in Chapter 4). What matters in our context is that to all intents and purposes the lower one-third of the black community is conceivably worse off today than it was when affirmative action first started.

It is not too late to turn the clock back. As affirmative action has evolved it has clearly misfired. The need for drastic change is apparent. The priorities would appear to be as follows:

- fundamental programs of inner-city structural renewal;
- determined efforts to upgrade all inner-city educational institutions to the standards ruling elsewhere;
- job training programs, linked to realistic public and private employment opportunities, that reflect the career patterns within mainstream society;
- drug policies which, if they can no longer effectively enforce prohibition, move towards giving serious consideration to legalizing at least the milder drugs;
- last but not least, an intensive attempt to harmonize the distinct black and white cultures, now sadly at odds with each other.

It would be naïve to presume that the precise qualities of past community life can ever be recreated. Social change has been too thoroughgoing and is moving too fast. Yet it may be equally unrealistic to propound the view that resegregation ('re-tribalisation' as Elshtain (1995) has termed it) is so absolute that essential aspects of the open society can never return. It is quite likely that while group adherence, thanks to affirmative action's open-handed approach, continues paying off, its hold may strengthen. However, once the diverse benefits are confined to those who need it most, the hold that group politics now exerts may substantially weaken, if not disappear. Even today, surveys reveal, 'the great majority of Americans are intermarried, participate rarely in the culture of their inherited ethnicity, do not pass their ethnic heritage to their children, and consider themselves in actual behavior, if not always in nostalgic reminiscences fully American' (Wolfe, 1996; 102). As Alba documents, a mere 2 percent are members of lodges and clubs by the third generation, while only a few of them are fluent in the language of their forebears (Alba, 1990). One may yet witness the rise of a new American exceptionalism that, uniquely combining the values of the open society with a multicultural manifestation all of its own, will serve as a model for all. For that to occur, the deep cleavages that currently characterize American society will need to be repaired.

REFERENCES

Alba, R., *Ethnic Identity: the Transformation of White America* (New Haven, Conn.: Yale University Press, 1990).
Borjas, G. J., 'The New Economics of Immigration', *Atlantic Monthly*, Vol. 278, No. 5 (November 1996), 72–80.
Brimelow, P., *Alien Nation: Common Sense About America's Immigration Disaster* (New York: Random House, 1995).
Danziger, S. and Gottschalk, P., *America Unequal* (Cambridge, Mass.: Harvard University Press, 1995).
D'Souza, D., *The End of Racism: Principles for a Multicultural Society* (New York: Free Press, 1995).
Ehrlich, P. and Ehrlich, A. H., *The Population Explosion* (New York: Simon & Schuster, 1990).
Elshtain, J. B., *Democracy on Trial* (New York: Basic Books, 1995).
FAIR, *Why Americans Should Support a Moratorium on Immigration* (Washington DC: The Federation of American Immigration Reform, 1994).
Fix, M. and Passel, J. S., 'Immigrants Do Not Cost More Than They Pay', in Hohm, C. and Jones, L., *Population; Opposing Viewpoints* (San Diego, CA: Greenhaven Press), 155–61.
Fredrickson, G. M., 'Demonizing the American Dilemma', *New York Review* (19 October 1995), 10–16.
Frum, D., *Dead Right* (New York: Basic Books, 1994).
Geyer, G. A., 'Travel Restrictions Miss Immigrants', *San Diego Union Tribune* (12 August 1997), B6.
Gitlin, T., *The Twilight of Common Dreams* (New York: Metropolitan Books, 1995).
Glazer, N., *We Are All Multiculturalists Now* (Cambridge, Mass.: Harvard University Press, 1997).
Glazer, N. and Moynihan, D., *Beyond the Melting Pot* (Cambridge, Mass.: MIT Press, 1963).
Gleason, P., *American Identity and Americanization* (Cambridge, Mass.: Harvard University Press, 1980).
Gramsci, A., *Selections from the Prison Notebooks*, 'The Intellectuals' (New York: Columbia University Press, 1992).
Grant, L., *A Beleaguered President, a Fizzled Economic Stimulus Package, and a NAFTA Time Bomb* (Teaneck, NJ: Negative Population Growth, 1993).
Hacker, A., *Two Nations: Black and White; Separate, Hostile, Unequal* (New York: Scribner, 1992).
Hardin, G., 'How Diversity should be Nurtured', *Social Contract* (1991).
Henderson, C., 'Myths of the Unloved', *New Republic* (25 August 1997), 14–15.
Himmelfarb, G., *The De-Moralization of Society* (New York: Knopf, 1995).
Hohm, C., *Population: Opposing Viewpoints* (San Diego, CA: Greenhaven Press, 1995).
Hollinger, D. A., 'Prosthenic America', *Contention*, 2 (1) (Fall 1992).
Huddle, D., 'Immigration Costs More than they Pay in Taxes', in Hohm, C., *Population: Opposing Viewpoints* (San Diego, CA: Greenhaven Press, 1995), 147–54.

Hudson Institute, 'The American Dream' (unpublished study, Indianapolis, 1994).
Isbister, J., *Remaking America* (W. Hartford, Conn.: Kumarian Press, 1996).
Jenks, C. and Peterson, P. (eds.), *The Urban Underclass* (Washington, DC: Brookings Institution, 1991).
Jones, M., *American Immigration*, 2nd edn (Chicago, IL: Chicago University Press, 1992).
Kasarda, J., 'Mismatches, and Emerging Mismatches', in Geary, M. G. H. and Lynn, L. (eds.), *Urban Change and Poverty* (Washington, DC: National Academic Press, 1988).
Kelly, M., 'The Great Divider', *New Republic* (7 July 1997), 6, 41.
Kennedy, D. M., 'Can We Still Afford to be a Nation of Immigrants?', *The Atlantic Monthly*, Vol. 278, No. 5 (November 1996), 51–71.
Lind, M., *The Next American Nation: The New Nationalism and the Fourth American Revolution* (New York, Free Press, 1995).
Lipset, S. M., *The First New Nation* (expanded ed. orig. 1963, New York: W. W. Norton, 1979).
—— *American Exceptionalism: A Double-Edged Sword* (New York: W. W. Norton, 1996).
—— 'Why No Socialism in the United States?', in Bialer, S. and Sluzar, S. (eds.), *Sources of Contemporary Radicalism* (Boulder, Co: Westview Press, 1977), 31–149.
Loury, G. C., 'Double Talk', *New Republic* (25 August 1997), 3.
Luttwark, E. H., *The Endangered American Dream* (New York; Simon & Schuster, 1993).
Madrick, J., 'In the Shadows of Prosperity', *New York Review* (14 August 1997), 40–4.
Magee, B., *Popper* (London: Fontana Modern Masters, 1973).
Magnet, M., *The Dream and the Nightmare: the 'Sixties' Legacy to the Underclass* (New York: William Morrow, 1993).
Marx, K. and Engels, F., *The German Ideology* (New York: International Publishers, 1960, orig. German edn 1845).
Massey, D. S., 'The New Immigration and Ethnicity in the United States', *Population and Development Review*, 21 (3)(1995), 631–52.
Mosley, A. G. and Capaldi, N., *Affirmative Action: Social Justice or Unfair Preference?* (London: Rowan & Littlefield, 1996).
Myrdal, G., *An American Dilemma* (New York: Pantheon, 1975).
Paine, T., *Common Sense* (New York; Penguin Books, 1986).
Piore, M. J., *Beyond Individualism* (Cambridge, Mass.: Harvard University Press, 1995).
Portes, A. and Rumbaut, R., *Immigrant America* (Berkeley, CA: California University Press, 1990).
Rosen, J., 'Affirmative Action: A Solution', *New Republic* (8 May 1995), 20–5.
Schlesinger, A. M. Jr., *The Disuniting of America: Reflections on a Multicultural Society* (Knoxville: TN: Whittle Direct Books, 1991).
Sen, G. and Germani, A., *Population Policies Reconsidered: Health, Empowerments and Rights* (Cambridge, Mass.: Harvard University Press, 1994).

Shelley, L. I., 'American Crime: an International Anomaly?', *Contemporary Social Research*, No. 8 (1985).
Simon, J., *The Economic Consequences of Immigration* (Oxford: Blackwell, 1989).
Sombart, W., *Why is there no Socialism in the United States?*, orig. German edn 1906 (White Plains, New York: International Arts and Sciences Press, 1976).
Tagaki, R., *A Different Mirror: a History of Multicultural America* (New York: Little Brown, 1993).
Talbot, M., 'Baghdad on the Plains; a Meltingpot Meltdown', *New Republic* (11 August 1997), 18–22.
The Economist, 'Europe and the Underclass; the Slippery Slope' (30 July 1995), 19–21.
—— 'A Question of Colour' (15 April 1995), 13–14.
—— 'Immigration: Does America Want Them or Not?' (19 July 1997), 25–6.
Waldinger, R., *Still the Promised City? African-Americans and New Immigrants in Postindustrial New York* (Cambridge, Mass.: Harvard University Press, 1996).
Walzer, M., *What it means to be an American* (New York: Marsilio, 1992).
Wilson, W. J., *The Truly Disadvantaged: the Inner City, the Underclass, and Public Policy* (Chicago, IL: Chicago University Press, 1987).
Wolfe, A., *The Marginalized in the Middle* (Chicago, IL: Chicago University Press, 1996).
Zelnick, B., *Backfire* (Washington, DC: Regenery, 1996).
Zuckerman, M., 'Where Have our Values Gone?', *US News and World Report* (8 August 1994).

3 Good Governance

1. WHY IS GOVERNMENT SO UNPOPULAR? CANDIDATES, CAMPAIGNING AND PUBLIC IRRESOLUTION

Good governance refers to the ability of government to deliver quality public service in terms of stated objectives while maintaining public confidence and trust in its leadership. It is vital to have effective government, both accountable and responsive to changing public interests and needs. Peter Drucker comments that: 'the new political theory we badly need will have to rest on an analysis of what does work rather than on good intentions and promises of what should work because we would like it to' (1995: 61). In most societies such a goal is never easy to define or maintain, but America's distinctive political culture poses special problems. As Lipset observes: 'The American Creed is something of a double-edged sword: it fosters a high sense of personal responsibility, independent initiative, and voluntarism even as it encourages self-serving behavior, atomism, and a disregard for communal good' (1996: 268). Governing a nation characterized by such contradictory individualistic values has invoked both admiration and disdain at different times in US history. This chapter examines the domestic and international constraints under which government operates, and the limited courses of action currently sanctioned by the voting public. The more the state can reinforce its legitimacy (by renewing its commitment to the 'American dream'), the more this enhances its effectiveness globally. Without the former, the latter will fall prey to internal and cross-party dissension, with the promise of globalization unrealizable.

In analyzing the nature of the American government in terms of its institutions and performance one is struck immediately by a paradox. The constitution written over 200 years ago is revered, the system of government widely admired and appreciated, with high expectations as to the role and mandate leaders are expected to pursue. Americans are patriotic and open in their declaration of support for the system of values that the US represents. Yet, and it is a big and growing qualification, many are now vociferously critical of the performance and standards they feel their leaders operate by. Public attitudes are fluid, confused and inconsistent. Many lament the lack or falsity of available political choices while others perceive the social contract formed between citizen and government as broken (Craig, 1996). The office of the president enjoys immense power and prestige. It is the one unifying national symbol of government which acts as a focus for the whole electorate, and perhaps above all, incorporates the hopes and aspirations of the majority of Americans. Past presidents have embodied the 'American dream', rising from obscure backgrounds and through dint of hard work or through success in war have enjoyed great public esteem. From Jackson, the war hero, to Lincoln's log cabin origins and now Clinton himself, all confirm that the self-made rule has validity.

However, since Nixon's forced resignation in 1974, prior to a potential impeachment hearing in the House, presidents have rarely commanded public confidence, with only Ronald Reagan, in his first term of office, enjoying much acclaim. But even he, a master of public communication, was unable to sustain the high expectations he had cultivated. During his second term his reported amnesia and deception surrounding the Iran-Contra affair was damaging to his integrity and that of his government. Officials, including high-ranking cabinet secretaries within his own administration, lied to Congress over their conduct in breaching rules expressly forbidding the funding of the counter-revolutionary Contras, a group of para-militaries determined to unseat the Marxist Nicaraguan government. The scandal involved the trading of arms for hostages held by Iranian terrorists with the surplus funds to be used illicitly, via Swiss bank accounts, to finance the illegal war in Nicaragua. The independent counsel appointed to preside over the débâcle wrote as follows: 'What set Iran-Contra apart from previous scandals was the fact that a cover-up engineered in the White House of one president and completed by his successor prevented the rule of law from being applied to the perpetrators of criminal activity of constitutional dimension' (Walsh, 1997: 531). President Clinton, by way of contrast, suffers from the 'character issue' with allegations of sexual misconduct, the misuse of campaign funds including the illegal use of White House property, and even of financial support from Chinese sources during the 1996 election. The never-ending investigation into his conduct as governor of Arkansas prior to becoming president, understandably wearies the American public and breeds cynicism.

Within Congress allegations against individual incumbents (including the House speaker Newt Gingrich, reprimanded and fined by the ethics committee in 1997 for financial irregularities) echo those made against the president and feed journalistic copy. The voter is angry and disillusioned not just with the conduct of their elected representatives, but also with the means by which they are elected. The decline of the old party machine and rise of candidate-centered campaigns with a plethora of primaries and other contested elections all needing money, feeds the belief that the public good has been sacrificed to the individual's need to get re-elected in any way possible. Inconsistent public attitudes, however, offer no clear guidance nor secure a hoped-for panacea.

To illustrate why the public is disillusioned, consider the forlorn attempts to clean up the conduct of campaigns and their financing. Reform has followed reform over the last quarter-century in an attempt to control escalating costs at all levels of the federal system. At first the targets were the 'imperial presidency' styles of Johnson and Nixon, which were seen as remote and disconnected from public opinion and the younger activists. In particular the candidate selection process and the cost of campaigning were disfigured by the wealthy patronage of the few, and an often unrepresentative and secretive candidate selection. Since the 1971 Federal Election Campaign Act, moves have been made to regulate financial contributions, with disclosure of sources and how funds are disbursed, including the availability of public finance for presidential campaigns. Strict limits were placed on individual contributions which, quite inadvertently, led to an explosive growth of political action committees (PACs) mostly supporting existing incumbents. Union members, political organizations and corporation employees have since 1974 enjoyed official sanction to pool their resources to create a PAC, thereby avoiding the individual limits placed on contributions. Their funding is, however, monitored and must be filed with the Federal Electoral Commission. Today they are viewed with much disfavor by the public as another source of lobbying and insider influence-peddling, with vast amounts of money at their disposal (in the two-year election cycle ending in 1992 total PAC disbursements exceeded $394 million).

Another anxiety concerns 'soft money': funds raised through 'special events' such as exclusive dinners with candidates, whereby unlimited amounts may be donated by the faithful or those seeking influence. Theoretically, any money raised was available only for state and local party activities and not to the candidates, but seepage into the presidential campaign is commonplace. 'Issue advocacy' stretches the rules even more whereby funded advertising supportive of issues, but not of candidates, acts by association to further the candidate's campaign. One commentator remarks: 'In the mid-1990s campaign finance laws do not limit expenditure, do not limit donations, do not limit the extent to which the very rich may finance their own political ambitions, and do not restrict the overall costs of publicly funded presidential campaigns' (Davies, 1995: 214). In these and a myriad other ways the original intentions to control campaign spending have been thwarted. *The Economist* reported that in 1996 the average winning Senate seat cost $4.5 million with overall campaign spending up 73 percent in the last four years (*Economist*, 4 October 1997).

Some argue for the public funding of all campaigns with only limited television time while admitting it may reduce political participation (Walzer, 1997). There are periodic attempts at reform within Congress to rectify the situation. Politicians decry negative TV advertising and the posing of simplistic 'solutions' and the narrowing of public debate. One concerned critic castigates what he terms the powerful and influential 'punditocracy' within 'insider' Washington who help define the national agenda and then assess its political stage-management and presentation. The punditocracy is defined by Alterman in the following terms as: 'a tiny group of highly visible political pontificators who make their living offering "inside political opinions and forecasts" in the elite national media. And it is their debate, rather than any semblance of a democratic one, that determines the parameters of political discourse in the nation today' (Alterman, 1993: 5). Acting like Broadway critics, he wryly notes, they 'will inform both the players and the audience the next morning whether the performance can be judged a success' (1993: 304). Meanwhile, the issues raised seem more and more remote from the affairs of ordinary Americans. Most political insiders, however, seem to have made a Faustian pact to continue with business as usual. In any case, as Davies remarks about earlier calls for change: 'The danger remains that the reform will be window dressing, the results will be limited, and the electorate will continue to be disappointed' (Davies, 1995: 216).

At an institutional level there are parallel criticisms. For some the political system is out of date; a constitution designed for a rural society seems hopelessly antiquated for the late twentieth century with its global markets and post-industrial society. Government can be easily paralyzed by filibustering individuals within Congress, or by the blocking activities of powerful committee chairmen. More ominously the problem of divided government and with it institutional gridlock is seen as a way of deterring effective decision-making. Along with divided government there has been a marked increase in partisan dealignment with more voters registered as independents and a growing tendency to ticket-splitting. The presidency won by the Democrats in 1992 followed with Congress becoming Republican in 1994, the first time the latter obtained majorities in both the House and Senate since 1948, a feat reaffirmed in the 1996 election. However, Gore Vidal ironically notes: 'Today the separation of powers is a useful device whereby any sin of omission or commission can be shifted from one branch of government to another' (Vidal, 1993: 961). Gridlock can be an excuse for inactivity and paralysis with one side blaming the other and competing teams of spin doctors rationalizing failure, while the real problems faced by the country suffer neglect. Americans were less than enamored during the partial shut-down of their government in December 1995, which followed a stalemate over the details of funding the federal budget for the following year. The situation seemed not only absurd and demeaning, but politically irresponsible. It backfired for the Republican leadership, viewed as being too inflexible and instigators of an unnecessary confrontation.

Current criticisms of government are, however, excessive, and tend to disregard the positive role government has played in its insistence on economic competition rather than protection, its support for health care, environmental protection and scientific research. Derek Bok in his 'state of the nation' summation lists how unfair many public perceptions of Congress actually are: it is responsive to the public will, the abuse of office is limited, there is less control by major interests, and gridlock is exaggerated. However, he acknowledges that government policy has led to unfortunate unintended consequences. These include the high cost and limited coverage of health care, and poor job training resulting in many areas where the US lags behind Europe. Government should be doing better and success tends to be where funding has removed barriers to individual talent thereby facilitating competition. Ideological differences are often over whether the public or private sector should deliver services, and so result in 'vacillating policies that end by satisfying no one' (Bok, 1996: 411). This produces inadequately funded programs often targeted on the poor who remain confused by overlapping bureaucracy. However, many problems do require collectivist solutions to achieve societal goals, such as eliminating widespread poverty, which needs both planning and coordination of activity. There is often a failure to cooperate with the private sector, which is viewed with suspicion, and so policy implementation becomes a recipe for inefficiency, formalism and poor public coverage. This is compounded by the entrepreneurial style of many in Congress anxious for federal largesse for their own constituents, but which produces a pork barrel of waste and duplication.

Bok concedes that government is the problem, but unlike conservative critics he claims that it 'must also be the solution' with reformed public administration providing practical solutions to furthering the social values that underpin American society – crucially, equality of opportunity. He concludes as follows: 'Advancing technology and global competition may be the primary forces that transform the world, but public policies will determine which nations (and regions within nations) can cope with these changes best and use them to greatest effect in furthering social goals' (Bok, 1996: 424). The widespread debates in Europe on combining social welfare (and social benefits such as public transport or national health care) with the role of the free market have found little resonance in the US, so axiomatic is the market's role in the public consciousness. Determining those future public policies, against such indifference, makes governance a problem and one handled only by skillful leadership.

2. UNDERSTANDING VOTER UNEASE: DIVIDED PARTIES AND WINNING MARGINS

One gigantic plus for Clinton and the key to his successful re-election in 1996 was the strength of the American economy. Political legitimacy rests above all on system effectiveness and with low levels of employment, inflation and sustainable economic growth he commanded a majority of 220 over his Republican challenger, Robert Dole, in the electoral college. He won 49 percent of the popular vote, some 6 percent higher than in 1992, when the intervention of the independent candidate Ross Perot championing trade protectionism and balanced budgets siphoned off 19 percent by way of protest. Many of these were 'free floating' Reagan Democrats, discontented blue-collar workers – the swing voters capable of determining election results, but still without a stable allegiance. However, the voter turnout in 1996 was only 48.8 percent, well down on the 55.5 percent figure recorded in 1992, reinforcing the long-term political decline which has marked so many elections since 1960. From the Second World War to 1960 the mood of the nation was optimistic. The USA, still the workshop of the world and motivated by a growing inclusive vision set to promote justice for all: for the segregated black community in the South, for the poor who had missed out in the economic boom, for women tied to domesticity and also, as befits the leader of the 'free world', assistance to other nations in their search for democracy. President Kennedy captured the mood brilliantly in his 'new frontier' speech of 1960. Since then, as Patterson convincingly argues, the mood up to 1974 turned sour as a result of political assassination, war in Vietnam, contested civil rights in the South and white resentment, urban riots and the ignominy of Watergate and a president's enforced resignation (Patterson, 1996). By the 1990s, President Bush admitted to having problems with 'the vision thing', thereby implicitly acknowledging the difficulties of defining new goals for his administration and governing what appeared to be a more fractious nation.

At state and Congressional level the results of 1996 were more mixed for the Democrats. They achieved some limited gains in seats, but control still lay with the Republicans in Congress and also at gubernatorial level, with their command of 32 states. As McKay notes: 'the election was a vote for the *status quo* and one where party realignment was confirmed only in the conservative South, now a Republican stronghold. Winners at all levels of government tend to be adroit campaigners, very much like the president himself' (McKay, 1997: 37). Clinton also possessed one further advantage shared by other leaders nominally on the left. The uncertainties of the new post-industrial era have led to a demand that basic entitlements – such as Medicare and social security – remain immune to cut-backs. Standing as a resolute defender of such basic institutions against the fulmination of the Republicans in Congress gained him electoral popularity, reflecting perhaps the wider concern of the electorate that further economic liberalization may only benefit the few rather than the many. Action to control rising expenditures (and public expectations) of these programs, widely acknowledged as a basic right of citizenship, has been put on hold for the moment. A dilemma Clinton was unable to resolve, despite public support, was the failure of his own initiative on health-care reform to widespread Congressional criticism. Ultimately a lack of political will and inability to articulate a progressive vision of where he wishes to lead his country proved damaging. Although adept at counter-punching against the right, Clinton is forced to fight within their ring on an agenda of tax cuts, welfare reform and limited government. A policy vacuum now characterizes much of the Democrats' agenda, with little sense of rearticulating new values for a new era.

America has unquestionably become more conservative since 1972. This is not just attributable to growing Southern influence and to Republican – at least at presidential level – patterns of voting. It also reflects a desire to reduce the scope of government, seen as too intrusive and costly, coupled with an elite losing touch with majority public sentiment worried by social and community disintegration. Even President Clinton acknowledged that 'the era of big government is over'. While enjoying the benefits of government the public resent its costs, and are often ill-informed as to the true source of their grievance. Susan Tolchin writes: 'The unifying theme behind the free floating anger of the 1990s is the target: government. Government has suddenly become the scapegoat for all that has gone wrong with society' (Tolchin, 1996: 6). The major beneficiary of this perception has been the Republican party. The majority Democratic party and the 'New Deal dynasty' have been in slow retreat, becoming increasingly divorced from much of their natural constituency. Samuel Freedman's *The Inheritance* graphically illustrates the drift away from the party since Roosevelt's time by focusing on three Catholic immigrant families, Polish, Irish and Italian, over three generations. Committed to the New Deal and what it stood for, the crunch came in the 1960s with the anti-war, counter-cultural movement, symbolizing to them an extreme form of anti-Americanism. The bitter divisions within the party over race and civil rights were seen as being at the expense of labor and ordinary working families, and rising levels of taxation funding new anti-discriminatory programs and welfare simply fed their resentment.

The roots of the current political revival on the right can be dated back to William F. Buckley's *National Review*, founded in 1955. Lind argues that the Buckleyites fused laissez-faire economics with Burkean moral traditional values by emphasizing personal responsibility, renewed religious faith and a contempt for welfare. Their target was the intellectual elite of the post-New Deal era, portrayed as being sympathetic to communism, and out of touch with the values of the patriotic common man. This cleverly diverted attention away from their own narrow economic agenda by suggesting that the Democrats had been captured (in the 1960s) by the radical left, and supported counter-culture values thereby ignoring the basic economic issues which were popular with the party's rank-and-file. By focusing on working-class resentment, the Republicans under Nixon's leadership turned populism into a fine art with their call to the 'silent majority' in 1972 (Lind, 1996).The decisive switch to Reagan in 1980, following Carter's victory for the Democrats in 1976, by representing 'outsider' values against the Washington elite in the aftermath of the Watergate scandal, was based on growing white Southern defection and increasing support amongst (now) suburban-based Catholics. In 1994 Catholics accounted for one-third of the total vote while comprising less than 25 percent of the population, thus making them instrumental in the Republican Congressional victory of that year. Ironically many of them were beneficiaries of earlier Democrat-inspired reforms.

Whether all this heralds a permanent shift to the right cannot as yet be determined. It does though indicate a problem which governments everywhere have to contend with – the problem of living within tight spending limits. Securing the benefits of a well-funded safety net at a time when people are anxious and insecure, seems an obvious and legitimate demand that government should satisfy. Yet demographic projections show people living longer and expecting a better standard of care in old age. The costs are daunting, and made more difficult if the public is not forewarned. The choices are: either to cut existing service provision covering the entitlement programs or to means test access, making it dependent on ability to pay. Alternatively, raise general taxes including social security to cover more fully rising projected future expenditures. Should government raise expectations or dampen them down, and can even existing commitments be satisfied as the dependency ratio widens? As Mackenzie and Thornton note: 'The entitlement monster is the critical macroeconomic problem that will confront policymakers over the next decade or more' (1996: 162). One day this issue will have to be resolved, as a politics of postponement is simply evasive of responsibility and leadership. The answer to this conundrum and whether it lies in a move to enhanced private provision, or a strengthening of the universal coverage that the state can provide, may well determine the future political direction of the nation.

Another shared difficulty for both parties is that neither is internally consistent in terms of their ideological appeal. Within the Republican leadership the early abrasive, hubristic style of Newt Gingrich has not won him many friends amongst the public at large, few of whom have read or seem to know much about the much-heralded 'Contract With America'. This document, unveiled before the massed ranks of 300 candidates in September 1994, acted as the unifying statement of the House Republicans prior to the election campaign. It prescribes a focused conservative program around such issues as balancing the budget, term limits, the line item veto and various tax cuts to individuals and families. Gingrich (and Dick Armey, the co-author), cleverly eschewed controversial social issues. On becoming Speaker of the House, Gingrich quickly asserted his control by streamlining the organization and composition of many of the existing committees, and was instrumental in gaining acceptance of all but one of the Contract's proposals. However, the Senate was not to be so obliging in similarly ratifying the proposed legislation. Furthermore, the party became embroiled with the president, initially placed on the defensive, but who cleverly out-maneuvered Gingrich by coopting some of his ideas (especially on welfare), while acting as defender of social security and Medicare. The Republicans, though instrumental in framing much of the policy agenda, are hesitant on how to proceed further.

The social conservatives, active since the mid-70s (Falwell's Moral Majority dates from 1979), are anxious to use state power to limit abortions, control pornography, appoint more police and, in general, revive family values and respect for tradition, notably that of white male dominance. One notable victory was their defeat of the equal rights amendment in 1982. They have a profound fear of social disintegration, with racist attitudes commonplace amongst their members. Although their fear of communism has receded, the populists amongst them favor economic nationalism and trade restrictions (Hodgson, 1996). Their support overlaps with the Christian Coalition (founded in 1989 by Pat Robertson and claiming 1.7 million members) and the TV ministries who have promoted obscure issues such as school prayer and tuition vouchers to a central place on the Republican political agenda, and have pushed the party further rightwards (Wilcox, 1996). Their disproportionate influence reflects the fact that religious feeling in America remains powerful. Active at a grassroots level and adopting a 'stealth strategy' they have had notable successes in the south and west. However, at a time when the influence of the Christian Coalition appears to be waning, other right-wing Christian groups have emerged. Bill McCartney's evangelical born-again Christian 'Promise Keepers' (PK), founded in 1990 and now claiming an exclusive male membership of one million, recruits across the barriers of race and class (though surveys indicate it is very much white, middle-income and middle-aged) by promulgating family values, asserting male dominance and responsible fatherhood within the home. It provokes virulent opposition from the National Organization of Women (NOW), who view it as a threat to women's hard-won political rights and 'a Trojan horse for the religious right', despite McCartney's denial (Dejevsky, 1997; Cohen, 1997). Ribuffo argues that earlier revivals, following a well-worn pattern, tend over time to moderate and already are 'edging away from inflexible male dominance' (Ribuffo, 1998: 13). Indeed the increasing moderation of PK and its avoidance of too strident a denunciation of the usual targets demonized by evangelical conservatives has seen a falling off in attendance since their successful rally in the Washington Mall in October 1997, when up to 700 000 gathered.

The difficulty for the Republican leadership is that such populistic and anti-feminist views, sustained by many well-funded groups on the right, offend more than they attract. This is especially true for women, who are so central to the labor market, and whose income is vital in sustaining family living standards and whose vote and support are essential. By way of contrast, the libertarian wing of the party, concerned with extending supply-side measures including the flat rate tax, is averse to any state control. Developing a program which satisfies both wings and yet appeals to the wider public is therefore somewhat problematic. One day, a Republican leader will have to stand up to the anti-abortion lobby, as their politicizing of the issue in a society where women comprise 53 percent of registered voters is, as opinion polls have consistently indicated, unpopular. The 1992 Republican nominating Convention in New York proved to be a public relations disaster with TV cameras showing the right-wing populist, Pat Buchanan, in full flow with his invective against abortion and other sensitive issues, all available at prime time. San Diego in 1996 was carefully orchestrated so that any contentious speech was effectively off-limits to prime-time coverage. A more moderate and socially balanced image was presented to the viewing public. In practice past Republican presidents have made sympathetic noises to the cause, but have failed to deliver concrete changes, knowing full well that this risks alienating much of mainstream opinion.

Michael Lind, a former leading conservative, is deeply critical of the Republican party for allowing right-wing populism to go so far unchecked, thereby potentially alienating the moderate center. In ignoring the legitimate economic worries of the middle class for a religious cultural invective, the party is in danger of becoming moribund. In articulating these worries by calling for economic protectionism, most vividly with his win in the New Hampshire primary in 1996, Buchanan exposed the party's economic elite to the contradictory nature of much of their blue-collar support (Lind, 1996). Further confirmation of the dislike the majority of Americans display towards politicized religion is provided by Wolfe, who suggests it extends even into the Southern Bible belt (Wolfe, 1998). Indeed, most Americans reject the idea of a culture war as a concoction of the media, are more tolerant and non-judgmental about women's rights, civil rights and religious diversity, and adopt a 'live and let live' philosophy in which they seek a middle way to life's complexities.

However, all is not plain sailing for the Democrats. The president and his vice-president, Al Gore, heir apparent in 2000, are part of the Democratic Leadership Council founded in 1985 as a more moderate counterbalance to the influence of Labor and the Rainbow coalition of Jesse Jackson. Clinton is a 'New Democrat' sympathetic to the claims of conservative Southern Democrats, Big Business and opinion on Wall Street. Their program, after a hesitant start in 1992, was to encompass – following the 1994 Republican triumph – a policy known as 'triangulation'. Devised by policy advisor Dick Morris, it distanced Clinton from old-style Liberal 'tax and spend' Democrats in Congress and the newly resurgent Republicans. The centrist agenda pursued was based on welfare reform including workfare, a defense of 'entitlements', slimming government agencies to make them accountable and efficient (including decentralizing power to the states), adopting the language of communitarianism and social responsibility, and in general advocating a pro-business low-tax environment. The most significant legislative victory for Clinton was the ratification of NAFTA (the North American Free Trade Agreement) which enjoyed crucial bipartisan support from the Republicans, and was bitterly contested by many leading House Democrats and the AFL-CIO lobby. So important was this to Clinton that one commentator has argued that a potential new consensus is emerging around free trade abroad and leaner government at home, with room for only minor small-scale forms of intervention (Walker, 1997). Former Labor secretary Robert Reich, a leading thinker in Clinton's team until his departure in 1996, confesses to some small achievements such as raising the minimum wage. Reich argues, however, that Clinton became a prisoner of seeking a budgetary deficit reduction as the number one priority, thereby foreclosing options such as improving public investment, and redefining an agenda that would tackle areas of public spending such as defense, plus corporate and farming subsidies which had long outlived their usefulness (Flanders, 1997).

Against this powerful appeal to the middle class, with an implied promise of tax cuts and 'entitlement' protection, old-style Liberal Democrats such as Richard Gephardt, and other elements of the Democratic House leadership have made populist appeals to the blue-collar worker threatened by corporate downsizing. Many American manufacturing companies and their workforces are located outside of the high-tech areas and are under competitive threat from low-cost foreign producers. They seek labor protection and higher tariffs through restricting the trade of those countries whose labor and environmental standards do not match those of the US. Equally, many countries lack open markets – being defended by hidden subsidy or licensing restrictions – and have built up vast trading surpluses through their export drives, and so would also be restricted on reciprocity grounds. These two wings of the party could yet unite in a progressive compromise. Recognizing that in the new global market a government committed to upgrading skills and securing good minimum standards, and acting in a facilitating or enabling role, could prove popular. It would have to prioritize public spending, adjudicate fairly between contending lobbies, and stay within existing spending limits, or if additional public investment proved necessary, legitimize it.

3. UNDERSTANDING VOTER UNEASE: GLOBAL MARKETS – A THREAT TO THE NATION STATE?

Since the 1980s, both government and people are becoming increasingly wary of the activities of the global market, realizing they do not necessarily lead to a harmonization of world interests, fostering democracy and the 'end of history'. The advent of 'neutral' technologies promoting worldwide economic integration by facilitating the movement of capital, goods, services and now even labor, may have deleterious consequences which may not be to the advantage of all nations. Within America, many workers are insecure as to their long-term future, fearful of either technological redundancy or of being unable to compete by further reductions in prices and wages in the highly competitive world marketplace. The transnational corporations (TNCs), in their pursuit of higher profits, can out-source production overseas where labor costs are low, thereby denuding the domestic economy of investment and jobs, and there seems little that organized labor can do about it. A strong suspicion exists that globalization redirects society's priorities to economic ends and markets which take precedence over politics and political accountability.

Even a powerful nation state such as the US apparently lacks adequate control in the face of such an unrelenting economic process. The adoption of market criteria as one basis of US foreign policy can lead to double standards with unfortunate consequences – at times turning a blind-eye to human rights and violations of democratic standards in support of regimes with dubious records. Thus Indonesia received favorable treatment whereas Cuba was vilified. Perceived inconsistencies in America's record limit her own global effectiveness. The IMF, seen by many as under American control, is viewed with unease by the Asian Tigers, who are currently dependent on loans to bail out their struggling economies and anxious that predatory American corporations will buy into their struggling financial institutions cheaply (Bush, 1997). Competitive nationalism bedevils global cooperation. Later chapters (Chapters 5 and 7) will explore the ramifications of this debate further, but a few preliminary observations are in order here. It should, however, be noted at the outset that state spending in the USA is roughly the same today as it was a decade ago, at about a third of GDP despite the accelerating pace of economic change. Much of the debate on globalization and its implied threat to the integrity of the state is exaggerated. In fact the world in many respects was as much 'globalized' a century ago, though under British financial hegemony, as it is today. The question still arises: what role should the state play, if any, to alleviate such fears and what would constitute the basis of 'good governance'?

The American government, like other nation states, has to contend with the growing power of the global market dominated by powerful TNCs, and the need to react to regulatory supranational institutions, such as the World Trade Organization. In a real sense power is shifting upwards (and outwards) to these new global bodies and also downwards to local, state or regional levels. One prominent commentator, Susan Strange, lists three limitations on government: 'the shift in power from states to markets; the increased asymmetries of state power; and the gaps in government' (Strange, 1995: 296). Governments, she argues, have to contend with a triangular diplomacy. This is not just dialogue with other states and corporations, but also the consequences of inter-corporate diplomacy (for example, developing new strategic alliances), with this latter component becoming the critical actor. States are pressed to conform to an external standard, be it the World Bank or foreign exchange markets, and to deal with growing transnational links many of which are non-governmental. The sort of issues dealt with range from environmental questions (Kyoto in December 1997), to international crime control (drugs and the Mafia). Also included are the more traditional great power diplomacy negotiations such as the grand coalition of nations, led by the US military, which evicted the Iraqi forces from Kuwait in 1991, but which were crucially legitimized by the United Nations.

Of great concern, however, have been the arguments over establishing regulatory authority over the global economy. Even the US, with massive structural power at its disposal, can still fall prey to external pressure in key commodity markets, such as its critical dependency on oil. On the other hand, US dominance by many new *private* technological companies gives it the chance to set the market standards that others must follow worldwide, including the American government itself. This can pose the danger of monopoly, recognized now by government in initiating legal action against leading US information technology companies. Also, states compete with each other to attract not just inward investment but also to domicile TNCs within their domestic economy by tempting tax packages. In this unequal struggle between states across territories, the traditional political role of government in allocating values is now shared with market operators, as their actions decisively alter the domestic social and economic order. This does not necessarily mean a crisis of the nation state, now theorized somewhat differently than in classic Weberian terms, but it does mean that freedom of action becomes more circumscribed by other actors pursuing different agendas.

Good Governance

A different example drawn from the European Union, and one that bedeviled the last Conservative government in Britain, concerned the regulatory powers of the European Commission in Brussels and worries over alleged loss of sovereignty. The single market requires a strong central commission with powers of rule enforcement which at times run counter to the interests of individual member states. In the US, a comparable example was the signing of NAFTA in 1993, an agreement which ceded some shared control to both Canada and Mexico. Domestically, powerful interests such as Labor and the AFL-CIO were fearful for the future of the manufacturing base, as it would be prone to severe wage competition from low-cost Mexico. The US, for many years, has been running a vast trade deficit, mainly of manufactured goods it needs to import, as it no longer produces them when other nations have successfully targeted its open domestic market. Irrespective of the merits of the argument, it has left a residue of suspicion and unease within key constituencies of the Democratic party and amongst the populist wing of the Republican party too.

The wider debate on whether the nation state is becoming obsolete, irrelevant and sidelined will be explored later. One self-professed globalist argues that the twenty-first century will be American, with an emergent world order based on free trade dominated by America's persuasive counsel. Dominance, however, rests not on crude military supremacy, but by exerting influence and control over the sinews of the world's energy, informational and financial flows, including audio-visual images, much of which already passes through Washington. The key to growth and prosperity lies in openness to trade, information, ideas and people. Washington is emerging as the HQ of 'World-America', although admittedly at the expense of a declining republic and nation state. The federal budget acts in a supportive role to the states and localities, but with a growing international clientele also dependent on its largesse. Crucially, America's ability to act as midwife to the new order rests on the experience gained from its unique domestic melting pot, which has provided a 'cultural syncretism' to deal with the differing domestic claims of identity. This familiarity is conducive to allaying the fears of other nations and cultures, as the US can act with sensitivity. The 'particularisms' which are such a defining feature of US culture will, through the power of its global mass media, project an American identity both admired and imitated. The imagery is that of a new but democratic Roman empire, in which the American military act as the Praetorian guard of a worldwide alliance. Furthermore, the American dream potentially embraces the world, and 'is kept alive by the massive arrival of new citizens, immigrants from all over the world' (Valladao, 1996: 193–4).

However, Valladao's optimism needs tempering somewhat with the self-evident limitations in white America's relationship to the black community and other minorities, many of whom remain locked outside the structures of opportunity. Indeed the promotion of the civil state and diversity since the late 1960s may weaken the national state. Schwarz argues that throughout much of American history '"Americanization" was a process of coercive conformity according to which the US was a melting pot, not a tapestry' (Schwarz, 1995: 62), and exporting this model overseas rests on a false myth of pluralist integration. He continues: 'A crusade in support of multi-national, multicultural tolerance abroad really seeks to validate it at home. But... we have not yet found a "reasonable" solution here, and that perhaps such a solution cannot be found' (ibid.: 67). Furthermore, many outside of the US remonstrate at the neglect of its international commitments, notably with regard to its limited and declining donations to developing countries' economic aid programs. There is also anger at US interference in the rights of countries doing business with countries the US disapproves of; specifically, the Helms-Burton Act limiting trade with Cuba has led to wide EU Commission protests. In Iran, French and Russian companies have reached agreement to develop offshore oil and gas fields at a time when Europe is once again in 'constructive engagement' with Iran, despite American hostility. Frustration is evident with the US over its tardy recognition of global warming, and its unwillingness to push sooner rather than later for tighter emission controls in the industrial sector. All of these examples demonstrate a recurrent feature of US foreign policy: the evident clash between idealism and realism.

In conclusion, clearly the new global economy creates new sorts of problems for governments to resolve. The US is perhaps uniquely positioned to benefit from many of these changes, but in doing so it has to win the hearts as well as the minds of the electorate. It is not enough to see the enrichment of the major corporations often at the expense of employees who suddenly find themselves surplus to requirements. To legitimize America's global ambition it is necessary, at the same time, to reinforce the social networks of support, acting through both public and private agencies, to capitalize on what Drucker has called the knowledge sector (Drucker, 1994). At the heart of this lies enhanced educational provision and an independent social sector, which can reconnect the citizen with the state. At many levels, precisely the opposite has been happening, with growing concern at fragmenting community, loss of trust and remoteness of government, not just in tackling the problem but in recognizing that one exists. President Clinton is aware of this need but so far has not been able to articulate to the wider public the attractions of this new world now opening. The nation state is still pivotal as it gives both a sense of local identity to its citizens (with respect to national sovereignty), who thereby provide the necessary legitimacy enabling the state to act as an intermediate element connecting them to the global community. However, as Strange rightly argues, there is no legitimate democratic opposition to the new forms of global governance, no 'negarchy' to offset the arbitrary powers of non-governmental organizations and their value allocating authority, including the menace of the Mafia. We lack a set of international rules in this historic shift to market power operating globally, and so far the US seems unprepared to become the new enforcing hegemon thereby enhancing good governance (Strange, 1996).

4. UNDERSTANDING VOTER UNEASE, DOMESTIC ISSUES: DEVOLVING POWER TO THE STATES AND CITIES WITH NEW WELFARE RESPONSIBILITIES

A second feature of the changes experienced by the nation state, lies in the moves to devolve power downwards to local, or regional assemblies. The new Blair government in the UK in September 1997 secured approval, following referendums, for the creation of new political assemblies in both Scotland and Wales, thereby loosening the tight grip that, in a unitary state like Britain, Whitehall has traditionally exercised. Though controversial, they have been broadly welcomed as a means of modernizing the British state. In the US, the process of further devolving powers to the states and localities, thereby extending the 'new federalism', has been given a boost with Clinton's welfare reform of 1996. This decision emerged in the summer months prior to his re-election. Despite vociferous criticisms from the left of his party, he signed a Republican-inspired Welfare Reform Act. In 1992, he had uttered the prophetic words 'to end welfare as we know it', mindful of how much this was seen as an affront to American values. Critics argued it created dependency, and supported deviant lifestyles with the stereotypical single mother (the illegitimacy rate is 33 percent and rising) wedded not to a partner, but to the welfare check. At a stroke, the federal entitlement to welfare for the poor, initiated in 1935, has been rescinded. The major casualty has been Aid to Families with Dependent Children, which at most captured 2 percent of the federal budget. Symbolically, 'welfare mothers' were an easy target, but not the major entitlement programs benefiting the middle class and business (Levine, 1996).

At the heart of the Act, time limits will be imposed on welfare recipients of two years' duration. Then they must seek employment, either through the private sector or through state schemes and undertake recognized retraining. Throughout their lifetime the maximum period recipients can receive benefits is five years. Crucially, however, each state has the option of exempting 20 percent of welfare recipients from the five-year limit, so some flexibility is built into the system in the case of those structurally unemployed or incapable of work. Currently, one in seven children and about four million single mothers depend on welfare. The new scheme will be designed and administered by the states who will receive a federal block grant. They can experiment to find the most suitable programs which will facilitate the move back into the labor market. Prior to the new Act, however, many states had been granted waivers by the federal government to run their own 'demonstration programs'. The results are on the whole modest. They are bedeviled by changes in local political leadership, by conflicting goals of administering welfare while acting as an employment office, and on top of which all is dependent on the buoyancy of the local economy. The real problem is not the myth of welfare dependency as such, but the deterioration of the low-wage labor market and changing family structures. Poverty in fact is a far wider phenomenon than those simply dependent on welfare as it includes the working poor, many of whom subsist below an adequate standard of living (Handler and Hasenfeld, 1997: 62–85).

In some states like Wisconsin, where full employment is the norm, the moves to ending welfare go back a number of years. Here an extensive workfare program is supplemented with generous schemes of child care support, free health care for the low paid, and assistance with transport costs, which have proven to be successful but expensive. By contrast, exactly how this will work within the most blighted inner-city neighborhoods, where all form of work is scarce, where public transport links to where the work is located are either non-existent or involve long journeys, and where educational standards and availability of child care are often inadequate, is anyone's guess. One concerned critic, Julius Wilson, calls for a New Deal-type 'Works Progress Administration', employing people on renewing the country's infrastructure. But the change of political direction and the scale of investment this implies has little chance of being currently realized (Wilson, 1996). Wilson's approach is for a class-based (there are numerically more poor whites than blacks) rather than a race-based proposal. President Clinton in 1997 called for a 'national conversation on race' as disadvantage still falls disproportionately on the non-white community. Of immediate concern is that some conservative Southern states may well take a punitive disqualifying approach to welfare, especially as many of the recipients are ethnic minorities, as a means to reducing state taxes further. Aside from the ethics involved in this legislation, the states will take on more responsibilities, as they are seen as being closer in touch and so more accountable to their own constituencies. This new direction could be the forerunner of other proposals.

The new responsibilities now being carried by the states are going to need careful monitoring. It will need more than enlightened bureaucracy, and may well involve the formation of the type of citizens' movements which have been so assiduous in promoting the needs of the Californian middle class since the 1970s with their effective use of proposition laws to mandate local changes. These, however, can act as a threat to representative government by restricting attempts to promote legislative action and establishing priorities, by limiting debate, and paradoxically acting to promote indifference or hostility to minority rights. Plebiscitary electronic government is often advanced by voter tax-paying groups who are keen to defend the status quo, mindless of their effects on the wider community (Schrag, 1998). Whether the equivalent moral concern can be mustered for poor and often inarticulate people remains doubtful. The proposed workfare element may involve more spending in the short term if its objectives are to be realized. Already there are signs that the politicians' Pied Piper of no increase in taxes is becoming dysfunctional at local level, inhibiting necessary public investment and paralyzing political choice and initiative. In some fast developing parts of the country (Fairfax, Virginia is one example), local business leaders are becoming worried by the evident shortfall in the quality of the local workforce due to poor schooling. They are demanding more public investment from the state. In Pittsburgh the local business elite, similarly worried, are prepared to kick-start the process by funding an Early Childhood Initiative for the poor, which they hope will act as a catalyst for the city and state government to follow through on (Vulliamy, 1997).

Changes of this magnitude create uncertainty, especially for the most vulnerable members of a society marked by widening income inequality. The Census Bureau's annual report on poverty and incomes (published in October 1997), noted that the typical household income in real terms rose marginally in 1996 but this was still 3 percent less than in 1989. For those in the bottom fifth, family income fell by 1.8 percent with the very poorest actually increasing in absolute numbers, and all this at a time when unemployment is at near record lows. Many commentators are as yet undecided as to how these changes will work and whether workfare will attain its objectives, although it will in the short run 'save' money and may provide the leverage necessary to help individuals re-enter the labor market. The American government's programs are already among the most parsimonious, and after an exhaustive analysis of public provision, Bok comments: 'Americans enjoy less security from the principal threats to their well being than the citizens of any other industrialized country' (Bok, 1996: 375). Conceding that the far more extensive welfare provision available in Europe is currently being curtailed due to economic cost he writes: 'In the end, therefore, if European welfare programs put prosperity at risk by doing too much, American social policies threaten to do the same, by accomplishing too little' (Bok, 1996: 399).

Given then the contrary pulls on the state from above and below to find resources (and locate taxes on mobile TNCs) at one level, and minimize expenditure at another, it is hardly surprising that many Americans feel a sense of bewilderment. For all the criticisms leveled at the state, much revolves around unfulfilled rather than diminished expectations, demonstrating both the limits of leadership and an all-inclusive vision. Since Roosevelt and the New Deal, a more personal and intimate relationship has been created between the White House and the public, fostered in part by Roosevelt's mastery of the radio and his 'fireside chats'. Roosevelt was prepared to act pragmatically in the classic American fashion and yet challenge established interests. Watkins remarks that this 'helps to explain why Americans still invest so much hope in the possibility of their presidents and their government and exercise so much anger when they believe either or both have failed them' (Watkins, 1993: 18). Despite recent economic success the gap separating the public from the political elite is wide and growing. Many problems can be resolved only by an active enabling government, but one which has internally reformed itself along progressive principles (Weisberg, 1996). An immediate priority is to grasp that opportunity.

5. CONCLUSION

This chapter has focused on both domestic and international political questions – the problems and constraints that require definition and make governance so complex. To renew faith in government the moves to clean up campaign finance with a determination to tackle other problems too will help. Equally, Americans realize they have lost their innocence, that a retreat into protectionism and autarky has long gone as a policy option, as they learn to cope with the outside world and its pressures. That is why it is important that political leaders articulate, not evade, the difficult choices that have to be made. Sound bites, focus groups and spin doctoring are no substitute for reasoned policy and vision. If the direction of policy and the use of power are evident to the public, then the modern paraphernalia of politics, with a focusing on personality at the expense of content (even ideology), becomes redundant. The Democrats lack a long-term vision of progressive reform, and are as desperate as the Republicans not to appear as tax raisers. This is irrespective of whether increased funding for the modernization of the public sector, including its infrastructure, may well be a popular initiative and intrinsically worthwhile. Furthermore, the Congressional Democrats, a majority of whom seem to favor economic protectionism (against the policy of their own president), could be sidelined in future electoral contests with a backward-looking economic program.

Politics often appears negative, with powerful interests exerting what appears to be a veto over government. The manipulation of images, of the 'feel good' factor, are insufficient in themselves to build a sustainable coalition of reform along expansionist lines. With widening domestic inequality exacerbated by global capital, Clinton's priority of expanding free trade is not being offset by any major investment in social goals which could help allay the anxieties and promote more opportunity. The state's role will be that of an enabler not a provider. It can, for instance, modernize the tax and benefits structures to selectively assist some groups, or offer incentives to others currently excluded from the opportunities now opening up. The emerging global market, with its costs and benefits to American consumers and workers, needs both explaining and legitimizing to the American public. It has produced both winners and losers, with a perception that much of the new wealth generated has not been fairly shared. So far there has been little concerted presidential justification for this new agenda, apart from a brief flurry of activity surrounding the (failed) fast track authority negotiations with Congress in November 1997, resulting in further splits for the Democrats.

As the US enters a new economic era at the close of the twentieth century, all that painful restructuring of companies and their labor forces (the technocratic language of 'downsizing', 're-engineering', 'outsourcing' and 'lean production') of the late 1980s and early 1990s, may pay off with the unbridled promise of future prosperity. Against this optimism, a note of caution needs to be registered. As the information age and what it means is digested, it becomes even more apparent that many Americans are, in the foreseeable future, incapable of sharing in its promise. For them the 'American dream' will remain elusive. Growing prosperity – albeit of a limited kind in wages and wealth for the majority – will need a concomitant response by government to develop new policies with new forms of targeting addressed to the social needs of the poor and excluded. This will be vital if social stability, legitimacy and social justice are to be maintained, and if government still sees itself as playing a meaningful role in the search for a better future society. A role, incidentally, that the public expects its government to pursue, and which if carried out successfully would constitute the basis of what we have called 'good governance'. In the UK, the creation of a Social Exclusion Unit based in the Cabinet Office and bringing in expertise from the police, civil service, business and the voluntary sector, is seen by Tony Blair as one of his administration's defining characteristics in tackling homelessness, unemployment and school truancy. The unit will be preventative, holistic and more personal in approach and will offer 'joined-up' policies, as the problems to be tackled are so multifaceted (Wintour, 1997).

A similar response may well be needed in the US. The state (in conjunction with the private and voluntary sectors) must therefore redouble its so far lukewarm response to social amelioration, with an inclusive drive to rebuild the cities and extend and secure more fully the pitiably inadequate social support networks. This will involve, for example, the retraining of redundant older workers left stranded by technological change, or developing new ways of tackling the marginalized and dispirited underclass. The inner cities cannot be abandoned as the problem reflects profound social attitudes as much as it does political economy.

In arguing against the moves to absolve or simply reduce too far the state's role in so many traditional areas of life, there is a danger that 'social capital' will be further eroded. One of America's leading intellectuals, Francis Fukuyama writes: 'The contemporary black underclass in America today represents what is perhaps one of the most thoroughly atomized societies that has existed in human history' (Fukuyama, 1995: 303). Within the inner city there are few functioning intermediate-level organizations vital to cohere the social order, such as churches, clubs or libraries. Life is the Hobbesian nightmare characterized by lawlessness and brutality, where no one trusts anyone else, and where communities rot through lack of work, investment, morale and opportunity. Without state investment the racial divide will only get worse. Disadvantaged communities have high transactional costs, such as policing and schooling, which must be borne by all of us. For all the criticisms leveled at Europe's social charter, it does provide civilized minimum standards below which no one should fall. It helps build that first vital rung by strengthening the social trust which ultimately binds us all together.

However, redistribution by reprioritizing within existing budget limits will be the norm, as there will be little new money available now that the balanced budget is accepted by all parties. This means that any enhanced spending depends on sustaining a growing economy which generates further extra revenue. The agency of redistribution and the means by which this is achieved is unlikely to be Washington. It is too remote and inflexible, so the states and cities will play a more pivotal role in future, along with a revitalized voluntary 'social sector'. However, this does not herald a return to small-scale conservatism with the concomitant danger, as Chomsky warns, that local states 'will simply make themselves more susceptible to influence and control by private power' (Chomsky, 1996: 120). The segregation by income of incorporated suburbs and townships, and the inner city has created vast differences in local tax bases which are supportive of better schools and environments to raise children and promote opportunity. The federal government's role will be crucial in setting goals, monitoring standards and allocating resources fairly across the nation. Information technology makes this a relatively easy task to accomplish today. Success may be accomplished by building on the non-partisan approach of several of the mayors of big cities – Riordan in Los Angeles, Giuliani in New York, Rendell in Philadelphia – who have more freedom to experiment pragmatically be it zero tolerance of crime in New York or wherever the local problem arises. As Steizer argues: 'For cities are where the political action is, the place where the citizens meet their government up close and personal, where experimentation is possible, and success or lack of it visible to all' (Steizer, 1997). Revitalizing the 'American dream' is a moral imperative, and if it not resolved, then American claims to being the harbinger of a bright new world will remain empty rhetoric, with other nations unwilling to follow her lead.

REFERENCES

Alterman, E., *Sound and Fury: the Washington Punditocracy and the Collapse of American Politics* (New York: Harper Perennial, 1993).
Bok, D., *The State of the Nation: Government and the Quest for a Better Society* (Cambridge, Mass.: Harvard University Press, 1996).
Bush, J., 'How West Cages Asian Tigers in IMF Trap', *The Times* (London: 24 December 1997).
Chomsky, N., *Class Warfare: Interview with D. Barsamian* (London: Pluto Press, 1996).
Cohen, D., 'Born-again Husbands – a Promise or a Threat?, *The Independent* (London: 7 October 1997), 11.
Craig, S. C., *Broken Contract? Changing Relationships Between Americans and their Government* (Boulder, Co.: Westview Press, 1996).
Davies, P. J., *An American Quarter Century: US Politics From Vietnam to Nixon* (Manchester University Press: 1995).
Dejevsky, M., 'The Promise People want Men Back in Charge', *The Independent* (London: 4 October 1997), 11.
Drucker, P. F., 'Really Reinventing Government', *The Atlantic Monthly*, Vol. 275 (February 1995), 49–61.
—— 'The Age of Social Transformation', *The Atlantic Monthly*, Vol. 274, No. 5 (November 1994), 53–80.
Flanders, S., 'Portrait: Robert Reich', *Prospect* (Issue 20, June 1997), 46–9.

Freedman, S. G., *The Inheritance: How Three Families and America Moved from Roosevelt to Reagan and Beyond* (New York: Simon & Schuster, 1996).
Fukuyama, F., *Trust: the Social Virtues and the Creation of Prosperity* (London: Hamish Hamilton, 1995).
Handler, J. T. and Hasenfeld, Y., *We the Poor People: Work, Poverty, and Welfare* (New Haven: Yale University Press, 1997).
Hodgson, G., *The World Turned Rightside Up: a History of the Conservative Ascendancy in America* (Mariner Books: Houghton Mifflin, 1996).
Levine, R. A., 'The Empty Symbolism of American Politics', *The Atlantic Monthly*, Vol. 278, No. 4 (October 1996), 80–4.
Lind, M., *Up From Conservatism: Why the Right is Wrong for America* (New York: Free Press, 1996).
Lipset, S. M., *American Exceptionalism: a Double-Edged Sword* (W. W. Norton, 1996).
Mackenzie, G. C. and Thornton, S., *Bucking the Deficit: Economic Policy Making in America* (Boulder Co.: Westview Press, 1996).
McKay, D., 'Campaigning and Governing: the 1996 US Presidential Elections', *Government and Opposition*, Vol. 32, No. 1 (Summer 1997), 25–38.
Patterson, J. T., *Grand Expectations. The United States, 1945–1974*, The Oxford History of the United States, Vol. 10 (Oxford: Oxford University Press, 1996).
Ribuffo. L. P., 'Promise Keepers on the Mall', *Dissent* (New York: Winter 1998), 10–13.
Schrag, P., 'Politics: California, Here We Come', *The Atlantic Monthly*, Vol. 281, No. 3 (March 1998), 20–40.
Schwarz, B., 'The Diversity Myth: America's Leading Export', *The Atlantic Monthly*, Vol. 275, No. 5 (May 1995), 57–67.
Steizer, I., 'Mayors Show how to Make America Work', *Sunday Times*, Business Section (12 October 1997).
Strange, S., 'The Limits of Power', *Government and Opposition*, Vol. 30, No. 3 (Summer 1995), 291–311.
—— *The Retreat of the State: the Diffusion of Power in the World Economy* (Cambridge: Cambridge University Press, 1996).
The Economist, 'All Aboard for Campaign Finance Reform' (London: 4 October 1997), 59.
Tolchin, S. J., *The Angry American: How Voter Rage is Changing the Nation* (Boulder, Co.: Westview Press, 1996).
Valladao, A. G., *The Twenty-First Century will be American* (London: Verso, 1996).
Vidal, G., *United States: Essays 1952–1992*, 'The Second American Revolution' (London: André Deutsch, 1993).
Vulliamy, E., 'Read Our Lips – Don't Cut Taxes', *The Observer* (London: 31 August 1997), 15.
Walker, M., *The President They Deserve* (London: Vintage Books, 1997).
Walsh, L. E., *Firewall. The Iran-Contra Conspiracy and Cover-Up* (W. W. Norton, 1997).
Walzer, M., 'Campaign Financing: Four Views', *Dissent* (New York: Summer 1997), 5–11.

Watkins, T. H., *The Great Depression: America in the 1930s* (Boston: Back Bay Books, Little Brown, 1993).
Weisberg, J., *In Defense of Government* (Scribners, 1996).
Wilcox, C., *Onward Christian Soldiers: the Religious Right in America* (Boulder, Co.: Westview Press, 1996).
Wilson, W. J., *When Work Disappears: the World of the New Urban Poor* (Knopf, 1996).
Wintour, P., 'Ghetto Busters to Tackle Poverty in Can-do Mood', *The Observer* (London: 7 December 1997).
Wolfe, A., *One Nation, After All* (New York: Viking, 1998).

4 The Underclass and Joblessness

1. UNEMPLOYMENT

In 1994, the Organization for Economic Co-operation and Development (OECD) published a 'job study' report which had a salutary effect. For some fifty postwar years, the western world had lived with the comforting presumption that the specter of unemployment had been laid to rest once and for all. Until the mid-1970s, that presumption had been largely correct. Thanks to the task of rebuilding shattered economies, pent-up demand, and when required, Keynesian intervention, accompanied with regular growth, held joblessness at bay. Under the impact of the 1970s' oil crisis – and, as we contend, even more so the gathering momentum of computerization – the situation started to change. Recession, deflation and the later stagflation put millions out of work. Yet the incidence was largely sporadic, confined to rust-belt, smoke-stack communities cut off from the mainstream, and wherever extensive considered to be of short-term duration. The OECD report put an end to such complacency (OECD, 1994). Mass unemployment had returned with a vengeance. Throughout the world's twenty-five leading economies comprising the membership of the OECD, the incidence of unemployment, previously confined to some 10 million people, was now affecting 8.5 percent of the labor force, and had risen to some 35 million. Moreover, taking account of the unrecorded additional millions who, disenchanted with prospects, had given up looking for work, the total would rise further still. An estimated additional 15–18 million people would need to be included, raising the actual total close to 13 percent.

Europe, comfortably above the norm with regard to affluence, fared the worst. There, unemployment levels were highest. In addition, long-term joblessness had taken root, while young people, especially males, were singularly affected. Whilst allowing for job mobility plus the residue of unemployables the 'normal unemployment' rate is considered to veer around 5 percent. Within the fifteen European Union states, the official rate had risen to 12 percent, as much as 15.8 percent in Ireland, and to 22.4 percent in Spain. As many as one-third of school leavers in some of the countries – above all in Spain and Italy – were unsuccessful in finding a job. Additionally, long-term unemployment, the surest indicator of consolidation, had established itself. More than one in four jobless persons had been out of work for more than one year, mounting close to 60 percent in Italy, Belgium and Spain (OECD, 1994: 9–14).

Other countries, by contrast, were doing relatively well. Japan, at that time still ranked as a successful buoyant exemplar, had a mere 2.5 percent rate of unemployment, while in the United States it amounted to no more than 6.7 percent, with long-term joblessness standing at 15.4 percent and 11.2 percent respectively. In the eyes of the OECD analysts, the cause for the divergent performance was not hard to seek. According to the OECD 'unemployment is probably the most widely feared phenomenon of our time' (OECD, 1994: 7) and that it 'creates insecurity and resistance to organisational and technological change, is de-motivating and self-reinforcing' (ibid.: 41). Furthermore, since unemployment jeopardizes the very democratic structure on which stability rests, the report delivered a stringent rebuke. Three prevailing assumptions were given short shrift. It was firmly denied that technological change, and imports from low-wage countries, or the intensity of competition as such, in any significant way carried the blame. The motto was, and is, 'adapt and survive' – an injunction that a few countries heeded, whilst others had not. The adherence to policies such as statutory minimum wages, generous unemployment benefits or job protection, when conditions had drastically changed, made European countries arthritic. Adverse employment effects can be cured only by reversing the role of the state: by reduced public spending, deregulation and especially benefit cut-backs plus the ending of job protection. 'Flexibility' – the new panacea – implying a retreat from welfare provision, for the first time made its presence felt on the world stage. When globally consumer demand had, more than ever, scope for expansion, worries about a new era of 'jobless growth' under the impact of technological progress were declared as unfounded. The United States, despite its low pay policy (or could it be, because of it?), where nearly one-fifth of all full-time workers were below the poverty line, was proclaimed as the paragon (OECD, 1994: 27, 33).

The report is invaluable for its comprehensive courage, and for opening up this crucial debate. We do, however, strongly dissent from its conclusions. Technological change, in the sense of advanced computerization together with the informatics highway, we consider, has dramatically transformed not merely labor markets, but modern societies altogether in virtually every dimension. As we will set out below, the still largely implicit impact for good or ill is immeasurable. Before turning to this, we will briefly review the changes in the unemployment position that have occurred in the meantime.

Between 1994 and mid-1998, there has been both consolidation and change. Japanese unemployment, though still remarkably low, has at 4.1 percent risen by almost one-third, while the two Anglo-Saxon nations, Britain and the United States, have notably moved in the reverse direction. At 6.4 percent, the British unemployment rate has fallen by well over a third, while the United States at 4.3 percent stands at a 28-year low, having declined by over 27 percent. Europe, however, has lapsed even further. The European Union average unemployment rate has risen to just over 10 percent, reaching levels of 12 percent in Italy and France, and still higher in Spain, at 19.6 percent. Even Germany, that vaunted bastion of general well-being and dedicated hard work, has not been immune. Its unemployment rate of 12.6 percent, with 4.8 million out of work (February 1998), represented a record high since the grim days of Weimar and one moreover that only just shows signs of receding. In eastern Germany, one in five remain unemployed despite massive investment with the Kohl administration's 'Alliance for jobs' delivering nothing. German trade unions claim that but for make-work schemes the real total would be close to 6 million. Vainly, *The Economist* goes on to observe that: 'In 1996 Chancellor Helmut Kohl pledged to halve German unemployment by 200 ... Spain's prime minister, José Maria Aznar, has promised that 1997 will be "the year for jobs" ... Jacques Chirac was elected president in 1995 partly because he offered to do most to cut French unemployment' (*The Economist*, 5 April 1997). Throughout the European Union, more than 40 percent of those jobless have been out of work for more than one year. In Spain almost one-half of those below the age of 24 are officially out of work, while in France and Italy, more than one-quarter of youths are unemployed, though faring a little better, and are similarly in dire straits.

The villain of the piece, as before, is purportedly the European reluctance to move with the times. Minimum wages, job protection plus term-less unemployed benefits, linked to the welfare state provision of universal medical coverage and public housing, are still charged with obstructing labor markets. While a formidable crutch to the employed labor force, conversely 'the poor are out of a job' (*The Economist*, 5 April 1997: 21). Americans are beginning to resuscitate the term 'Eurosclerosis' symbolized by the French lorry drivers' dispute in November 1997, itself a re-run of one a year earlier, as: 'the favourite symbol of economic perversity, barricading the road to US style prosperity' (*The Times*, 11 December 1997). By way of contrast, America is viewed as the ideal model. There, with 138 000 new jobs created in one single month, the message now is that 'anyone who wants to work pretty much can ... Employers are increasingly having a difficult time finding unemployed people who want to work' (*San Diego Union Tribune*, 7 June 1997: A1). In President Clinton's 'State of the Union' address delivered on 27 January 1998, he spoke of the 14 million new jobs created since he became president in 1992, adding: 'Our leadership of the world is unrivaled.' The fact that a mere 11 percent – one-quarter of the European proportion – have been out of work for more than one year, serves as a reinforcing factor of vindication. 'Flexibility' is the mantra even more than before. Respond to – or better still, anticipate – the rapidly changing conditions, and all will be well. Technology, as the OECD report presaged, creates as many jobs as it takes away. Remove the inhibiting obstacles, and the path forward is clear.

Reality, however, is somewhat less rosy. Bare statistics tend to conceal as much as they reveal. Observers have for some time spoken of the United States as a dual economy, divided, on the one hand, between those in regular full-time employment, and on the other, what has come to be known as the growing 'discretionary labor force'. The former typically enjoy regular hours and pay, occupational benefits, access to union representation, and generally the prospect of progressive careers. Conversely, discretionary workers – made up of part-timers, casuals, home workers, and increasingly subcontractors converted into involuntary 'independent contractors' – are devoid of security, social provision, union affiliation and progressive careers. The current trend has been in one direction. The regular labor force has steeply declined, while the co-discretionary element has consistently risen. There are no hard and fast rules of measurement, but the contrast between the United States and Europe is marked. Whilst it is true that America 'creates and destroys jobs with a verve Europe gawps at' (*The Economist*, 30 July 1994: 20), they are overwhelmingly in the arena of contingent employment.

Already by 1993 temporary workers comprised 15 percent of the US labor force, while the Manpower temp-agency with its 600 000 contingent (compared to 400 000 for General Motors) had grown into the largest private employer. In March 1994, the largest monthly job gain was recorded in the past six years. Out of the 465 000 jobs created, a full 349 000 – more than three-quarters – fell into the contingent employment category (Chomsky, 1994: 13). As a general rule: 'temporary jobs accounted for two of every three new private-sector jobs' (Rifkin, 1995: 191). The 1997 Census Bureau data revealed that three out of ten Americans – 34.5 million people – are now in 'non-standard jobs', with average earnings some one-quarter lower than in their previous employment. They may or may not be 'pseudo-workers in pseudo-jobs' – the oft-cited hamburger flippers – but as Will Hutton contends, 'after all, if you include the inactive and part-time workers looking for full-time work, US unemployment stands at 14 percent' (Hutton, 1996).

The contrast with Europe is startling, engendering a new form of American exceptionalism. Europe, alongside a well-protected and highly paid labor force, has developed a workless contingent assisted by generous social benefits plus unemployment provision. They have assumed a decisive self-consciousness by asserting that 'people should be able to choose for themselves to work or not', disdaining the American pseudo-work pattern, and claiming new rights 'to do decent and useful work, to fulfill themselves and develop on the job' (Engbertsen et al., 1993: 121). Whilst a potent factor in the continent's growing stagnation and loss of competitiveness, their role is insidious, forming the core of resurgent neo-fascist political movements in countries like France, Germany and Austria – and a grim reminder of the interwar years (Weisskopf, 1996: 378).

The USA so far has miraculously succeeded in converting the bulk of the newly dispossessed into adherents of the American dream. In the first place, due to greater advance in promoting advanced automation, the contingent labor force not only comprises the manual lesser skilled, but has bitten far deeper into the ex-managerial ranks, already inured in the mind-set of individualistic success. As Kuttner observes: 'Far from cherishing their experienced employees, some Fortune 500 corporations today literally invite their experienced workers to bid to keep their jobs by taking pay cuts... Large corporations are pursuing strategies of retaining as few core employees as possible, pursuing the maximum possible degree of flexibility in how they take on labor. Consultants offer seminars on how to convert a large portion of the work force from permanent staff to contingent employees... The new information technology facilitates this shift. Business can use temp agencies, independent consultants, or subcontractors to increase or decrease their payroll, day by day... In this new economy, everyone is a capitalist, whether as an owner of a firm or free-lance' (Kuttner, 1997: 75).

Thanks to a fortuitous sleight of hand, the United States has avoided the pitfalls that blight Europe today. Not only does the nation once again enjoy near full employment plus prosperity, but the occupationally dispossessed remain firmly ideologically aligned. Competitive, eager and ready for compromise, their allegiance to the American dream is, if anything, stronger than before. Yet for all that, *The Economist*, a publication which routinely commends 'the American way', arrives at the baleful conclusion that, in regard to social disruption, America has already 'passed the point of no return' (*The Economist*, 3 July 1994: 19). The cause is the new underclass, a phenomenon intrinsically different from the European scenario. It incorporates not the mainstream downsized and unemployed, but overwhelmingly racial minorities, predominantly comprising an inner-city black community and to a lesser extent newcomer Hispanics, many of whom remain marginalized, polarized and confined to decayed ghettos. These people are isolated from the mainstream, and increasingly mobilized within a counter-culture that, while still strangely quiescent, prospectively poses a threat to the very structure of civic society.

2. THE UNDERCLASS

It is important to note at the outset that the underclass concept is highly contested, and that consequently discussion needs to be qualified. Historically the concept, however terminologically defined, has always been a metaphor applied to the urban poor and their family pathology (Katz, 1993: 469). Today's stereotypical underclass is composed of diverse groupings, labeled and stigmatized in an undifferentiated way, but with the highlighted elements of 'the social outcasts' constituting the major component in public presumption. Thus, Gans defines the stratum as follows: 'A large group of people who are more intractable, more socially alien and more hostile than almost anyone had imagined. They are the unreachables: the American underclass' (Gans, 1995: 32). Much of the debate has been framed by the right. Charles Murray blames the easy availability of welfare, regarded now as a right and no longer a stigma, for removing the distinction between the deserving and the undeserving poor. It acts as a disincentive to work, promoting feckless social behavior together with irresponsible family attitudes (Murray, 1984: 182). Rising illegitimacy and the culture of poverty produce crime, he contends, with growing numbers of dysfunctional families headed by single female parents, often still in their early teens, as a consequence. The solution advocated, and finding an ever more eager echo in federal policy as well as public support, is simple: cut welfare with its 'dependency', promote opportunity, and support those already in work. The Clinton 'Personal Responsibility Act' of 1996 embodies much of the spirit of the new right.

The left's response, partly disarmed by the actions of the Democratic president, has been mixed. Pointing to the fact that amongst all social classes single parenthood had increased, or that drastic welfare cuts had not induced a tapering off in demand (Jenks, 1991), has done little to diminish support for the policies now being pursued. Other variables are equally significant: the change in the labor market with greatly fewer jobs for the lower-skilled; the massive deindustrialization, strengthening the move to a service economy requiring a higher entry level education; dismal inner-city schooling; and the increasing racial residential re-segregation, with inner-city blacks now extensively polarized, have all reinforced the rise of the underclass (Wilson, 1987, 1996; Massey and Denton, 1993). The 'problem' thus needs to be viewed less in behavioral or cultural terms focusing on deviants and the anti-socials, but more emphatically in a structural perspective where educational disadvantage, racism and self-perpetuating poverty play a primary role. Welfare recipients, of whom only a minority are black, are in fact only one-third of the total formally defined as being in poverty (Handler and Hasenfeld, 1997).

Were it not for the fact that a significant proportion of the underclass is typically out of work, it would be apt to speak of America as a triple economy. Approximately one privileged half of the labor force is in regular full-time employment, while the other half is divided between a larger discretionary labor force and the mainly black underclass. Rifkin offers an interesting variant upon the prevailing premise which relates the emergence of the underclass directly to the downsizing of the lower-grade industrial workforce undertaken since the early 1970s. As Rifkin perceives the situation, its origin dates back to the arrival of the mechanical cotton picker in the South in 1944 which, at a stroke, put many thousands of sharecroppers out of work and compelled them to seek their fortune in the factories of the North (Rifkin, 1995: 71–7). For some twenty-five years, they were prospering economically. During the growth years there was ample work and pay was quite good. Yet even then, in the days of relative well-being, the omens were there. In the inner-city slums to which they migrated, their destiny was essentially predetermined by low-grade housing, failing schools, lack of facilities, together with racial prejudice and discrimination. Within a few years the suburban flight of many whites ensured their polarization. Chronic unemployment followed, with mass lay-offs in local factories and other places of work, which rapidly aggravated the crisis. The black underclass became an established fact of American life.

The most explicit analysis comes from Ralf Dahrendorf, one of Europe's leading intellectuals, who in reference to the 'precarious balance' bluntly admits that 'some people are – awful as it is even to put this on paper – simply not needed ... they are a cost to the rest, not a benefit' (Dahrendorf, 1995: 25). Nothing could better describe the fate of the American underclass. Technological change in the shape of machine intelligence has upended the nature of work. Thanks to advanced automation, work is becoming a scarce commodity, and those with modest skills are simply redundant. Indeed, faced with overseas low wage competition in older traditional industries such as textiles, steel and apparel, their fate, and not just for the underclass, is perilous. Within the context of the prevailing individualistic ideology, they are left to fend for themselves. We consider the issue of machine intelligence to be of primary importance as the century moves to its end. We will consider its reverberations in this chapter's last section, and will turn to it once again at a later stage. Meanwhile, for setting the scene, it is appropriate to consider some of the sociological implications of the underclass.

Black life expectancy is 6.4 years lower than that of whites. Infant mortality is greater by a factor of three, the incidence of unemployment is more than double, and the child poverty rate is 2.7 times greater (Mishel and Bernstein, 1993: 39, 227, 286). Comprising 12 percent of the national population, blacks account for three-quarters of the long-term unemployed, and two-thirds of children born out of wedlock. One in four black males is either in prison or out on probation, while nine-tenths assert they have never been married – explaining the fact that the bulk of welfare recipients is composed of young women (Magnet, 1993). In a number of communities, one-half of blacks, particularly the young, are out of work (Yates, 1994: 64). And in New York which, as Cockburn reminds us 'was supposed to be a pioneer from the old manufacturing base to a "world city", 1.8 million are on welfare, with black youths' labor market participation down to one-tenth. One in four New Yorkers is a pauper, in the Bronx the rate is 40%' (Cockburn, 1994: B7). Luttwark argues that in the inner cities prevailing conditions approximate third world standards in terms of housing conditions, homelessness, schooling or public hygiene (Luttwark, 1993). In Washington, the nation's capital, 42 percent of black men aged 18–25 are either in jail, out on parole, awaiting trial or being sought by the police (Rifkin, 1995: 77–8). Altogether, with more than one-half of young black males jobless and also more likely to end up in jail rather than college (O'Hare, 1991), it is tempting to speak of 'Two Nations' between whom – as Benjamin Disraeli, Queen Victoria's favorite prime minister observed – 'there is no intercourse or sympathy, who are as ignorant of each other's habits, thoughts and feelings as if they were dwellers in different zones or inhabitants of different planets' (*New Republic*, 13 April 1994: 30).

For all that, with the exception of a few periodic outbursts such as the 1992 Los Angeles riots, the black underclass, in its inner-city ghettos, has been remarkably quiescent. The counter-culture of crime, drugs and work allergy has been virtually self-contained and inner-directed. That is to say, the huge cost of containment apart, they have barely spilled over into white communities. Hard metal music, modes of clothing or even their overt non-conformist lifestyle have barely penetrated into the value pattern of white youth. Of course, the soaring financial and social costs of containment of the drug scene are stupendous: '14 000 dead each year; a soaring prison population; indirect costs put at $67 billion each year' (*The Economist*, 15 November 1997: 36). However, that vast network is activated primarily by consumer demand – who takes all that heroin or sniffs all that cocaine? – a vicious circle of law defiance in which black underclass youths become mere dispensable underlings.

Were it not for the rumblings in other directions, it is perfectly possible to image a world where this state of affairs could endure for a number of years. After all, at some 4–5 million the black underclass is only a minuscule proportion of the national population, at just under 2 percent. Given a modicum of reward, such as a regular flow of social welfare benefits, some job training, infrastructural improvements plus – were administrators creative enough – diversions in leisure, sport, entertainment and gaming, the situation remains confinable. Add to this strict law enforcement, including such draconian policies as the 'three strikes and you are out' policy, extensive incarceration in prison, whilst, for the ambitious, disguised forms of affirmative action offering an escape route into the middle class, and the imbalance could be maintained, with the black underclass effectively insulated in their ghettos.

Latterly, however, a potentially more disturbing phenomenon has arisen. Its organic roots reaching back into the civil rights struggle, the 'Nation of Islam' consciousness is gathering strength in several dimensions. This 'movement' was originally the preserve of militant hotheads, who for both functional as well as symbolic ends were committed to methods of violence, with their alienation from the indigenous core notably marked. The part-conformist, part-evangelical new wave of the black middle class is resurgent. The extremist Louis Farrakhan wing, both ultra-black nationalistic, separatist and linked to white fascists such as LaRouche (Marable, 1998), has been partially eclipsed by the evident ardor of such as the Million Men March and its subsequent women's counterpart. It is as yet a fundamentalist type of eruption – to paraphrase, 'conformists without a cause' – with, so far, decidedly nowhere to go. Injunctions such as 'brother love brother' or 'sister buy from sister' may make striking headlines, but pragmatically do not seem to offer programs for change, neither in personal let alone social terms. The connection between an overwhelmingly middle-class composition and a black underclass – or to express it somewhat differently, signs of a common black consciousness – have so far not been made. The resegregation movement that in the 1990s visibly turned the clock back upon the American *e pluribus unum* cohesion, has failed to reach across the intra-black class divide. There are still separate black middle and underclass schools, churches, residential neighborhoods, family patterns and, even more significantly, adaptations to mainstream society that stand in the way of forging unity.

Islamic fundamentalists have traditionally risen to power by marrying the aspirations of the urban insurgent intelligentsia to the potency of the dispossessed. America may not have a direct parallel. Nationally an intelligentsia in any authentic sense is lacking. The leadership input will need to come from a currently amorphous group of the prominent, characteristically beneficiaries of affirmative action, yet for all that resentful at real or imagined racial constraints. At the opposite end, the masses are waiting. As in other fundamentalist situations, inhabitants of the ghetto – economically redundant, inured to violence, indifferent to their own lives no less than others – are at the same time supremely equipped with a simulacrum of the very flexibility which, it is alleged, is the pathway to grace and favor in the legitimate world.

As yet, the balance of probabilities is highly ambivalent. As the supreme open society, America might well find a key to fully integrate the black middle class within all levels of the wider community: breaking through the final glass ceiling, just as other impediments have been left behind. The easy manner in which professional blacks have risen among the senior levels of political life, the judiciary, the military, corporations and academia – culminating in 1996 in the real possibility of a first American black president in the person of Colin Powell – bodes well in its promise of a new form of multiculturalism within which even the black middle class may find full acceptance. On the other hand, the prevailing winds of individualist non-interventionism diminish the likelihood of providing the positive strategies needed to uplift the underclass from its ongoing plight. With liberal reformism in headlong retreat, there is no sign whatever of a New Deal to integrate the dispossessed – and now economically unwanted – from their marginalized state. Pleas from Julius Wilson and others to recognize the claims of the 'ghetto poor' go largely unheeded. Wilson's approach remains universalistic, however, committed to federal involvement and stressing the need for political alliances across the racial divide, as poverty and low skills extend beyond the inner city into suburban and rural areas. He wants to focus on 'the relationship between employment and education and family support systems and, in the metropolitan context, the relationship between cities and suburbs' (Wilson, 1996: 569). The type of Commission to resolve racism invoked by President Clinton in 1997 could only make a slight remedial difference to the evident schism at best. Relief will certainly not come from the opposite side of the political spectrum. The most likely candidates to espouse the cause of the black underclass, now that Jewish support has been alienated, is and must remain their ethnic middle-class peers, the very social group now heading in the direction of fundamentalist affiliation. Militancy rather than reintegration, were this to occur, must objectively appear the more likely prospect. For all the pain and rancor this may entail, it at least offers one positive sign of relief for the underclass.

One final comment is apt. In a recent study Roger Waldinger dissents from the 'mismatch' thesis which accounts for the imbalance between the demands of the labor market and the available labor supply (Waldinger, 1996). Originally propounded by Julius Wilson, and now the prevailing premise, the mismatch thesis points on the one hand to the burgeoning gulf between the demand for knowledge-intensive skilled people, as against the minorities who lack the qualifications required by the information-producing industries, and so cannot find work (Wilson, 1987). Accordingly, consolidated within an undifferentiated underclass, the thesis maintains, minorities are caught equally in the same net. Pointing to the wide array of affluence-determined lower grade service jobs sprouting in the inner cities and drawing his evidence from New York, Waldinger rebuts this presumption. The Chinese, Koreans, Taiwanese, Vietnamese, and increasingly the entire gamut of Latinos – forming an ethnic hiring queue – do not share the blacks' record of worklessness. By dint of hard work and dependability they are, slowly to be sure, inching their way up the ladder to full assimilation. What they possess and the blacks lack is the tight network of co-ethnic settlers to whom the newcomers flock and who then become instrumental in hosting their work through facilitating 'ethnic niches'.

The black community is doubly handicapped. In the first place they are devoid of the conduit leading to lower grade jobs, and secondly as long established citizens, they look upon the lowly paid menial jobs as being intrinsically worthless and with utter disdain. Though possibly good enough for third world newcomers, they are well beneath the dignity of native Americans and so are ignored. When forced to such work by exigencies that are viewed as inherently status-debasing amongst their own peer groups, then only overt self-destructive contempt can restore their prestige. The manifest ease with which many non-blacks negotiate their way up the social scale lends weight to Waldinger's argument. If in any way accurate, this further depreciates the black underclass situation. With public employment, their traditional preserve, it had somewhat ironically recently placed middle-class blacks negotiating sensitive welfare proposals with the black poor. In any case many such jobs within a declining municipal welfare state will themselves be under threat making them potentially the outstanding victims of the continuing immigrant open-door policy. This would ultimately line them up in direct opposition against their former allies. Before weighing the full implications of this further inhibition, we will briefly consider the issue of inequality next.

3. INEQUALITY

America has historically been an exceedingly unequal society. Wealth distribution is twice as heavily concentrated compared to France and trebly to Britain (Wills, 1996: 16), while income distribution follows an equally disparate path. The quest for success has, in what is held out to be a classless society, always been given a major priority. Inherited status is less valued, while riches confer social honor with alacrity. Even questionably acquired wealth is rapidly legitimated. The ground rules are known and generalized: fortune favors the brave; effort and enterprise are duly rewarded. Equality of opportunity, with the starting point equal for all, is naturally presupposed.

For some fifty years, the New Deal mitigated the strict market focus. Social legislation protected the weak, the sick and the indigent in some measure against the vagaries of unrestrained competition. Redistribution, further promoted through the tax system, notably narrowed the gap. Then, in the 1980s under the Reagan regime, the safeguards were gradually set aside. Supply side economics, with the emphasis on deregulation and the market as the ultimate arbiter in resource allocation, made a comeback. Its philosophy was that policies of low taxation, freedom of enterprise, plus non-intervention would, as a rising tide, lift the level for everyone. Trickle-down economics was to ensure prosperity for the poor as well as the rich.

Clearly this has not happened. Except for a minority of the privileged who have done extraordinarily well, the outcome has been one of stagnation. Not until well into 1997 did incomes begin to rise in real terms for the first time in a decade. In October of that year, average incomes in real terms had risen by 1.5 percent over the previous year. However, as 5'1" Robert Reich, Labor Secretary during the first Clinton administration, reminds his audiences, averaging his height with that of the 7'1" Laker superstar, his average height becomes 6'1". Averages, in other words, can be misleading. In the past ten years, the rich have benefited from market exigencies extensively, while at the lower end of the income scale, conditions have drastically declined. 'In the shadow of prosperity' as Madrick terms it (1997), the 73 million blue- and white-collar labor force workers have gained a nominal income rise of 142 percent in real money terms, in the face of an inflation rate of 183 percent. Thus, in practical terms they have lost a quarter of their purchasing power (made up typically by dual household employment as against the previous sole male breadwinner of the past). Against that, the 'compensation' of the higher paid executives has ballooned by 951 percent, at five times the inflation rate, moving the authors of *America, Who Stole the Dream?* to claim that: 'the American dream of the last half-century has been revoked for millions of people – a dream rooted in a secure job, a house in the suburbs, the options for families to live on one income rather than two, a better life than your parents had and a still better life for your children' (Bartlett and Steele, 1996: 7–8). On the other hand, the households who in today's dollars report a million-plus annual income have risen five-fold to 68 000 since 1979. 'By the early 1990s', Madrick postulates, 'some Wall Street money managers were earning $100 million and eventually even $1 billion in a single year' (Madrick, 1997: 42). By way of contrast, even the official poverty rate of 13.8 percent apparently does not entirely reflect the state of affairs at the opposite end of the spectrum. As many as 28 percent of the population – some 90 million Americans – according to Hacker deserved to be rated in the deprived category (Hacker, 1997). Statistically, the top 20 percent of income earners, taking home 45 percent of the national income, receive eleven times the pay of the bottom 20 percent (compared to only 7.5 times in 1970), whose share amounts to a mere 4 percent (*The Economist* 1994: 19). During the past two decades' 'silent depressions', the typical worker's buying power has declined by 15 percent (Heilbroner, 1995: 81).

Wealth ownership is even more skewed whilst its impact is of even greater significance. Wealth confers power as well as compliance. It becomes consolidated via inheritance, while actively promoting accumulation towards even greater wealth-holding. Like income, the postwar redistributive trend has been reversed. In today's United States, according to Sklar (1995: 113), 'the richest one percent of American families have as much wealth as the entire bottom 95 percent. Such obscene inequality befits an oligarchy, not a democracy. Manhattan's income gap is worse than Guatemala's.' Fewer than 1 percent of the population own 48 percent of all national wealth (compared to 39 percent in 1989), while the top 10 percent lay claim to 70 percent (Krugman, 1994). Yet even the remaining 30 percent shared amongst nine-tenths of Americans, is similarly skewed. Vague as such projections are bound to be, it is estimated that close to one-half of Americans possess a net worth of nil, or even a negative balance. That is to say, were they financially to be wound up, their net assets would be less than their outstanding debts (Bradley, 1997: B9).

Among this welter of inequities, it will hardly be surprising that the ethnic minorities fare the worst. One-third of Afro-Americans and a similar proportion of Latinos are living below the poverty line, while in the past twenty-five years the average black income has fallen by 24 percent (Rifkin, 1995: 180). Compared to a white family's median income, the earnings of a typical Afro-American family today are even lower than twenty years past (Hacker, 1997).

The 'winner take all' society that radical capitalism promotes is widely denounced for its pitiless austerity. For all its euphemistic terminology, 'downsizing' means millions losing their jobs, 'flexibility' implies submitting to the harsher realities of the discretionary labor force, while 'competition' and 'enterprise' can be seen as the topside of the 'everyone for himself' philosophy of rational choice. Yet modern societies are in a quandary. Progress is universally equated with more and more growth, and economic growth emphatically works better in a market society. Michael Parenti, an overt sympathizer, recounts how 'rewarding inefficiency' came to be institutionalized in the state-controlled ex-Soviet system. Non-accountability led to the flagrantly wasteful use of material and human resources. Technological progress was thwarted by controllers' fear of raised quotas, whilst the *nomenklatura* rewarded mediocrity and stability rather than merit. Labor and material were massively hoarded against hypothetical shortages. At every level, with 'nobody minding the store', the unending proliferation of 'the tricks of the trade' turned job performance into a farce. The notoriously surly restaurant service, for example, with its unpalatable miserly meals, allowed the staff to idle and take the food home. Slack maintenance, rents uncollected, wholesale pilfering and rampant bribery, as much as anything else, led to the downfall of the regime (Parenti, 1997: 59–65). As the old joke had it 'you pretend to pay us and we will pretend to work'.

When weighed against the rampant materialism that now pervades the capitalist world, the scales are uneasily poised. On the one hand, extreme inequality induces social division and wastes human resources, causing avarice and crime. On the other hand, in terms of productivity, innovation and general standards of life, the market system indisputably remains supreme. The United States' head-start in technology, productivity and enterprise is, if anything, lengthening further. Furthermore, America scores similarly well in other dimensions. The Human Development Index – an amalgam of education, life expectancy, health, sanitation and female status with the economic variables of GDP and adjusted real incomes – spanning some 137 nations puts the USA a close second behind Canada, with Japan in third place. Similarly the 'Misery Index', a composite of unemployment and inflation, is only half as high as in Germany or France (*The Economist*, 25 October 1997: 114). Possibly more significant still, in regard to the 'fun for the masses' the United States is appreciably ahead. Leisure, historically the preserve of a tiny elite, has become democratized. In all its various facets, the masses are participants to a remarkable degree. According to a recent study recreational spending, extending to all, now accounts for 8.5 percent of national consumption, having in the past year risen by 7.7 percent as against the 5.5 percent for consumer spending as such. 'By lowering the price of entertainment' one report concludes, 'technology has improved the standard of living of those at the lower end of the income scale' (*The Economist*, 2 August 1997: 62).

Yet such benefits should not blind one to radical capitalism's dark underside. Rising levels of inequality, the inevitable by-product, are socially divisive and corrosive to public morale. For all its success in job creation, the American model of laissez-faire deregulation is deleterious to integration and social accord. Ostensibly the 'two-third society' in which the affluent upper tier is waxing rich, may well induce a spirit of complacency that dismisses the fate of misery and deprivation that the lower one-third experience as inevitable and self-deserved (Habermas, 1994). Democracy is a fragile structure that cannot for long endure social neglect. The prejudicial behavioral pattern of the underclass in respect of early school leaving, teenage pregnancy, crime, drugs and work allergy is potentially contagious. The incipient undercurrent of social conflict inherent in such extremism, though embryonic, now prevails widely and is a signal of prospective disruption that, once active, may not be easily stilled.

The political process itself is made a mockery of when the way in which money buys office is flagrantly daily displayed. In the 1996 election, candidates with the largest purse – primarily incumbents relying on donors' war chests – won 88 percent of the Senate and 92 percent of the House contests, while less than 1 percent of the population funded $597 million out of the total $734 million that was spent altogether. Steve Forbes, one of the Republicans who fell by the wayside in his presidential bid, alone spent $37.4 million of his own money on his abortive campaign. Political life has never been spotlessly clean. The gross civic distortions, increasingly evident, that rising inequality is laying bare must give rise to serious concern. Graver still, we believe, is the growing job deficit to which we will next turn.

The November 1997 European 'Job Summit' predictably ended in a 'hot air about jobs' stalemate. Despite leaders' upbeat declarations of 'new directions', the building of 'a social Europe' or the overplayed 'historic turning point', when it came to resolving the issue of joblessness, the achievement turned out to be nil. 'How not to make jobs in Europe' *The Economist* dubbed its failure to deregulate, make labor markets more flexible and start to trim welfare (*The Economist*, 29 November 1997: 52). All of that, the USA has done with reckless abandon. Labor markets are infinitely flexible, there are no constraints on deregulation, while welfare trimming is currently underway. Yet job creation, breaking new records month after month, has turned into a mere numbers game. Temporary jobs, as noted earlier, typically account for two out of three of every new private-sector job (Rifkin, 1995: 191). The more jobs that flow out of the pipeline in ascending profusion, the greater the proportion of the 'reserve army' pseudo-type jobs. Jobs that look good in public statistics, but for those compelled to take them are devoid of benefits, possess no security and all too often do not pay a living wage. In both arenas – America as well as Europe – the dual economy reflects a 'two-thirds' society that inexorably wends its perilous way. The conclusion that '"while jobs, jobs . . . jobs" is regarded as the solution to crime, homelessness, hunger, education, and loss of revenue' and that 'if jobs are the solution, we are in big trouble' (Aronowitz and Difazio 1994: xi–xii) cannot be avoided for ever. One is reminded of the Nottingham hand-weavers who, some two centuries past in rapidly industrializing England, vainly tried to turn the clock back, setting out on their nightly trysts to destroy the dreaded machines that had wiped out their trade. Their attempt tragically ended in shootings, mass arrests plus executions, but hardly deterred the process. Within a few years their cherished jobs had become history, the machine loom a universally used means of production.

One wishes neither to be judgmental, nor to suggest that technological determinism is predominant. Nevertheless, in conditions where the materialist imperative is ascendant, productive advances will sooner or later come to hold sway offering the prospect of a third Industrial Revolution. Having made itself master of the universe and now capturing space, mankind stands on the brink of approaching its most cherished dream: the conquest of scarcity and with it the conquest of toil and social injustice. Machine intelligence might take us as close to universalization as interactive constraints could allow. Marx once famously put the context of liberated society as well as anyone when he stated that in: 'Communal Society where nobody has one exclusive sphere of activity but each can become accomplished in any one branch he wishes, society regulates the general production and thus makes it possible for me to do one thing today and another tomorrow, to hunt in the morning, fish in the afternoon, rear cattle in the evening, criticise after dinner, just as I have in mind, without ever becoming hunter, fisherman, shepherd or critic' (Marx, 1846, quoted in Tucker, 1978: 160).

Clearly such utopian projection might never materialize. Twentieth-century events would make one chary of projecting perfectibility under any conditions. Yet, given social effort combined with open-mindedness, a reasonable approximation stands within grasp. For pragmatic purposes Judith Schor's analysis graphically points the way. As she observes: 'Since 1948 productivity has failed to rise in only five years. The level of productivity of the U.S. worker has more than doubled. In other words, we could now produce our 1948 standard of living (measured in terms of marketed goods and services) in less than half the time it took that year. We actually could have chosen the four-hour day. Or a working year of six months. Or every worker in the United States could now be taking every other year off from work – with pay. Incredible as it may sound, this is just the simple arithmetic of productive growth in operation' (Schor, 1991: 2).

Yet, at the same time, while the intervening years have brought further productive advance, Americans are working longer hours with greater job stress, longer commuting and fewer benefits. A majority of households are impelled to dual employment, escalating house prices, less upward mobility, in fact harsher conditions than at any time since the depression (Newman, 1993). Americans,

Rifkin summarizes, 'are working longer hours today than forty years ago at the outset of the information-technology revolution ... More than 15 percent of all full-time workers put in forty-nine or more hours on the job each week' (Rifkin, 1995: 223).

Meanwhile the 'two-thirds' societies' Luddite response to the artificial intelligence revolution follows its merry course. The flow of technological progress within the advanced world that ought to substantially raise living standards all round is inhibited by one means or another in the two western power blocs. Within continental Europe, high social benefits, indefinite unemployment entitlement plus the consolidated resistance of the well-paid, discourages the downsizing that the United States and Britain were free to launch. Within the latter two, particularly America, corporate capital is sufficiently dominant to effect downsizing, thereby casualizing labor, while pocketing the enhanced profits that accrue. In both instances, ultimately the broad spectrum of the tax-paying middle class bears the actual burden. In Europe, taxes are high to pay for the 'welfare state'. While in the US ostensible taxes are appreciably lower, the public at large confronts the hidden costs of social neglect: a large contingent of lowly paid without health or pensions coverage, and even more drastically the huge rising costs of the underclass. The conservative *Business Weekly* in its survey on 'The Crisis of Urban America' postulates that the cost of providing for the underclass amounts to a staggering $230 billion per year (*Business Weekly*, 18 May 1997: 38). Yet for all that, while the 'haves' get by comfortably in largely settled lifestyles and progressive careers, decision-makers still preach the mantra of 'jobs, jobs ... jobs' seemingly unaware of what the future portends. Even Robert Reich, the Clinton administration's former Labor secretary with the most enlightened of credentials, follows the wrong track. His 'New Social Compact' calls on the corporate world to return to the socially responsible standards they ostensibly practiced in the postwar 'golden age'. Then, as he recalls, their workforce enjoyed not only secure employment, thanks to corporate goodwill, but equally all manner of social benefits. In this he seems sadly mistaken. Acute labor shortage plus expanding demand, in the context of restricted productive resources, impelled a corporate 'social conscience', like nothing else. Benevolence can play no part in corporate management. Competitively, those who indulge in it will go to the wall. Management is beholden to maximize stockholders' returns, with social engineering not their concern. When downsizing linked to labor casualization offers the best returns, then this becomes corporate policy.

Two events might disrupt the prevailing complacency: a consolidated consciousness on the part of the underprivileged one-third; or the possibility of one leading nation or regional body unilaterally breaking the restrictive mold. Within the United States, the discretionary labor force and the underclass remain two different entities, ideologically barely on speaking terms, while socially facing different ways. Transformed into para-capitalists and enrolled into the American individualist dream, the contingent labor force remains solidly anchored within the mainstream. The underclass, however, has become notably culturally deviant. It may take a while for the two to unite, and were this to happen, the more likely prospect is a proto-fascist alliance along nativist lines, rather than the desired progressive stance. Indeed the problems of constructing progressive alliances are immense, given the social and political changes of the last twenty years and made more difficult, as Wilson notes, because 'working class whites are more likely than middle class whites to express their hostility in blatantly racist terms and behavior' (Wilson, 1991: 477). The underclass has remained relatively quiescent, but the rising cost of policing and social control includes the latent possibility one day of a 'violent reaction' (Galbraith, 1993: 171).

As 'the new thinking machines make their way up the economic pyramid, absorbing more and more skilled jobs and tasks along their way' (Rifkin, 1995: 88), the underclass could one day extend into white suburban groups. Were this to happen, their mobilization potential would be greatly enhanced. The black underclass would find the leadership they presently lack, while new white recruits would mobilize the very masses that characteristically serve as the shock troops in right-wing revolt. Meanwhile the doctrine that 'government is the problem and not the solution', linked to the power of capital, inhibits the vanguard role in the third Industrial Revolution that, in view of its structural and technological primacy, America so richly deserves. At the same time there are signs that Europe is stealing a march. Despite critics contending that one of the reasons for Germany's high unemployment is due to their having the lowest annual working hours in Europe (Britain has the longest but one of the lowest rates of unemployment), Jospin's socialist government in France is sympathetic to the institutionalization of the thirty-five-hour week. Whilst Britain is initiating policies to integrate the 'social exclusion' minority, who according to Tony

Blair comprise 'people who do not have the means, material or otherwise, to participate in social, economic and cultural life' (*The Economist*, 6 December 1997: 59), they could become the first to actualize the incipient promise of the new age.

At the end of the line stands the proverbial 'free lunch'. The current imperative of 'there is no free lunch, you get what you pay for' is compelling. Were non-work to become fashionable as well as well-paid, the non-work ethic would stifle all effort, destroy incentive and jeopardize change. Who would do all the menial work, keep the streets safe, pay taxes? The answer is simple: the armies of our newly acquired mechanical slaves. Virtual-thinking computers, never recalcitrant, unwell or tired, doing our bidding, abundantly producing the goods and services that we require while we are busy in other directions – to develop our talents, help the community, socialize, have fun or sleep. Even if no further progress has taken place in the 1990s, Schor's analysis shows what could have been done. Transcending the watershed we could be working a half-week, a half-year of half of a lifetime transposing disposable labor into disposable free time while inanimate labor continued creating the output to maintain or enhance our wealth. There would be no loss in common wealth, quite the contrary, while new factors of production increasingly take over the tasks we once performed.

That such dramatic change cannot come about all on its own is palpably evident. Leaving it to the play of market forces alone, with work now a scarce commodity, would result in the most qualified, determined and incumbent seizing the lion's share, leaving the now 'excluded majority' to fend miserably for themselves. Governmental intervention alone, whatever its character, can resolve the conundrum: imposing constraint, sharing out work while, with national wealth accumulating by leaps and bounds, helping in the provision of outlets for voluntaristic, participatory, expansive effort. Toil, scarcity and social injustice could prospectively be consigned to the past.

Toffler's warning of 'some dystopian fantasy in which two percent of the population use robots and perform all the work, while 98 percent do none' stands as a somber warning of what could occur (Toffler, 1983: 29). André Gorz's extrapolation of the universal 20 000 hour per lifetime work voucher converts the dystopian vision into feasible pragmatic terms. 'Twenty thousand hours per lifetime represents 10 years' full-time work, or – a more likely choice – 40 years of intermittent work, part-time alternating with periods for holidays, or unpaid autonomous activity, community work, etc.' (Gorz,

1985: 41). Concomitantly, 'the free development of individuals, perhaps the most abiding element of human prevision, lies within reach within a society of free time' (Gorz, 1993: 353). Barry Jones, Australia's former Minister of Technology, charts the progression from the post-industrial to the post-service society. Having solved, he presumes, the problem of material subsistence that had always exceeded all else, humankind stands on the brink of replacing *homo laboraces* – the worker – by *homo ludens* – universalized humankind at play. Liberation from scarcity opens the vista of going well beyond the all-encompassing 'money culture' that, as Keynes argues, debases all in its path. Within the 'Convivial Economy' the opportunities for self-enhancement, historically the preserve of a tiny minority, will lie open to all (Jones, 1984: 94–9).

One would not want to be carried away by such visions, nor expect that heaven on earth would arrive overnight. When and how this will happen, who is to take the decisive initiative, how to administer vouchers – who is likely to volunteer for the task of care for the geriatrics or sewer maintenance? – what post-scarcity society would look like or how it would effectively function are still enigmas beyond our present resolve. Nor are we unaware of the many variegated obstacles to overcome. From public inertia to vested interests, the lobbies, or blockages within the decision-making bodies themselves, the status quo would be stoutly defended. Nor must one forget that these projections are confined to a privileged western perspective. From the vantage-point of some three-quarters of humankind, debate over particulars of 'artificial intelligence' or the 'Convivial Economy' are perceived as a chimera confined to the overfed. Hypothetically, our boundless materialism converting wants into needs, could run on for ever. Issues of finite resources, ecological depredation, demographic realities or generalized nuclear threats follow closely behind. None of these would, *deus ex machina*-like, be resolved by the advent of machine intelligence all on its own. Within the present context we have tried opening up the vista of what might be done. We will return to the theme of the Convivial Economy within the context of artificial intelligence, particularly in Chapter 7, 'Learning Curves'.

REFERENCES

Aronowitz, S. and DiFazio, W., *The Jobless Future and the Dogma of Work* (Minneapolis, MN: University of Minnesota Press, 1994).
Bartlett, D. L. and Steele, J. B., *America, Who Stole the Dream?* (Kansas City: Harvard University Press, 1996).
Bradley, W., 'When Cynicism Meets Money, It's Politics Now', *Los Angeles Times* (9 October 1997).
Chomsky, N., *New World Orders Old and New* (New York: Columbia University Press, 1994).
Cockburn, A., 'Ministers admit 60 percent of young black men are jobless', *Los Angeles Times* (12 December 1994).
Dahrendorf, R., 'A Precarious Balance: Economic Opportunity, Civil Society and Political Liberty', *The Responsive Community*, 5(3), (Summer 1995).
Danziger, S. and Gottschalk, P., *America Unequal* (Cambridge, Mass.: Harvard University Press, 1995).
Engbersten, G., Schuyt, K., Timms, J. and van Warden, F., *Cultures of Unemployment* (Boulder, Co.: Westview Press, 1993).
Galbraith, J. K., *The Culture of Containment* (London: Penguin Books, 1993).
Gans, H. J., *The Underclass and Antipoverty Policy: the War against the Poor* (New York: Basic Books, 1995).
Gorz, A., *Paths to Paradise: On the Liberation from Work* (London: Pluto Press, 1985).
—— 'The Condition of Post-Marxist Man', in Docherty, T. D. (ed.), *Postmodernism: A Reader* (New York: Basic Books, 1993).
Habermas, J., *The Past as Future* (University of Nebraska Press, 1994).
Hacker, A., *Money: Who Has How Much and Why* (New York: Scribners, 1997).
Handler, J. F. and Hasenfeld, Y., *We the Poor People, Work, Poverty and Welfare* (New Haven and London: Yale University Press, 1997).
Heilbroner, R., *Visions of the Future* (New York: Oxford University Press, 1995).
Hutton, W., 'Keynes still has the best measures', *Guardian Weekly* (7 April 1996).
Jencks, C., 'Is the American Underclass Growing?' in Jencks, C. and Peterson, P. E. (eds.), *The Urban Underclass and the Poverty Paradox* (Washington: Brookings Institution, 1991).
Jones, B., *Sleepers Wake! Technology and the Future of Work* (New York: Oxford University Press, 1984).
Katz, M., 'Reframing the "Underclass" debate', in Katz, M. (ed.), *The Underclass Debate: Views from History* (Princeton, NJ, Princeton University Press, 1993).
Krugman, P., *Peddling Prosperity* (New York: Norton, 1994).
Kuttner, R., *Everything for Sale: the Virtues and Limits of Markets* (New York: Knopf, 1997).
Luttwark, E. H., *The Endangered American Dream* (New York: Simon & Schuster, 1993).
Maddox, B., 'America's "Eurobashing" possesses the power to cause a bad headache', *The Times* (London: 11 December 1997).

Madrick, J., 'In the Shadow of Prosperity', *New York Review* (14 August 1997), 40–4.
Magnet, M., *The Dream and the Nightmare: the Sixties Legacy for the Underclass* (New York: William Morrow, 1993).
Marable, M., 'Black Fundamentalism', *Dissent* (New York: Spring 1998), 69–76.
Marx, K., 'The German Ideology' (1846), in Tucker, R. C. (ed.), *The Marx–Engels Reader* (New York: Norton, 1978).
Massey, D. S. and Denton, N. A., *American Apartheid, Segregation and the Making of the Underclass* (Cambridge, Mass: Harvard University Press, 1993).
Mishel, L. and Bernstein, J. (eds.), *The State of Working America, 1992–93* (Armonk, New York: M. E. Sharpe, 1993).
Murray, C., *Losing Ground: American Social Policy, 1950–1980* (New York: Basic Books, 1984).
Newman, K. S., *The Withering Away of the American Dream* (New York: Basic Books, 1993).
O'Hare, W. P., *African Americans in the 1990s* (Washington, D.C.: Population Reference Bureau Books, 1991).
Organization for Economic Co-operation and Development, *The OECD Jobless Study: Facts, Analysis, Strategies* (Paris: OECD, 1994).
Parenti, M., *Blackshirts and Reds* (San Francisco: City Light Books, 1997).
Redclift, N. and Minione, E. (eds.), *Beyond Employment* (Oxford: Blackwell, 1985).
Rifkin, J., *The End of Work, the Decline of the Global Labor Force and the Dawn of the Post-Market Era* (New York: G. P. Putnam's Sons, 1995).
Schor, J., *The Overworked American* (New York: Basic Books, 1991).
Sklar, H., *Eyes Right* (Boston, Mass.: South End Press, 1995).
Stonier, T., *The Wealth of Information: a Profile of the Post-Industrial Economy* (London: Thomas Methuen, 1983).
The Economist, 'Europe Isn't Working', 5 April 1997.
Toffler, A., *Previews and Premises* (New York: William Morrow, 1983).
Waldinger, R., *Still the Promised City* (Cambridge, Mass.: Harvard University Press, 1996).
Weisskopf, T. E., 'Marxian Crisis Theory and the Contradiction of Late Twentieth-Century Capitalism', in Lippit, V. D. (ed.), *Radical Political Economy* (Amonk, NY: M. E. Sharpe, 1996), 368–91.
Willis, G., 'A Tale of Two Cities', *New York Review* (3 October 1996).
Wilson, W. J., *The Truly Disadvantaged: the Inner City, the Underclass and Public Policy* (Chicago: University of Chicago Press, 1987).
—— 'When Work Disappears', *Political Science Quarterly*, Vol. 111, No. 4 (1996–7), 563–95.
—— 'Public Policy Research and *The Truly Disadvantaged*' in Jencks, C. & Peterson, P. E. (eds.), *The Urban Underclass and the Poverty Paradox* (Washington: Brookings Institution, 1991).
Woirol, G. R., *The Technological Unemployment and Structural Unemployment Debates* (London: Greenwood Press, 1996).
Yates, M. D., *Longer Hours, Fewer Jobs* (New York: Monthly Review Press, 1994).

Part II New Times

5 Globalization

1. INTRODUCTION

Globalization is fast becoming the battleground for a new ideological division within the social sciences as similar facts can be reconfigured and interpreted in many different ways. With the ending of the Cold War, the last major barrier obstructing worldwide economic cooperation along capitalist principles was finally within reach. Globalization, however, conjures up either fear and opprobrium based on widening inequality within and between states, or alternatively the promise of a future golden era. Supporters argue that the new and globally available information technologies will raise the living standards of even the poorest nations, who are potential beneficiaries in a global free trade arena where comparative advantage prevents a zero-sum outcome. Free trade can be a conduit for conquering authoritarianism by facilitating the spread of new modernizing ideologies (Ohmae, 1996; Naisbitt, 1994; Bergsten 1997). Critics argue that it ushers in a 'false dawn', with the 'Washington consensus' of laissez-faire capitalism and liberal democracy obliging countries to compete for foreign direct investment, resulting in internal disruption to their traditional way of life with social cohesion sacrificed on the altar of rapacious western corporations seeking new markets and profits. From this perspective, the unregulated global market constitutes a threat rather than a promise and undermines the integrity of the nation-state (Gray, 1998; Peter-Martin & Schumann, 1997; Greider, 1997).

Love it or loathe it, the world is moving towards greater economic integration through the momentum of the international capital markets. The leading sponsor is the USA, sometimes acting with hesitancy and confusion, but propelled nevertheless by the prompting of its major corporations and business leaders who see the benefits as axiomatic. There is, to be sure, much internal political opposition within the US and elsewhere (notably in the Tiger economies buffeted by collapsing currencies and banking systems), and though the ultimate denouement is unknown, the process appears unstoppable. Bit by bit, American insistence on free trade, albeit in conjunction with the international agencies of world trade, is globally prising open the protectionist locks of other nations. Though advantageous in the short term, the problem of resource constraints may be ultimately destabilizing, and US promotion of its own economic interests and global vision could prove counter-productive. Protectionism is no solution but neither is unfettered trade. Markets need rules, and while global regulatory frameworks slowly emerge, expectations inevitably run ahead of international agreement leaving current anxieties unresolved.

A second contested area lies in America's promotion of cultural 'soft power'. The cultural values promulgated by the US induce other nations either to positively embrace them or to recoil from them in distaste, with some powerful Islamic states rejecting outright 'the great Satan'. Huntington posits a future 'clash of civilizations', with western culture and America in the vanguard, threatening traditional societies so that their ancient and absolutist cultural differences revive (Huntington, 1996). The latter remain fearful of losing their indigenous culture and sense of national identity to the sorts of values promoted by international tourism, global marketing and the reach of international companies such as Disney. Resistance to globalization is also widespread in Europe and can take many forms: from a defense of regionalism or even national film industries, to ultra nationalist movements of separatism. Domestically, America is embroiled in its own mini version of a 'culture war', lacking what Vaclav Havel calls 'a climate of social concord' based on a settled moral order of interpersonal relationships, with its image abroad reflecting this inconsistency and conflict. Critics observe, for example, Hollywood and the global ubiquity of the US mass media flattening and homogenizing world cultural standards through a commercial logic downgraded to the lowest common denominator of public taste, reinforced too by their growing control over global distribution outlets. Concurrently, a more positive and enduring vision is also projected: the values of tolerance, multi-culturalism, democratic government and individual self-fulfillment, the exemplars of the 'American dream' understandably attractive to other nations, but which all too often become equally traduced and prey to the values of the marketplace.

Globalization equally encompasses new forms of military development and diplomatic cooperation. The US, as the only remaining nuclear superpower, projects its forces globally, and currently faces no major threat in the 'new world order'. It has inherited the world's sheriff role, a position it finds both flattering and ambiguous, not least in its relationship to the UN. However, it has found that conflict is still endemic worldwide, that unreason holds sway with abuses of human rights and threats from 'rogue' states a constant worry unlikely to disappear. In promoting the extension of Nato eastwards by incorporating the former Warsaw pact allies of the Soviet Union – Poland, the Czech Republic and Hungary – its new military borders will abut those of Russia herself. The attendant danger, not least for a newly emerging European identity, lie in a weakened and humiliated Russia construing the changes negatively. The US can also appear insensitive to the needs of smaller nations, oddly limited by the powerful military-industrial forces at her command. A recourse to force or covert means forecloses other diplomatic options, all too evident in America's 'backyard' of Latin America. Current efforts to reach a pan-American free trade zone by 2005 could falter over worries of democratic abuse and renewed military sales to the region. This leads to internal political dissension, a sense that domestic politics drives policy and an incoherent strategy confusing to America's allies.

2. ECONOMICS AND GLOBALIZATION

Historically it is worth remembering that prior to the outbreak of the First World War comfortable Edwardian Britain lived off its vast overseas assets accumulated earlier. Two world wars, competitive devaluation and protectionism in the 1930s, plus the loss of empire, shattered that complacency, and it has taken many years for confidence to be built up with other nations again prepared to open up their markets to international competition. America has the world's largest domestic market and most productive economy to cushion worldwide shocks, but as its economy has become more internationalized it will not be immune to the economic cycle and, perhaps one day too, a military rival. Globalization does not necessarily mean a harmonization of world interests nor the fostering of democracy, but can exclude ordinary citizens who lack the resources of the powerful elites and interest groups, including the corporate lobby. It can also mask real domestic decline in the US whilst maintaining the appearance of invincibility. It is easy to be deluded that there is an inherent logic to this process of a neutral technology promoting worldwide economic integration, thereby inducing restraint and mutual benefit. After all, the First World War was fought between nations whose economies were interlocked by major trading interests. Or to take another example, China's self-interest may lie in mercantilism rather than free trade whilst pursuing the role of regional hegemon in south east Asia (Beinart, 1997). There is no inherent logic as to why China should pursue the global free trade option nor can we suppose that the Pacific Rim economies will necessarily pursue a common cause with the US as some anticipate (Kim, 1996).

Kenichi Ohmae, a leading prophet of the information age, suggests the nation state is becoming defunct and is an obstacle to progress with Keynesian-style interventionism both wrong and futile. He argues that the onset of new information technologies operating within border-less markets, limits the state's activities to those of a mere 'night watchman'. The state and its self-interested bureaucracy intrinsically gravitate towards protectionism. This both conserves its power and makes regulation and taxation easier, but distorts trade flows which often prefer to by-pass the center through promoting regional or city alliances (Ohmae, 1996). By contrast, Hirst and Thompson insist that a more regulatory interventionist role is both possible and desirable, as the markets and multinationals are still largely 'embedded' in their own domestic base, permitting the state some leeway. For them, ideal governance involves negotiating independent agreements with the major states and supranational bodies, between regulatory trade blocs (such as NAFTA), and between national and regional levels. The key is coordination of the major trading blocs with the state acting as a neutral mediator (Hirst and Thompson, 1996). However, new situations evolve which redefine state sovereignty and authority by offering new challenges. For example, the Internet makes state control difficult. Its activity in a virtual market goes unregulated, but this deters many users from fully trusting its operation until the problem of encryption and Internet governance is sorted out, thereby limiting its future scope. States or trusted third parties could provide public guarantees and regulatory control to eliminate potential fraud, but only in a situation where cross-national guarantees have been earlier secured.

(a) Limits and Dangers

One problem with the globalization thesis is that many accounts tend to be ahistorical. The beginnings of the international economy under British hegemony at the end of the nineteenth century and up until the First World War were in some ways more open in terms of capital and labor mobility. There was a higher proportionate volume of capital exports from Britain (twice that of Japan today, currently the world's leading creditor nation) helping to finance the railways and other leading industries of the then developing world, including the US. Now, most TNCs tend to be home-based rather than homeless, with business extending from a dominant national market which is the focus for their production and trading. Capital tends to be internationalized rather than globalized, with foreign direct investment (and bonds) concentrated in and between the developed economies, with newly industrializing countries' participation a not very significant exception to the rule (Hirst and Thompson, 1996). The vast majority of investment (some 90 percent) is still domestically financed within the emerging markets. In addition, fears that competition with the developing world is destroying jobs in the advanced economies are premature, as trade is still of only minor significance (Krugman, 1996).

The Economist, quoting from the UNCTAD study on globalization, notes that the income differences per capita between the seven richest and poorest nations has nearly doubled from 20 times in 1965 to 39 times in 1995 (*The Economist*, 20 September 1997). The world's 200 largest multinationals' sales made up 28.3 percent of the world's GDP in 1997, up from 24 percent in 1983. Being global offers the advantages of economies of scale and of vertical integration, but paradoxically according to Naisbitt, it need not be to the disadvantage of small companies or individuals who may more easily exploit the opportunities opened up by the global Goliaths not least through the acquisition of relatively cheap information technology (Naisbitt, 1994). Of the world's top 100 economic entities only 49 are countries; the remainder are multinationals with a wide geographic diversification and spread of risk for potential investors reluctant to enter the new developing markets. As Brian Tora observes: 'Virtually all these major multi-national portfolios are located in the US, Japan and Europe. The combined value of the stock markets in all these countries accounts for 84 pecent of total world capitalization. However only 14 percent of the world lives in these regions' (Tora, 1997). Since the Uruguay round of negotiations at GATT were concluded in 1993, the US has pushed further for the opening up of the telecommunications and information technology markets worldwide. These are sectors where the American lead is considerable, and where there have been huge corporate mergers in the telecommunications market as companies jostle to develop global alliances and achieve further economies of scale. Further consolidation is now occurring within the banking and motor industries. These developments are reciprocal as European and Japanese companies buy into the US market. Worries over globalization and the reach of capital markets are perhaps overstated for the present, but trends are being established which give cause for future concern. There is no single world interest rate, nor an integrated global capital market, though it is developing with concentration greatest amongst the advanced economies.

Floating exchange rates (and short-term capital flows) are destabilizing, as the British government learned to its cost when forced out of the Exchange Rate Mechanism of the European Union in September 1992. Government macro-economic policy with regard to setting domestic interest rates (in the US the responsibility of the Federal Reserve), fiscal policy and banking controls, are becoming constrained and subject to a performance evaluation by international financiers. During the 1980s, the dollar rose and depreciated alarmingly, making international trade a lottery for American exporters. Attempts by governments to 'buck the market' can be costly and several have called for capital controls. Witness the anger of politicians in Thailand and Malaysia in the autumn of 1997 against the international financier, George Soros, who had himself warned earlier of the dangers of unregulated markets. The more the Asian crisis spread, engulfing South Korea and later Indonesia in its wake, the more it became apparent that its roots lay in endemic structural weaknesses, inadequate banking regulation and control, bad loans 'guaranteed' by government, informal deal-making, crony capitalism and over-borrowing, all hidden behind regimes lacking accountability and openness. The net result has been collapsing currencies, mass bankruptcies and plummeting stock markets, with the humiliation of asking the IMF for emergency bail-outs. Though Japan has not been directly involved in the crisis, her present banking problems, stagnant economy, ineffective political leadership and 'inability to shift to internally based growth strategies' leave her vulnerable (Thurow, 1998: 26). This does not necessarily spell the end of the Asian model, but it does for the moment lay bare the hubristic claims made on its behalf.

Projecting beyond the current situation, it may well be the case that when the necessary reforms have been effected the 'Asian Tigers' will be even more formidable competitors to the west based on their well-known strengths. These include a high savings ratio, strong family and communitarian networks based on trust, relatively closed markets and strategic investments in future growth industries, including strong support for education. However, it seems likely that the prodigious economic growth rates of the early stages of industrialization are difficult to sustain long-term, as a more mature economy takes shape. Whatever the outcome of their current difficulties, unless the west is prepared to act with decorum and restraint this will only stoke up further resentment and limit future cooperation. Already the humbling of their national attempts to leap-frog the west are being sought in finding suitable scapegoats. Many ASEAN politicians criticize what they perceive as western-dominated global institutions, such as the IMF and World Bank for not doing enough to help, while implicitly forcing them to recognize their own shortcomings (*The Economist*, 28 February 1998). Indeed the crisis and the speed with which the international markets punished miscreants suggests how supine the national state has become, including even alliances of states such as the ASEAN bloc powerless to withstand the attacks on their currencies and markets.

Critics suggest the need for international reform either by specific controls on short-term capital in emerging markets (Stiglitz, 1998) or through more ambitious efforts involving a global economic summit, extending beyond the G8 (the eight major industrial economies) to include those developing countries threatened by further marginalization, and to allay domestic worries within the advanced economies (Sutherland and Sewell, 1988). Currently fears are growing over the proposed Multilateral Agreement on Investment (MAI) under consideration by the richest twenty-nine economies, with the US in polar position, with the aim of deregulating global investment. It is a charter, one critic argues, for a 'one-sided bill of rights for corporations and wealthy investors, not the human rights of individual citizens' allowing corporations extensive rights to sue governments in an international trade tribunal (Moberg, 1998). Many of its provisions on environmental standards and labor guidelines are voluntary and would even limit existing US standards.

As goods, services and labor begin to follow capital movements more freely across borders, William Greider poses a crucial question: 'The nation-state faces a crisis of relevance. What remains of its purpose and power if authority over domestic social standards is yielded to disinterested market forces?' (1997: 334). He argues the central global problem is one of excess investment, underconsumption exacerbated by declining wages, and high unemployment. His global solution is to abandon the orthodoxy of laissez-faire and to tax capital instead of labor, reform the terms of trade, raise low wages, write off bad debts on poor countries, support a pro-growth regime and refocus national agendas on work and wages (1997: 322–8). Yet, as productivity improves wages increase (witness the rising living standards of the Asian Tigers), enabling countries to benefit from specialization in the international division of labor. Equally problematically, Greider refuses to acknowledge that the financial markets have a positive role to play. Admittedly this can be erratic, but they penalize states which engage in over-borrowing or running a severe trade deficit, often instigated by politicians who are seeking their own short-term popularity, discounting the effects of their profligacy on future generations. Krugman pours scorn on those theorists of world glut and deflation arguing this is 'tilting at windmills' and concludes, reassuringly, that the capacity of the human imagination to develop new needs is unlimited (Krugman, 1997). But Greider's strictures on those who see the problem as one of technical adjustment only, and not one of politics and democratic control, is apposite.

(b) The US and Globalization

Free trade espousal is the prerogative of the leading economic power, encouraging others to follow its lead. Since the Second World War, attempts to manage the world economy more coherently (such as Bretton Woods), reducing trade barriers – including the abolition of capital exchange controls by the USA in 1974 – and developing multilateral regulatory institutions (Marshall Aid, the IMF, World Bank, GATT and now the WTO) were all designed along American nostrums – a commitment to free trade and openness. The exercise of what Nye and Owens have called 'soft power' – the attractiveness to outsiders of the values of American democracy and free markets – plus the use of the 'information umbrella' where the US lead in crucial technologies is overwhelming, has been instrumental in preserving US ascendancy which, they argue, needs to be selectively shared with others. They write: 'This new political and technological landscape is ready-made for the United States to capitalize on its formidable tools of soft power, to project the appeal of its ideals, ideology, culture, economic model, and social and political institutions, and to take advantage of its international business and telecommunications networks' (Nye and Owens, 1996: 29). Certainly culture is crucial to economic development, though whether other nations respond appropriately, benefiting from their own changeable comparative advantage in an unequal trading situation, is an open-ended question (Landes, 1997). Doubts exist that the pluralistic American state could play an even-handed role in negotiations fostering control over the global market, as international capital interests are deeply embedded in its lobbying and decision-making forums.

Two European critics point to the paradox that within the US, criticism and concern over globalization have gone further than elsewhere. Positing a future nightmarish 20:80 society (with the lower figure referring to the employed working technical strata) it is vital, they argue, to assert the primacy of politics. They suggest that a democratically reformed and activist European Union could one day seize the chance afforded by American recalcitrance (Peter-Martin and Schumann, 1997). Two domestic critics argue that America has developed a twin-track economy in which the highly profitable, fast-growing and protected export sectors prevail (according to the WTO, in 1997 US merchandise exports at 12.6 percent of the world total were by far the highest of all exporting countries), at the expense of a shriveling under-capitalized domestic base. They write: 'In the era of the New World Order, the U.S. state diverts resources from the national enemy, favors speculative over productive capital, and provides incentives that promote the growth of U.S. overseas capital. Thus as the imperial economy grows, the domestic economy disintegrates' (Petras and Morley, 1995: 56). In effect, Wall Street prospers at the expense of Main Street. There is concern too at the lack of elite renewal. Phillips characterizes a 'permanent Washington' dominated by an 'interest group centrism' subverted by the 'arrogant capital' of Wall Street and the federal executive, with the 'financialisation' of the economy sacrificed to short-term profits (Phillips, 1994). This discernment promotes voter discontent, unease and apathy, and limits America's options. However, Washington ostensibly ignores these concerns in pursuing further global market deregulation.

Without proper democratic accountability of the 'stateless corporation' and global market, citizens feel they have meager economic protection so further eroding faith in government. In the US, both trade unionism and the many non-wage benefits it once secured have declined. A fear that jobs will migrate lies behind much anxiety, as the trade in jobs is unlike that of commodities. Increased immigration and low-wage imports are responsible for some of the growing wage inequality. Also greater elasticity in the domestic demand for labor as a result of global market changes limits labor's bargaining strength with capital. As one notable commentator argues, free trade redistributes its benefits to the rich and undercuts the public sector, thereby threatening social legitimacy (Rodrik, 1997). As the new plutocracy takes shape within the US, so they become an integral feature of the emerging global elite. They are feted on television, their movements recorded in fan-type magazines which they largely own and which justify their lifestyles. Further down the social scale, the fast-growing contingent labor force struggles to keep its head above water.

Fred Bergsten, a leading exponent of free trade, writing by invitation in *The Economist* (27 September 1997), advocates a more active US role in regional and global trade deals. It is the only power with the authority, at least until the European Union sorts out its single currency, that can push forward more liberal trading measures. To help facilitate this role, Clinton is seeking fast-track authority from Congress (in fact denied in November 1997) to negotiate and build on past successes, such as APEC (Asia Pacific Economic Cooperation) and the FTAA (Free Trade Agreement of the Americas), with both bodies and the WTO (World Trade Organization) active in restricting any moves to protectionism. Some economists suggest that (regional) preferential trade agreements create trade diversion, are discriminatory to outsiders and only genuine multilateral agreements should be pursued (Bhagwati, 1997). However, Bergsten makes the vital point that these new agreements like NAFTA 'represent a convenient proxy for the vast impersonal forces of the contemporary global economy that continue to produce deep anxieties in many Americans, notwithstanding the length and depth of the current expansion.' He continues (our italics): '*The government has been weakening its already-inadequate safety-net just when increased support is needed to alleviate fears of displacement. Better education and training are of course the constructive answers... but... our educational system is highly decentralized and will take many years to repair*' (Bergsten, 1997: 27).

To compound problems further, the appearance of the so-called 'weightless economy' makes taxation problematic for governmental revenue-raising. It is becoming more difficult to locate and tax profits at source, with intellectual piracy and breach of copyright, for example, costing governments and companies billions of dollars in lost taxes and profits. Of equal concern is the use of offshore tax havens and the transfer pricing system used by the TNCs and their subsidiaries to avoid national tax regimes. Coyle argues that 'weightlessness' (with production literally physically lighter, communications simplified and productivity rising) drives income inequality and insecurity, creating the 'hollowed out' western industrial system with companies gravitating to low-cost countries. Future employment growth will be within the high-tech spin-offs, the social economy (voluntary and paid) and personalized services based on seemingly invisible wealth generating activity (Coyle, 1997). With hopes of a new 'economic paradigm' emerging predicated on low inflation and sustainable growth, supporters outnumber critics in this new global marketplace. But, as Davies argues, low inflation is attributable to exceptionally low GDP growth, creating the high unemployment of recent years. Since 1990, the US has grown fractionally under 2 percent per annum (despite significant recent improvement), a figure hardly enough to allay the concerns of many American citizens (Davies, 1997).

The US is developing a substantial world lead in high technology, in computing, software and chip production, and in their practical application, creating new industries and altering the manner in which older industries operate. The productivity gains from these changes are still less than previous industrial breakthroughs (averaging only 1.2 percent per annum in the 1990s). But one beneficial consequence has been the generation of many types of employment previously unknown, especially in the booming service sector. Competition is keen over personalized and customized products where novelty and quality count, requiring vast supportive servicing of an increasingly fickle and satiated customer now that the era of simple standardized mass production is over. As Madrick observes: 'The modern economy ... may be returning to a high-technology version of a crafts economy, based on worker skills, thinking and inventiveness, rather than the muscle of large scale factories and distribution networks' (Madrick, 1998: 32). The development of personalized services maintains a competitive advantage, but it does not feed through into rising productivity and living standards. Company profits rise and revenues grow, but the need to employ more labor on low wages to satisfy fickle customer taste and loyalties has depressed overall living standards and productivity gains, producing a 'treadmill economy' (Uchitelle, 1998). The good news is that jobs are available. Whether they are intrinsically rewarding, capable of maintaining adequate living standards, and are reasonably secure is debatable. What is apparent is that the physical problems of production seem resolved with employment falling steadily, so that the strain of maintaining employability will fall ever more on service sector differentiation.

As other nations benefit from inward investment and outsourcing by TNCs, so the physical production of many goods will gravitate overseas, where environmental and labor standards can be ignored with a degree of impunity impossible within the US. The design, marketing and high-tech component, the high value-added aspects may well remain within the domestic economy so blurring the distinction between servicing and manufacturing, but much else will migrate to Mexico or further afield. As these countries develop and are drawn further into the logic of global competition and the supply chains of the TNCs, so in time they will be outbid by others competing on an even lower cost base. The Chinese have a vast and relatively homogeneous population of 1.2 billion, offering a pool of compliant labor easily mobilized and self-sacrificing in their understandable desire to 'catch up'. Since Deng Xiaoping's reforms of 1978, dismantling the commune system, unemployment and partial employment have inexorably risen to 27 percent (191 million people) mostly comprising rural workers desperately needing labor-intensive investment (Rojas, 1998). Many of the more 'traditional', older industries of the US now struggling to survive must either invest massively in new plant and machinery, or suffer a further degradation of labor standards and reliance on new forms of contingent labor. The situation can continue, perhaps indefinitely, but at an ever-rising global cost in environmental degradation, exploited child labor, resource constraints inducing political conflict over oil and other vital scarce resources, global warming and so on.

The ruling dogma is 'economism', the reductionist mantra that the market knows best and public involvement is wasteful, bureaucratic and self-defeating. One recent critic excoriates the revived doctrine of corporatism, associated not with the state, as in the past, but with the now unrivaled remit of the private market. The managerial elite and other powerful self-appointed interests that dominate the huge corporations, along with their armies of specialists, become insulated from ordinary concerns, and unconsciously suppressive of individual initiative and the notion of a public good (Saul, 1998). Despite growing nationalist antagonism towards the US and its market domination, the total commitment to the market paradigm forecloses thinking on other possibilities and narrows the range of choices deemed permissible. Indeed much of this thinking reflects the implicit premise behind Huntington's thesis propelling a future clash of cultures. The global economy cannot be left rudderless, and only the US has the present political clout to advance economic cooperation and regulation, building stability and mutual global benefits. Nationalism at home and abroad is a danger. Determined political leadership, tackling the entrenched special interests in Washington coupled with a commitment to a new philosophy of social justice underpinning global regulatory mechanisms, should be a priority of US policy.

3. CULTURE AND GLOBALIZATION

The US emphasis on individual rights, including the anomalous right to bear arms, creates internal discord over prevailing levels of crime, violence and family breakdown. Violent crime in grossly unequal America is five times its European equivalent. The sources of this contagion even embrace Hollywood which is vilified as the arbiter of popular cultural standards projecting, at times, to outsiders a dystopian vision of a commodified, selfish society where material success rules, pursued by any means necessary. This infuriates European film-makers envious of her commercial success, and repels fundamentalist nations appalled by the lax moral standards displayed in film and television. Of course this vision is a parody of American society, but one ironically which critics across the political spectrum concur with, as they too are unhappy with the direction the country is moving in. The 'culture wars' are testimony to this conflict and symbolize a struggle for control of the heart of the nation. Much that was new and radical in the 1960s was later legitimized and absorbed into the mainstream. Co-opted by commercial interests, it represented little more than a pyrrhic victory for progressivism. Hollywood has both rejected and promulgated some of the 1960s' values although critical mainline films are still the exception to the rule. However, one prominent critic, Robert Bork, argues that: 'Hollywood which once celebrated traditional values, has become a propaganda machine for the political outlook and permissive morality of the sixties generation' (Bork, 1996: 52). An essentially classless image celebrating notions of family, motherhood, integration of the outsider and patriotism, effortlessly bequeathed by Hollywood since the 1930s, is now in danger of being dissipated. The warm nostalgia for yesterday has been replaced by films reflecting a more brutal and savage era. Unfortunately many 'traditional' fundamentalist societies self-selectively perceive this negative imagery of America and reject it and all things western.

Culture is contested and has an ideological-political dimension now that the politics of the center hold sway. Provoking both passion and debate, cultural and religious conservatives clash with the politically correct in competing for the support of those broad acres of 'middle America'. Value politics rule and Washington, so remote and removed from much of American life, is reaffirmed, challenged and brought alive through the operation of the media. However, what is portrayed may be filtered in terms of form and content to conform to prevailing notions of rightness, constantly evolving within the pluralistic contours of American society. This internal struggle has its external reference point in Huntington's clash of civilizations.

(a) The Counter-culture of the 1960s and Conservative Reaction

From the late 1950s, an emergent cultural force associated with youthful rebellion redefined the idea of individualism itself, so central to the Puritan heritage, by pre-empting it as a symbol of non-conformity and a source of social revolt against rational, faceless, technocratic bureaucracy. A search for spiritual enlightenment and a call for democratic participation became central values of youthful rejection. Politically, the burgeoning student movement, galvanized by opposition to the war in Vietnam and support for civil rights in the South, stumbled upon new forms of protest in what came to embody the counter-culture. American culture could no longer be characterized, if it ever could, in unitary terms as new and submerged forms of cultural activity became widely accessible. Cultural pluralism became the ideal as first black literature and then feminist writers gained wider prominence. The former offered a critique of white American cultural imperialism both at home and abroad, while the latter targeted patriarchal domination. In both cases there was condemnation of the lack of democratic accountability and a desire to revolutionize the national cultural narrative to include their own repressed histories.

The holistic nature of the wider protest was exemplified by recasting the personal, so that: 'politics, art and personal life were all components of an interactive movement aimed at transforming the way people lived' (Bloom and Breines, 1995: 275). At times naïve and utopian, and dismissively portrayed as a 'culture of narcissism' by the prominent writer Christopher Lasch, critical of its demands for instant gratification and a tendency to public disengagement, the 'movement' nevertheless had a lasting impact, though not all of it positive. Reform followed reform, as American laws on civil rights, abortion, homosexuality, censorship, feminism, ecology and conservation reached the statute book. The sexual revolution was coupled with a cultural 'loosening up' of prevailing standards. However, the 'movement' increasingly fell prey to internal division – cultural rebellion or political radicalism – and overwhelmed by the complexity of the problems it had raised lost its direction.

The reaction was not slow in coming, at first ineffectively articulated by Nixon, but later more convincingly by Reagan, who when governor of California in 1966 invoked 'the rest of us' against the movement's apparent anarchy and hedonism. Significantly, many avant-garde cultural components were easily absorbed into mainstream consumerist culture, as the hippie style and youth culture became fashionable with cultural freedom becoming the rage. One critic argued: 'The U.S. establishment could ultimately accept cultural revolution because sex and rock-and-roll were so eminently marketable' (Steigerwald, 1995: 186). Cultural repression, such as it was, when challenged could hardly ever comprise the basis of the nation's power structure. In 1968 Nixon became president, but of equal import was the third party challenge of George Wallace pointing the way to future Republican success by his careful targeting of the white disaffected northern working-class vote. A decade later, the film character Rambo, with his long hair, empathy with nature, dislike of state and bureaucracy but not of country, could be appropriated by the right as a way to relegitimize the Vietnam War; emblematic of the radical conservative populism of the Reagan era with its reassertion of 'traditional values' and opposition to growing cultural fragmentation and decline. It is not for nothing that Kellner defines media culture as 'a contest of representations that reproduce existing social struggle and transcode the political discourses of the era' (Kellner, 1995: 56). However, the legacy of the

1960s was ambiguous, with no clear winner emerging, although conservatives clearly recognized in it a crisis of moral authority supportive of anti-social norms and behavior. A leading postmodernist critic on the left, by way of contrast, laments the litany of broken promises, as the 'good life' became unrealizable, as political ideas became detached from a failing economic base and as the modernist hymn to wider opportunity became a dream for the few (Woodiwiss, 1993).

(b) The Propaganda Model and Media Concentration

The media help to reconcile the diverse communities of the US by acting as significant agencies of socialization into national values, invoking that unitary sense of belonging. However, the problem of representation within a culture of commercial choice, and the manner in which choices (including political ones) are over-determined by the media giants through their control of television and the press, has become a source of concern. 'As democracy is diminished to the language of consumer choice, general feelings of disengagement are described as problems of consumer recalcitrance', write Ewen and Ewen. Civic instruction is reduced to the sound bite, photo opportunities replace public reason, spin doctors script the political process, 'infomercials' replace debate, and critical thinking becomes nullified by 'compliance professionals' reworking political stereotypes to elicit the appropriate emotional response so that 'the public begins to consume an image of itself as the abstract embodiment of visceral attitudes, authenticated and confirmed by the announced results of opinion polls' (Ewen and Ewen, 1992: 202, 215). The political role of the mass media and the semiotics of influence are a major preoccupation of many cultural critics. Lazere notes that: 'The basic problem of culture under capitalism is that capitalism is needed to finance it... virtually any right wing cause, no matter how loony, can find either a profitable market or backing by capitalist ideologues' (Lazere,1987: 17) The left, by contrast, remains to a degree impotent and marginalized in the face of such a concentration of resources. There is no institution comparable to the BBC. Though publicly funded, it enjoys great public esteem, expresses a wide variety of views nationally while acting as a central reference point by articulating a common cultural heritage.

A further defining feature of the mass media in the twentieth century is their interdependency. Television stations are owned by newspaper interests which control film studios. Thus, the radio network RCA also owns the Hollywood studio RKO. Rupert Murdoch controls not just a chain of newspapers but also a major TV network and Hollywood studio, with his empire global in scope. The media conglomerates through their diversified and extended cross-holdings have a profound impact on defining the consciousness of ordinary Americans but one determined within quite narrow boundaries of what is acceptable. Today, we have become acclimatized to 'faction' or 'infotainment' on film or TV whereby 'the process of turning the incoherent data of daily life into conventionalized dramatic modes' becomes commonplace (Vasey, 1993: 236). Michael Real estimates that Hollywood and the 'consciousness industries' are worth about $250 billion annually, noting that: 'Ideologically, Hollywood is one of the major instruments of the capitalist-consumer status quo' (Real, 1996: 152).

This in itself should hardly be a cause of surprise, but according to Herman and Chomsky, the role of the media, including Hollywood, is more overtly ideological. They write: 'the mass media of the United States are effective and powerful ideological institutions that carry out a system-supportive propaganda function by reliance on market forces, internalized assumptions, and self-censorship, and without significant overt coercion' (Herman and Chomsky, 1994: 306). The direction of ideological distortion is from political right-wing pressures, especially on TV and radio, and in the general management of news itself. Positing a 'propaganda model' – dependent on the vested interests of power and money – acts to filter news, whereby dissent and minority views are marginalized, with government and private interests receiving priority in getting their message relayed. The operative 'filters' mediating the raw uncooked news to make it fit for public consumption are a concentrated media ownership and the need for profit based on advertising income. There is too much reliance on government sources, business and 'experts' – what Alterman calls the 'punditocracy' – for information and analysis. 'Flak' makes news digestible and 'newsworthy' within the accepted discourse while anti-communism acts as the ultimate controlling benchmark. They back up their arguments by a systematic reading of the news coverage associated in particular with the Vietnam war. The right attributed this defeat to negative news reporting which undermined US morale but which they conclusively reject.

A commonly leveled accusation is that the conservative right is unable to accept any unpalatable truths about society. Capitalism and business are the 'givens' of the system that are rarely criticized. The right has managed to convince the majority of the inherent bias within government, education and the media because: 'American consciousness is skewed so far to the right that conservative bias is not even generally recognized as such but is accepted as the norm of neutrality' (Lazere, 1987: 92). In consequence the left can only mount a holding operation and is permanently on the defensive. One recent critical analysis by Miller depicts the US as narcissistic and egotistical – offering a quick fix of psychotherapy designed to promote individual 'empowerment' of the megaself in a society negatively depicted as 'egotopian'. He argues that the centrality of the shopping mall experience and of consumerism is quintessentially representative of public consciousness, while the cities and moral order which once underpinned public sensibility collapse. Real communal values are now overladen by a private carapace fundamentally at odds with America's core values (Miller, 1997). This type of criticism is understandable, but seems redolent of an earlier industrial era. It fails to recognize the sheer exuberance and creativity of the electronic information age, and the way in which new forms of leisure are becoming interlinked with the world of work dominated now by the handling of information flows. There is indeed much that is crass and shabby. Yet the inability to see anything of value within the culture vitiates much of his analysis and other critics as well.

(c) The New Right, Hollywood and Cultural Stalemate

The New Right apportions the blame for the current spiritual crisis, moral confusion and falling standards of behavior, not to the concentration of media ownership as such, or a 'propaganda' model, but to left-wing subversion of America's cultural institutions, including most of the media and Hollywood, which have been infiltrated and networked from within. Michael Medved accuses Hollywood ('the poison factory') of being a one-party Liberal state with an addiction to violence, a rejection of religion, an attack on the family and fixation on foul language and ugliness in its general denigration of all things American (Medved, 1992). The reality is that it will develop counter-cultural films if it believes there are exploitable market opportunities, and so will follow consumer demand. In any case, in a democratic society it is difficult to criticize public taste in a consistent manner, as there is equally a growing audience for excellence with challenging and even controversial material. Diversity and choice are central. In assessing Medved's claims, at the time of his book's publication, the top grossing films were the soporific *Aladdin*, *Home Alone* and *Falling Down*. Biskind argues that his claims are simplistic and factually incorrect. His assertion that Americans support traditional values needs treating with a degree of skepticism as 'the reality is that outside of a few right wing diehards, traditional values have become a luxury, which is why George Bush retreated so quickly from his convention's family values platform' (Biskind, 1992). Studios are not interested in promoting values, but in the box office. In 1997 the Southern Baptists even censured Disney, that repository of wholesome family values, for allegedly inserting subliminal messages of a sexual nature into their cartoon films, *The Lion King* and *Aladdin*. Sex apparently is feared more than portrayals of violence on screen. Powers and Rothman argue that film does influence and gradually change public attitudes. With the break-up of the major studios, most Hollywood films are in practice made by a small and highly creative elite whose personal politics are if anything liberal, so film content today is more critical of corporations and the establishment. However, the films they base their assessment on are the top grossing ones (those pre-selected by popular appeal), and so the problem remains that film-makers may simply have struck it lucky by reinforcing existing public sentiment rather than actually changing it as such (Powers and Rothman, 1996).

Today, critics are wearying of the endemic cultural conflict, rejecting both contestants' claims as counterproductive and myopic. The left is hooked on minorities, 'cultures of resistance' and separate identities; the conservatives on unattainable family values, rhetorical nationalism, and exploitation of white middle-class anxiety. These incompatible 'mind-sets' desperately need to reaffirm the commonality of a shared culture, what Gitlin calls 'the commons', while the real centers of power remain uncontested. What holds us together now that the unity once forged by the cold war has ended?, he asks. 'If America is the dream, then in a certain sense the end of the dream portended the end of the nation' (Gitlin, 1995: 81). There is equal criticism of the 'dumbing down' of America during the Reagan years, but also of self-righteous politically correct intellectuals accused of a 'fraying of America' (Hughes, 1994); while a 'betrayal of history' through shortened, simplified and one-sided interpretations in school texts is further cause for concern

(Stille, 1998). A rough stalemate ensues, but one achievable in terms of mutual contempt. The problem of a lack of balance of never seeing anything of value within American culture vitiates much of the culture wars debate, and this tendency was apparent right from the outset.

Given the nature of the controversy over culture, the media and Hollywood, and the projection of 'soft power' abroad, it is hardly surprising that 'fundamentalist' nations fearful of being co-opted by these standards reject wholesale everything America represents. They fear the advent of a consumerist culture as a way of defining lifestyle which leaves little space for religion. As culture becomes more universalized (indeed globalized by American corporations), so the values which underpin it tend to greater abstraction, yet permit far more cultural differentiation than ever before (Waters, 1995). Thus, religious ideas need fundamentalist reinforcement in a secular and relativist culture, and this perhaps explains the ferocity of much of the right's reaction domestically with some 'traditional' societies correspondingly wary. Similarly, 'to the extent that value-commitments are badges of identity, to the extent that politics is the pursuit of lifestyle, and to the extent that organizational constraints and political surveillance are displaced in favor of reflexive self-examination' (Waters, 1995: 156), so these innovations burst the boundaries of the traditional nation state and its values. The US stands at a threshold where the overcoming of scarcity and a reconfiguration of its values towards twenty-first century realities is now possible, yet scarcely realizable, within a consumerist culture. What could constitute the basis of this transcendence will be explored in the final chapter.

4. GLOBALIZATION AND 'THE NEW WORLD ORDER'

There is no 'big idea' underpinning US foreign policy now that communism has collapsed. No manichean struggle now that the former bi-polar world context has given way to multilateralism and acting through the UN. Americans like to see themselves as defenders of western civilization in which democracy and freedom, free trade, globalization and security are its underlying principles. In the implementation of these values, reality often forces unpleasant compromises so the US at times supports authoritarian nations which abuse human rights. The question of whether the US should act unilaterally in support of its 'friends' however dubious their record (the realists), or pursue a human rights foreign policy (the idealists), has informed discussion for many years although America, in any case, tends to dress its policy in the language of morality. Whatever course of action it follows, a retreat into isolationism, as Seitz argues, is inconceivable (*The Economist*, 27 May 1995). With well over a million troops available, America is uncomfortable using its military forces for political purposes and feels compelled to act only where there is a clear violation of international law, such as in the Gulf War of 1991, legitimized by the UN. America does act unilaterally on occasions, but the need to contain costs, limit casualties and have a clear exit strategy faced by an often suspicious and skeptical Congress limits her options further. The 1993 'bottom up' defense review argued the US should be capable of dealing with two regional wars/crises simultaneously. In the 1997 review this was downgraded to fighting 'in close succession' rather than simultaneously, with China not seen as a threat till 2010, and the US military budget constrained by the 'peace dividend'. However, the rapidly growing power of China has projected it into being the main hypothetical adversary, with the US characterized as suffering from 'enemy deprivation syndrome'. The basis of these chauvinistic fears should be rejected as they are grossly inflated, lack empirical support and amount to 'a substitute ideology to legitimise the power of the (US) elite' (Harries, 1997: 33). Republicans are currently calling for increased military spending. In 1996 it was 3.6 percent of GDP, nearly halving since Reagan's 'evil empire' days, with massive cuts effected in troop numbers in Europe from 1991, following START 1 and limits to the 'Star Wars' project.

One of the leading historians of the Cold War era, John Lewis Gaddis, maintains that the threat of nuclear war and annihilation disciplined both sides in their struggle for global mastery. From the Cuban missile crisis in 1962, to Vietnam and Afghanistan, both recognized the constraints within which they operated with an occasional resultant loss of face. However, he admits nuclear weapons prolonged the Cold War, as they were perceived as the ultimate source of national virility, rather than economic and social power, with the Soviet Union's economic malaise remaining undetected and undisclosed. At the same time Kennan's 'containment' of communist expansionism was made possible through the threat and improvement of such weapons until the Soviet state collapsed under its own failings (Gaddis, 1997). Now that this era is thankfully over, the US can take the lead in limiting the spread of nuclear weaponry, and also to removing the 'poor man's' weapons of destruction – the recourse to chemical and especially biological ones. These weapons are cheap to produce, can be easily transported, and favor those who seek salvation through martyrdom. The poison gas attack by Aum Shinrikyo in Tokyo illustrates the threat clearly. 'American activism to guarantee international stability is, paradoxically, the prime source of American vulnerability' as it is the only nation policing outside its own region thereby incurring the hostility of others (Betts, 1998: 28). Vietnam demonstrated the limits of the nuclear option as the US was rendered impotent. Despite rising numbers of 'body bags' and pressure from sections of the military to 'go all out', politicians recognized the moral abhorrence and national divisiveness this would create. Currently the nuclear stockpiles are being decommissioned in a piecemeal way, but their very existence creates 'envy' amongst other powers anxious to join the nuclear club while the newer threats posed by simpler but deadly weapons goes unanswered. The US could defuse this by its promotion through diplomacy of shared geopolitical responsibility for global management, thereby delegitimizing further the putative threat posed by rogue states.

At Helsinki in April 1997, Clinton saw an opportunity to rebuild a better world, lost since 1945. The proposed expansion of Nato eastwards is viewed as enhancing stability and democracy, promoting trade and security, and strengthening civilian control over the armies of the new democracies. The need to reassure Russia was symbolized by the earlier 'partnership for peace' idea of joint peacekeeping exercises with their own observers in Nato itself. However, the decision to expand the alliance before exactly determining what the alliance is for, now that the threat no longer exists, is illogical and economically costly, with one critic irresponsibly recommending the dismantling of Russia into a loose federation of semi-independent states (Brzezinski, 1998). American fears of rising nationalist sentiment within the Russian Duma could destroy the foundations of the fledgling democratic order emerging, and one exacerbated by declining army morale and loss of 'great power' status. Russia desperately needs targeted western economic assistance and easier access to Europe's markets to bolster her economy, and repair state damage after the years of communist misrule, with currently little forthcoming (Skidelsky, 1995). The architect of containment, George Keenan, suggests it is a 'fateful error' squeezing Russia when she is relatively weak. This will create a divisive new line across Europe. Others presently excluded – notably the Baltic states – are anxious to join Nato or remain isolated and defenseless. One unfortunate consequence is that Russia will retaliate by vetoing western initiatives in the UN Security Council. This was already apparent in Kosovo where initially only toothless sanctions could be imposed on Milosevic of Serbia. Even more significantly the Duma is refusing to endorse the Start 2 treaty which proposed the halving of its nuclear stockpile. Nor can Russia be relied upon to help prevent nuclear proliferation, or the selling of military armaments to America's bitterest enemies Iraq and Iran.

An opportunity has gone begging for a rethinking of the US military role. This would involve strict nuclear controls, including the full inspection of all countries with actual weaponry or the means for developing them, with the eventual goal of denuclearization. Despite the endorsement of the General Assembly of the UN to the Comprehensive Test Ban Treaty in September 1996, it is not fully operational nor likely to be until the five major powers of the Security Council give a lead. As they have not taken any significant measures towards eliminating nuclear weapons any agreement would simply freeze the present nuclear club (Arnold, 1997: 163). Proliferation continues as witnessed by India's nuclear testing in May 1998, followed within days by Pakistan (another 'threshold' state) retaliating with her own tests thereby plunging the region into instability.

In the Middle East, continuing US support for Israel, despite her lack of implementation of the Oslo peace treaty concerning withdrawal from the occupied West Bank territories, has led to a loss of trust and the charge of double standards by the Arab states towards her role as mediator. The PLO–Israel policy is in disarray with the Israeli Prime Minister Netanyahu stoking the fires of the powerful domestic Jewish lobby in Washington and embarrassing the president. This was reflected in Arab reluctance to further sanction the US military-led intervention against Saddam Hussein in early 1998. A notable 'rogue' or 'backlash' state which while being repressive, authoritarian and unpopular domestically and internationally, was yet able to counteract US resolve by successfully portraying America as the aggressor, a bully intent on unleashing its military might against a defenseless civilian population. Critics of the US role argued that Iraq posed no threat to the US, so there was no 'self-defense' justification, that it would strain relations with Russia further, and bombing would not obtain the objective of eliminating the chemical and biological facilities which prompted the crisis in the first place. A wider problem for the US was the charge of inconsistency and hypocrisy. The US would never allow similar inspections on her own territory, nor are other states with chemical (or nuclear weapons) threatened, such as Syria or the Chinese (with their violations in Tibet). Indeed the logic of bombing may have resulted in the unintended consequence of shoring up support for the Hussein regime. This is not an argument for doing nothing. A program of selective sanctions with the goal of ending the embargo if compliance with the UN's mandate was forthcoming (as ultimately negotiated by the UN Secretary-General), helped in defusing the crisis. The all too ready reliance on the military option may have been self-defeating for the US. The grudging acceptance given to the eventual diplomatic resolution where the US became a sidelined spectator was indicative of bad faith. By contrast, it was only concerted US diplomatic resolve (with the implied threat of military action), despite earlier vacillation, that eventually brokered the 1995 Dayton peace settlement in Bosnia.

China poses the biggest threat to American hopes of a new world order although its 'most favored nation status' was renewed in 1994, despite human rights abuses and mounting US anger over the trade deficit, currently standing at $30 billion annually. The US is fearful of losing access to the world's largest emergent market. The APEC meeting in Seattle in November 1993 gave additional testimony to the importance of the Pacific Rim to the US economy. Debate centers on whether China should be 'engaged' or 'contained' (as the pre-emptive display of force over Taiwan in 1996 suggested), and also whether Japan, as the major economic power in the region, should assume more responsibility for regional security thereby reducing the substantial commitment of US forces there. There are, for example, 36 000 US troops in South Korea, and if the US pulled out this could precipitate a regional arms race. Samuel Huntington operates with the paradigm of eight major historic civilizations, of which notably three – the West, Islam and the Sino communities – are set to vie for dominance in the next century. Of the three, he awards the Sino civilization the leading chance of emerging dominant. China, above all, in conjunction with Japan and the ex-Tigers, constitute a bloc of decisive power and influence that on its own or possibly joined with Islam, can successfully outface the west. The west – adrift, indecisive and fragmented – will only overcome its natural disadvantage, he argues, by rallying closer together (Huntington, 1996). In critical rejection of this thesis, the west's continuing ability to universalize its ideas is more because it can 'mix and merge cultures rather than set them against each other', based on a reciprocity in which the west adapts and learns from others too. The spread of 'westernistic' influence is not premised on the submergence of other cultures in a zero-sum confrontation, but ideally on an acceptance of multiculturalism and openness (Buzan and Segal, 1997: 19).

5. CONCLUSION

The Huntington scenario appears intimidating, yet is fanciful. Asian diversity and increasing wealth may just as easily dissolve their iron resolve with old regional hostilities resurfacing. The US could economically ally with the Pacific Rim to mutual benefit or to a growing European Union linked by the common bonds of history, culture and politics. In both cases, an alliance would be premature. The former lacks objective reality and popular domestic support within the US, while the latter is embroiled in much internal division over such issues as the Euro currency, unemployment and expansion eastwards which could yet put the whole project into reverse if economic problems remain unresolved. The US position should be one of leading from the front by eschewing new alliances, promoting demilitarization and global inspection through the UN and its diplomatic efforts, thereby outlawing the 'rogue' state threat as the US threatens no one by its actions. In coordinating new international controls over the global economy including the taxation of footloose capital, or in other international concerns such as the fight against drugs, the active cooperation of smaller states is vital and would act to reassure them. However, recent efforts, for example to create an international criminal court to end, as Kofi Annan expressed it, 'the global culture of impunity', have encountered the reluctance of the US (and others) to grant it proper autonomy, and are perhaps indicative of the difficulties ahead. America's role would be facilitated by less moralizing of the failures of others when its own cultural and political standards remain so indeterminate.

In the new transnational era unfolding, US reaffirmation of the nation state and politics, and of the possibilities of exerting meaningful economic control may be at the expense of its own powerful military-industrial lobby. The nation state, despite its changing role, still has the advantage of longevity and acts as a focal point for the multiple loyalties that citizens now increasingly take for granted. With the workless revolution underway, and the threat this poses to internal stability, it could offer a new way forward matching economic globalization with a commitment to international respect for human and social rights. Uniquely among all the advanced nations, it has been spared the class divisions others inherited from their servile pre-industrial past. The values of individual liberty, communal cohesion, risk taking and enterprise are as much needed now as in the past. Whether a new and progressive vision can fully develop will be explored in the final chapter 'New Visions'.

REFERENCES

Arnold, G., *World Government by Stealth: the Future of the United Nations* (Basingstoke: Macmillan, 1997).
Beinart, P., 'An illusion for our time: The false promise of globalization', *The New Republic* (20 October 1997).
Bergsten, F., 'American Politics, Global Trade', *The Economist* (London, 27 September 1997), 25–8.
Betts, R. K., 'The New Threat of Mass Destruction', *Foreign Affairs*, Vol. 77, No. 1 (January 1998), 26–41.
Bhagwati, J., 'Fast Track to Nowhere', *The Economist* (London, 18 October 1997), 25–7.
Biskind, P., 'Drawing the Line', *Premiere (USA)*, Vol. 6, Issue 4 (December 1992), 47–9.
Bloom, A. and Breines, W., *Takin' it to the Streets: A Sixties Reader* (New York: Oxford University Press, 1995).
Bork, R., *Slouching Towards Gomorrah* (New York: Regan Books, 1996).
Brzezinski, Z., *The Grand Chessboard* (New York: Basic Books, 1998).
Buzan, B. and Segal, G., 'A Western Theme', *Prospect*, Issue 27 (London, February 1998), 18–23.
Coyle, K., *The Weightless World: Strategies for Managing the Digital Economy* (Oxford: Capstone Books, 1997).
Davies, G., 'New US Paradigm is Really Just an Old Bugbear', *The Independent* (6 October 1997), 19.
Ewen, S. and Ewen, E., *Channels of Desire: Mass Images and the Shaping of American Consciousness* (Minneapolis: University of Minnesota Press, 1992).
Gaddis, J. L., *We Now Know: Rethinking Cold War History* (New York: Oxford University Press, 1997).

Gitlin, T., *The Twilight of Common Dreams: Why America is Wracked by Culture Wars* (New York: Metropolitan Books, 1995).
Gray, J., *False Dawn: the Delusions of Global Capitalism* (London: Granta Books, 1998).
Greider, W., *One World Ready or Not: the Manic Logic of Global Capitalism* (London: Allen Lane, Penguin Books, 1997).
Harries, O., 'The Anti-China Syndrome', *Prospect*, Issue 21 (London, July 1997), 30–5.
Herman, E. S. and Chomsky, N., *Manufacturing Consent: the Political Economy of the Mass Media* (London: Vintage, 1994).
Hirst, P. and Thompson, G., *Globalization in Question* (Cambridge: Polity Press, 1996).
Howell, D., 'Policy Makers are Losing their Grip on the Weightless Economy', *The Independent* (18 June 1997), 26.
Hughes, R., *The Culture of Complaint, the Fraying of America* (London: Harvill, 1994).
Huntington, S., *The Clash of Civilizations and the Remaking of the World Order* (New York: Simon & Schuster, 1996).
Kellner, D., *Media Culture: Cultural Studies, Identity and Politics between the Modern and Post-modern* (London: Routledge, 1995).
Kim, Y. J., *The New Pacific Community in the 1990s* (Armonk, New York: M. E. Sharpe, 1996).
Krugman, P., *Pop Internationalism* (Cambridge: MIT, 1996).
—— 'Is Capitalism too Productive', *Foreign Affairs*, Vol. 76, No. 5 (Sept./Oct. 1997), 79–94.
Landes, D. S., *The Wealth and Poverty of Nations: Why Some are so Rich and Some so Poor* (New York: Norton, 1997).
Lazere, D. (ed.), *American Media and Mass Culture: Left Perspectives* (Berkeley: University of California Press, 1987).
Madrick, J., 'Computers: Waiting for the Revolution', *New York Review* (26 March 1998), 29–33.
Medved, M., *Hollywood vs America: Popular Culture and the War on Traditional Values* (New York: Harper Collins, 1992).
Miller, J., *Egotopia: Narcissism and the New American Landscape* (Tuscaloosa: University of Alabama Press, 1997).
Moberg, D., 'Power Grab', *The Progressive*, Vol. 62, No. 3 (March 1998), 24–6.
Naisbitt, J., *The Global Paradox: the Bigger the World Economy, the More Powerful its Smallest Players* (London: Nicholas Brealey Publishers, 1994).
Nye, J. S. and Owens, W. A., 'America's Information Edge', *Foreign Affairs*, Vol. 75, No. 2 (March/April 1996), 20–35.
Ohmae, K., *End of the Nation State: the Rise of Regional Economies* (London: Harper Collins, 1996).
Peter-Martin, H. and Schumann, H., *The Global Trap: Globalization and the Assault on Democracy and Prosperity* (London: Zed Books, 1997).
Petras, J. and Morley, M., *Empire or Republic? American Global Power and Domestic Decay* (London: Routledge, 1995).
Phillips, K., *Arrogant Capital: Washington, Wall Street and the Frustration of American Politics* (New York: Little Brown, 1994).

Powers, S., Rothman, D. J. and Rothman, S., *Hollywood's America: Social and Political Themes in Motion Pictures* (Boulder, Co. & Oxford: Westview Press, 1996).
Real, M., *Exploring Media Culture: a Guide* (Thousand Oaks, CA: Sage, 1996).
Rodrik, D., *Has Globalization Gone Too Far?* (Washington D.C.: Institute for International Economics, March 1997).
Rojas, R., 'The Other Side of China's Economic Miracle: Unemployment and Inequality', (London, http; // www.soft.net.uk/julio, 1998).
Saul, J. R., *The Unconscious Civilization* (London: Penguin, 1998).
Skidelsky, R., *The World After Communism: a Polemic for our Times* (London: Macmillan, Papermac, 1995).
Steigerwald, D., *The Sixties and the End of Modern America* (New York: St. Martin's Press, 1995).
Stiglitz, J. E., 'Boats, Planes and Capital Flows', *Financial Times* (London, 25 March 1998).
Stille, A., 'The Betrayal of History', *New York Review* (11 June 1998), 15–20.
Sutherland, P. and Sewell, J. W., *The Challenges of Globalization* (Washington D.C.: Overseas Development Council, 1998).
The Economist, 'Assembling the New Economy' (London, 13 September 1997), 105–11.
Thurow, L., 'Asia: the Collapse and the Cure', *New York Review* (5 February 1998), 22–6.
Tora, B., 'Lots of Power in Few Hands', *The Independent* (19 July 1997).
Uchitelle, L., 'America's Treadmill Economy', *New York Times* (8 March 1998).
Vasey, R., 'The Media', in Gidley, M. (ed.), *Modern American Culture: an Introduction* (London: Longman, 1993), 213–38.
Waters, M., *Globalization* (London: Routledge, 1995).
Woodiwiss, A., *Post Modernity USA: the Crisis of Social Modernism in Postwar America* (London: Sage, 1993).

6 Civic Society

1. COMMUNITARIANISM

Communitarianism, established in the early 1990s with its focus on community decline, rapidly attracted elite support. 'We are all communitarians now', declared *The Economist* in its survey of global trends (*The Economist*, 18 March 1995: 16). In the course of his European lecture tour, Amitai Eztioni, George Washington university professor and the movement's unquestioned guru, filled large halls to overflowing. Leading politicians the world over came forward averring support. President Clinton, together with Vice-President Gore, publicly acknowledged their interest. Helmut Kohl, Germany's long-serving chancellor and the doyen of Europe's political elite, has equally joined the communitarian ranks. While Tony Blair, then leader of the opposition and now Britain's prime minister, at the last pre-election Labour Party conference, felt impelled to mention 'community' eleven and 'responsibility' fourteen times in his keynote address.

A glorious future promised. Communitarianism was bringing forward the cause of civic society in its quest for community life, now avowedly sadly foregone. It promised to restore the 'American dream' by relocating community at the heart of national discourse. Yet, just as swiftly as it had risen to prominence, communitarianism has suffered equally rapid decline. Within a few short years it has virtually disappeared from the public agenda. True enough, 'community' and 'responsibility' have passed into the lexicon of all parties' public debate, but as a distinct movement, with its own unique message, it seems to all intents and purposes moribund. Even Etzioni's most recent contribution to the debate, *The New Golden Rule*, departs substantially from his previous central concern (Etzioni, 1996). The emphasis is now on 'order' and 'autonomy', as the leading concerns of American society today – issues that incidentally bring him considerably closer to the standpoint of civil society. Yet, though sharing more common ground, the concepts still differ fundamentally in their underlying orientation. While communitarianism looks for impromptu moral regeneration, and politically comes to terms with the status quo, the civic society ideal regards structural reform as essential, before moral self-regeneration, on any significant scale, can begin. The present chapter will initially point to the diverse social deficiencies that are presumed to afflict modern society and that communitarianism is set to address. It will then turn to the advanced remedies, and analyze the main reservations. Following on from this it will examine the characteristics of civic society in its diverse manifestations, before finally turning to the various offshoots of critical thinking that have recently surfaced under the same general heading. Issues of inequality, machine intelligence and discretionary time, all relevant to the debate, will also receive consideration.

Ferdinand Tonnies' famous dichotomy between *Gemeinschaft* and *Gesellschaft*, with the former analogous to 'community' and the latter most resembling the context of 'association', was framed by him in the late 1880s. At the time, his home country Germany was still in the birth-pangs of industrialization (roughly three-quarters of a century behind England, but much in step with the United States), and this remains integral to an understanding of communitarian analysis (Tonnies, 1995; orig. 1887). As Tonnies defines it, *Gemeinschaft* applies to small-scale communities predating industrialization, where relations were primary and face to face. Values were stable, norms freely shared, standards respected, and deviance was rare. *Gesellschaft*, the adjunct of modernization, by contrast comprises a condition where chaos prevails. Relationships have turned specific and formal, interests have typically become antagonistic, while roles are volatile. Norms are both divergent and incessantly subject to unforeseen change. Anomie, atomization and alienation are endemic. As relationships flounder, and conflicts disrupt daily life, civic bonds dissolve. While the guileful and ruthless prosper, those who falter in life's contest are crushed and despised.

Modernization, with its corollary of urbanization, stratification and rationalization, has universally been the foundation stone of communitarian critique. Earlier versions, such as Nisbet's 1953 analysis, have tended to seek the recreation of small-scale community life as an alternative to the power of the national state. Reflecting an era where multiculturalism has emerged as a realistic threat to the identity of the national state, Etzioni's framework, by way of contrast, perceives communitarianism as an instrument to buttress the nation state via the vehicle of moral regeneration. Nisbet asserts that: 'The Quest for Community will not be denied for it springs from some powerful needs of human nature – needs for a clear sense of cultural purpose, membership, status and continuity... It is very difficult to maintain the eminence of small, local units when the loyalties and actions of individuals are consolidated increasingly in the great power units represented by the nation states of the modern world... Neither moral values nor fellowship can easily flourish apart from the existence of diverse communities each capable of enlisting the loyalties of its members' (Nisbet, 1953). In the intervening two generations, matters have drastically changed. The threat now is not of national power repressing group identity, but in excessive group identification where individualism has run amok. As Etzioni contends: 'The eighties tried to turn vice into virtue by elevating the unbridled pursuit of self-interest and greed to the level of virtue... But it has become evident a society cannot function well given such self-centered, me-istic orientation. It requires a set of do's and don't's, a set of moral values, that guides people toward what is decent and encourages them to avoid what is not' (Etzioni, 1994: 24). What is needed now is 'part change of heart, part renewal of social bonds, part reform of public life' (ibid.: 245). From the right of the political spectrum, Robert Bork, as noted earlier, locates the decline to 1960s-style liberalism: 'the Sixties generation's fixation on equality has permeated our society and its institutions, much to our disadvantage. Their idea of liberty has now become license in language, popular culture and sexuality' (Bork, 1996: 54).

In the light of such scathing critique, the proposed communitarian remedies are modest:

- reducing the cost of running for office;
- a more open process of public scrutiny;
- rebuilding communities and those vital intermediate associations necessary for stability and social cohesion;
- the strengthening of family life.

All are admirable in their own way, but are unlikely to reverse the baneful effects. Communitarian colleagues substantively echo their leader's prescriptions. According to Spragens, 'civic friendship within a flourishing community, will be sufficient to heal social breaches' (Spragens, 1995: 47). While Elshtain, a prominent spokesperson, maintains: 'while "social contract" has torn communities apart, voluntaristic "social compact" will effectively relocate power at the grass roots' (Elshtain, 1995). In short, there is no need to address such grievances as inequality, polarization or social division by treading on toes. Self-regeneration alone, it is thought, will be enough to heal the wounds.

It is little wonder that *The Economist* – not by any stretch of the imagination a hotbed of radical dissent – feels impelled to characterize communitarianism as a form of 'nostalgia for a partly imaginary past'. It dismisses the communitarian program as a mere 'love thy neighbour' fanciful injunction that, in the light of harsh reality, will dissolve into random 'do-goodism' unable to confront opposition and typically leading nowhere (*The Economist*, 18 March 1995). If moral exhortation could resolve social ills, then the Ten Commandments alone should have brought about an earthly paradise. Certainly, the 'solidaristic virtues' of extended family life, of neighborliness and social stability were, by all accounts, more strongly accented within pre-industrial communities than now. 'The world we have lost' is past and will not be easily regenerated. Western societies, having gone through the rigors of industrialization, urbanization and now globalization, are offered a vista of widening opportunities, but also new challenges that need to be faced. Unless societies are willing to confront them in a spirit of experimentation and innovation, undaunted by vested interests and social taboos, the incidence of crime, violence, family breakdown and social disruption is liable to further aggravation before it improves.

The kindest comment on communitarianism is that it implies 'reformism without reform'. Some would go further. Coote cautions that its basic anti-liberal rhetoric, while doing nothing to tackle the problems of unequal power in its diverse dimensions, will negatively affect human rights (A. Coote writing in *The Independent*, 23 June 1995). While Atkinson charges that in promoting the rise of voluntary associations over elected bodies, the inherent hierarchical autocracy of tight-knit self-appointed communities will be revived (Atkinson, 1995). Graver charges come out of the socialist camp. Derber characterizes communitarianism as being guilty of avoiding confrontation with the impact that economic capitalist institutions have upon the social environment. 'The linked crises of race and urban poverty . . . [and] the communitarianism of the middle class', he goes on to say, 'is flawed mainly by his [Etzioni's] inattention to the contribution of the elites to our moral crisis' (Derber, 1995: 198). The rot, in other words, starts at the top.

To his credit, Etzioni has not stood still. His more recent emphasis on 'order and autonomy', where 'a good society requires both a moral order and a bonded community' (Etzioni, 1995: 34), comes closer to the real source. He is not unaware that the two concepts are on opposite ends of the same pole. 'The more order', he goes on to say, 'that is imposed on us, the fewer choices we have, and vice-versa – the more liberties we take, the less order there will be' (ibid.: 34). Yet to him the concepts represent a symbiotic relationship while, in the harsh reality of today, they more closely resemble a zero-sum game. The balance is fine. Tilt the scale only slightly in one direction or the other, and order can be transformed into authoritarianism, even tyranny, while autonomy can lead to excessive permissiveness, license or chaotic dissension – the very pathologies that many claim to perceive in modern society. Etzioni's recipe, however, continues to adhere to non-intervention on the part of central authority. Moral self-regeneration, as before, will be enough. This is in marked contrast to Bork and other social conservatives, who strongly advocate state intervention on questions of morality and values.

The communitarian movement merits praise for having brought the demise of community life to the public's attention. However, for all its success (or possibly, for this very reason), it has left the task of redefining remedies largely undone. What has damaged community life is not the loss of moral fiber, but the fact of social decline: specifically, the widening gap between rich and poor; the plight of inner-city ghettos; rampant materialism; plus labor market decline. One cannot turn the clock back. The nostalgia for small-scale rural community life is surely misplaced. Nor will mere exhortation provide the needed remedy. Structural reform alone, boldly tackling the prevailing ills without fear or favor, might lead to success. This task the communitarian movement has signally failed to attempt.

Experience alas points in a different direction. Untrammeled 'free enterprise' (a misnomer when corporate welfare, on a grand scale, persists), will not give everyone their due share. The haves are not merely more wealthy, but also more powerful in every sphere. They have vastly superior access to the political elite, exercise control over resources and benefit by the ethos of command and subordination. Nowadays they control the informatics network to such an extent that the invisible hand of power and privilege, though seemingly weaker, has become even more powerful. Without governmental protection – be it central, regional or local – the scales will tilt further. Etzioni's Mark 2 communitarianism, though more subtle, is basically the same prescription. Civic society, in taking the next step by recognizing that structural reform must be tackled, constitutes a more rigorous approach.

2. MODELS OF CIVIC SOCIETY

The watchword of civic society is 'participation'. Democracy, it is claimed, can never thrive if citizens confine their civic duty to the occasional filling in of a ballot form, and then slink back into apathy. 'Power corrupts' in Lord Acton's famous dictum. If ever appropriate, it is doubly valid now. The control of the purse strings with vast fortunes in corporate as well as in private hands, plus media profusion, and the promise of untold rewards to those who hold office in return for favors done – all of this has undermined the qualities of integrity and accountability on which democratic order relies. The public has become so case hardened that betrayal of trust, even within the elite, barely raises an eyebrow when disclosed in the United States. Politicians' drive towards amassing huge war chests to survive the electoral process, the facility of the side-open 'revolving door', plus the vast unseen power of lobbies gravely impair the democratic ideal. Even such self-evident measures as the containment of killer weapons, or the protection of nighttime convenience store workers, have run aground in the face of the lobbies' bankrolls. Scandals are normalized, spin doctors perform magical sleights of hand that turn issues upside down, while the media have trivialized public discourse to an extent that the dividing lines between public affairs and show-biz, let alone right or wrong, are blurred. This is the public perception, despite the careful rebuttal noted earlier of Bok and Tolchin, and voters remain angry and disillusioned. It is idle to expect the cuckoo to clean up its nest. Perhaps, in the manner of the Greek polis, when the grassroots repossess the power that rightly belongs to them, the prevailing polarization and apathy will be overcome. Yet civic society cannot be effective while the chasm between the public and private sphere is allowed to persist (Cohen and Arato, 1992).

In the post-communist societies of Eastern Europe, civic society adherents take a quite different stance. Vaclav Havel, once a dissident hero and now the Czech president, keeps the discourse alive (Havel, 1997). Their model allows the public sphere – corrupt and self-seeking – autonomy. Salvation lies in the private sphere of civic order that, however adverse external conditions may be, can flourish on its own. It is taken for granted that central power will always be predatory and unjust. The powerful – in terms of Paretian analysis, possessed of the guile of the fox or the strength of the lion – as much as they have already, will always reach out for more. Whatever its transitory ideological guise, the public sphere will forever remain their domain. Yet ordinary citizens ('the man in the street'), need not be daunted. The private sphere, too lowly for the mighty to know or transcend, offers compensation. All manner of associations, clubs, networks, interest groups or informal gatherings permit scope for 'belongingness', meaningful contact, self-expression, as well as community life. Indeed, the more stark the repression (as the Stalinist era attested), the stronger will be the incentive to combine in the interest of community renewal.

Western traditions are different. There, the Kantian principle of universality regards the good life as essentially indivisible. Bad government precludes the formation of civic society; while under just and moral rule, civic life flourishes. This premise is fundamental to all versions of civic society prevalent in western democracies. Within the United States, there are presently four dominant versions, politically parallel between two on the right and two on the left. They are: right of center; left of center; radical right; and radical left – itself subdivided into two different versions. The two centrist positions subscribe to the market as the ruling arbiter of resource allocation. They are uncompromisingly pluralist, anchored within the individualist capitalist mode, while emphasizing the imperative of competition and enterprise. The two radical viewpoints are both populist libertarian, though pointing in opposing directions. They are at one in defining government power as anathema. Beyond that, they strictly part company. The radical right, by and large, subscribes to Social Darwinism in its viewpoint. Might is right, in their book. Whatever the system, the strongest and most able justly rise to the top. The idle and shiftless, on the other hand, if they spurn available opportunities will find their own level. The radical left is less unitary in its philosophy, and is in fact split into two. The radical socialist/communist wing accepts that even with the coming of economic democracy, there will still be a need for a formal structure: if no longer the traditional chain of command, at least a modicum of central authority. The anarchist view rejects authority in its entirety, arguing for unconditional personal autonomy and voluntaristic cooperation, with at most a bottom-up form of governance, as essentials.

The centrist conservative model basically refers back to Durkheim's concept of 'organic society', in which each functioning part is an integral element of the entire society. Power is implicit rather than overt (Durkheim, 1964). A central element is religion, which acts less as a transcendental concept but is functional in setting the moral precepts to which all subscribe. Margaret (now Lady) Thatcher most successfully tied her faith in the market economy to a wider ethical scheme in which Christian duty, with a more secular stance, stands in the forefront. 'Most Christians', she holds, 'would regard it as their personal Christian duty to help their fellow men, and women... These duties come not from any secular legislation passed by parliament, but from being Christian' (Willetts, 1997: 16). Reference to Christian values is never far from the precepts of the moderate right. John Gray, David Selbourne and David Willetts in Britain, and Robert Nisbet, Daniel Bell and Jean Bethke Elshtain in the United States appear as the leading voices. The state has now withdrawn from the economic arena, where the market nexus provides fair shares for all. Its role, however, is far from diminished. The moral sphere, where permissiveness is threatening to damage the social fabric beyond repair, needs moral intervention more than ever; interventionism not in the form of autocratic coercion, but more in the mode of a constitutional monarch setting the boundaries and pointing the way. When Willetts contends that 'the real threat to civil society comes not from the market but from the state' (Willetts, 1997: 17), he has that very construct in mind. Get the state out of the spheres where it does not belong – and these are not merely planning or ownership, but equally in jobs, pay and entitlements – and not only will enterprise flourish but its hands will be clean. In re-enacting the virtues of old – focused upon the family, the nation and the community – this will restore social cohesion to the extent that civic society can flourish. 'Conservatives', Willetts observes, 'are more interested in communities that have backbones – namely institutions' (Willetts, 1997: 16). Too long has the Big Brother state spread its tentacles in every direction, decrying thrift and effort to the extent that a sense of duty is all but foregone. Concurrently, the plethora of open-ended entitlements consecrates idleness, while fostering dependencies that only a return to free enterprise can end. They want social contract, not status conditions. Nor rights without duty, where freedom and opportunity are given free reign, and where the consumer is sovereign with merit bringing its just reward.

That some – far fewer than now – will not make the grade, and might if left unaided fall by the way, is not denied. As it was in the past, private charity enacted by religious orders as well as through private bodies and individuals (once referred to by George Bush as 'a thousand points of light'), will spontaneously step into the breach. Where succor has ceased to be enforced by dictate, communities will not fail in their duty of common humanity. 'Real institutions', organically arising from within the community, will be better equipped to restore the unfortunates than a depersonalized activist state. Indeed, the very act of assisting the unfortunates will strengthen mutual ties. Fukuyama's notion of trust, integral to the flowering of civic society, lends a further dimension. Where envy and discord prevail, mutual trust suffers demise. Remove the long arm of the state, and by and by the organic seedlings of civic society will take root again (Fukuyama, 1995).

In his recent gloomier approach, Fukuyama has lost faith in the potency of trust as a cure. Now 'The End of Order' imminently threatens. In a few short years, with warnings unheeded, matters have gone from bad to worse. The social dislocation caused by family breakdown, itself aroused by the random permissiveness of the liberal state, has brought the United States to a condition of chronic disorder (Fukuyama, 1997). In a somewhat less apocalyptic vein, David Selbourne in Britain projects similar sentiments. 'What is missing', he states, referring to the increasing precedence of rights over responsibilities, are 'the duties of the individual to himself and to fellow members of the civic order to which he belongs' (Selbourne, 1994). Pretending to stand for social justice and civic rights, the left, he contends, are inducing an invidious apparatus of social control. 'The demand for a return to civic society', argues Daniel Bell, with reference to the United States, 'emphasizes voluntary associations, churches and communities, arguing that decisions should be made locally and should not be controlled by the state or by bureaucrats' (Bell, 1996). For the conservative right, the battle lines are explicit. Civic society can only flourish where the moral order is impaired neither by coercive government nor by the licentiousness that the demeaning of values entails. Optimism mingles with gloomy prediction; indeed, a characteristic that all versions, in their own way, tend to share. For the right, unquestionably in the ascendancy these past two decades, the trend is surprising. After its prolonged travail, the left is now re-emergent and imbued with new ideas, and seems ready to seize the concept of civic society and take command of the social agenda once again.

The left's agenda has become decidedly muted in the past two decades. Both the disastrous end of the Soviet Union, with its revelations of corruption and decay, as well as the pathologies that arose in the mixed economy 'welfare states' of the west, have impelled drastic retrenchment. The confident expectation of 'the final crisis of capitalism' delivering power into their hands, has finally been abandoned. Equally so, has been the insistence on the common ownership of the means of production, plus the pursuit of equality as a principal aim. The United States, while devoid of a socialist movement, has been similarly affected with the dreaded 'L' (liberal) word expunged in the interests of getting elected. Overall, throughout the industrialized world, the parties of progress stand where the Conservatives once stood in the last generation. Gone is the reliance on statism, the power of unions, and the quest for equality that progressivism had advanced in the past hundred years.

The left's vision of civic society has not been exempt from criticism. The primacy of the market as the fully-fledged arbiter of resource allocation is almost unchallenged. The rampant individualism, liable for the climate of avarice and self-seeking now claimed to predominate, has come in for decisive critique. So have aspects of modernization, technological determinism and globalization that allow corporations and governments to plead ulterior forces whenever convenient to their own cause. The rise of the underclass is deplored, polarization is charged with having destroyed community life, while the crass materialism of the post-industrial age vitiates what civic society implies.

The universal watchword is 'participation'. Power needs to be brought down from the Olympian heights of privilege to the grass-roots. Failing that, apathetic indifference is bound to spread further. The fact that less than one-half of the American electorate chooses to exercise their democratic duty of voting in presidential elections speaks volumes. Yet even were turnout to approach the level of comparable western democracies it would be insufficient. Turning out once every few years to fill in a ballot slip cannot sustain the social fabric on which cohesion depends. One needs to look beyond formal bodies, even if regional or local, to the intermediate levels of association once held out as democracy's saving grace in the early postwar era. The vital element is direct personal involvement in civic affairs, all the way from the choosing of political delegates to participation in matters such as school boards, communal security or voluntary bodies of all possible kinds. Practice makes perfect. Habits of involvement and participation will give even the meekest the confidence to argue his or her point. Differences and divisions are bound to arise. Yet debate, deliberation and coming to terms with opposing viewpoints will affirm the spirit of empathy and compromise without which civic existence will be unable to thrive. Bottom-up deliberation and decision-making, even were it to take longer (although as one is now able to witness at first hand the tortuous routines of horse trading that characterize deliberation at the uppermost counsels of state, this seems open to doubt), would be worthwhile. For democracy to function, the ordinary citizen cannot be transformed into a mere passive digit in a computer printout. She/he needs to be rescued from the heavy hand of anonymity that now rules.

Jean-Jacques Rousseau, long denounced as the arch-apostle of totalitarian populism that empowered Hitler and Stalin, has remarkably been intellectually cleaned up into some form of half-way position. In his magisterial three-volume study, Maurice Cranston denies that the 'general will' acts as a tool of oppression. Instead, he claims, it as essential to achieve a synthesis between the private and the public realm (Cranston, 1996). The premise of the general will is that freedom for all is incompatible with the head-counting practice of 'democratic society' and can only be realized 'in the individual participation in the exercise of legislative power... to be involved in the laws that serve the common good, laws which inevitably restrain the liberty of some' (Krammick, 1997: 42). Walzer's definition of true civic society fits both wings of the left. He speaks of 'a centralized democratic socialism, a strong welfare state run, in part at least, by local and amateur officials; a constrained market; an open and demystified civil service; independent public schools; the sharing of hard work and free time; the protection of religious and familial life; a system of public honoring and dishonoring free from all considerations of rank and class; workers' control of companies and factories; a politics of parties, movements, meeting, and public debate' (Walzer, 1990: 23).

The 'social market' mechanism plus 'the stakeholder economy' are widely held out as effective measures to level the score. The social market concept implies governmental withdrawal from public ownership or direction, while retaining constraints that redress the problems the market system creates in its wake. This involves income redistribution by means of progressive taxation and/or a meaningful capital tax; worker participation plus the establishment of co-ownership enterprise; corporate responsibility for the damage that market operations typically leave (amongst those would be the deterioration or destruction of human capital through overuse, excessive toil, or noxious conditions); compensation for 'externalities'; making good the social costs of environmental degradation; and the usage of roadways, transport and educational facilities of every kind. Transferable pension rights to facilitate labor mobility and protection are equally considered essential (Schweickart, 1996). On this latter point, the new Labor government in the UK are currently developing a 'stakeholder pension', a second-tier scheme built on the existing state one.

Rhoda Howard charges modern society as being 'characterized by materialism, competitiveness, excessive individualism, and breakdown of community' (Howard, 1995: 5), thus promoting individualism in the place of responsibility and social harmony. According to Ignatieff, the absolute triumph of the market nexus – not just with the economy but equally prevalent within the political, social and cultural spheres – has implanted a double standard of middle-class affluence juxtaposed to a polarized underclass where concepts of participatory democracy remain confined to 'the tenured communitarians on the political philosophy guild' (Ignatieff, 1996: 44).

On a more sanguine note, Hilary Wainwright offers a cogent critique. Having co-opted the moral agenda, the New Right simplistically maneuvers laissez-faire critics into defenders of state tyranny, obscuring the alternative that modern conditions provide. Potentially, she contends, with the opening up of the communicative network, the role of voluntary cooperation can be made more extensive than ever before. Social movements of the left such as feminist pressure groups, educational networks, consciousness-raising formations, self-managed cooperatives, or most actively the Transnational Information Exchange bringing together working people from across the world, provide alternatives that, beyond narrow margins, have hitherto remained unexplored (Wainwright, 1996). The fact that quasi-informal bodies such as Rotarians, trade associations, charities and church organizations more typically thrive within conservative circles, must raise reservations as to whether their promotion would primarily further the progressive cause. Organizational skills, spare time and funds normally characterize the privileged classes unless allocation drastically changes.

The radical right manifestation, though less explicit in the United States than in a number of European countries, is nevertheless worthy of interest. It is dominated by religious self-assertion, from Pat Buchanan's political supporters to Jerry Falwell's fundamentalist Moral Majority and then beyond to the very influential Pat Robertson's Christian Coalition founded in 1989 with Ralph Reed as its first director. This latter organization has brought together not only fundamentalists but Evangelical and Charismatic voters, organizing them from the roots up and targeting its politics directly at the Republican party hierarchy. The mutual relationship is manifestly equivocal, as the 'country club' Republicans resent their tactics and ideological zeal, and yet are wary of upsetting them thus forfeiting the activist power they represent and their access to funding. The Christian Coalition is now deeply entrenched within the Republican party where, despite its narrow support, put by Wilcox at some 10–15 percent for whites, they exert significant influence. They have been clearly effective in the rightward drift of the party especially on pro-life family issues and also 'promoting some issues from obscurity to a central place on the agenda... school prayer, tuition vouchers and other proposals' (Wilcox, 1996: 145). For all that, their attempt to unwind the 'godless liberalism' of the 1960s, plus their embodiment of the values of the Puritan family, centered on small-scale community circumstances, has so far failed to yield meaningful change. Their idol, Ronald Reagan, cleverly manipulated them, but without endorsing significant legislative change on social and moral issues.

The militants, both black and white, lurk on the outer fringes. The perspective for all the radical right is quite simple: you are either for or against us; what is national is better than foreign, and what is parochial is better still; what is altogether untainted by outside influence is considered the best of all. As long as evil abounds, law and order is a primary consideration – again, the more local the better. Militia outfits typically take localization to the point where their own sheriff is perceived as the ultimate source of legal authority. Any attempts to generate an imposed equality, in the face of obvious divergent aptitudes and personal characteristics (they assume), flies in the face of reality. The strongest and fittest are destined to rule, the rest must learn to comply. Miscreants, deviants and criminals, if refusing to conform, have to suffer the consequences of their vicious actions. While this description most aptly befits the militant wing, in some measure it is generalized amongst the radical right.

Potentially the most ominous sign of the times appears in the upsurge of such populist mass movements as Louis Farrakhan's

'Million Men March' and the now even more popular Promise Keepers. At the drop of a hat, close to one million men (male exclusivity is the operative term) descend upon the nation's capital to proclaim unconditional obeisance to their leadership, to prostrate themselves before their deity forswearing all future sins, to vow self-regeneration, while reaffirming the values of old. The underlying subtext of exclusivity and fundamentalist intolerance does not seem to worry the media at all. One need not reflect all the way back to Mussolini's Blackshirts or to Hitler's Stormtroops for critical parallels. Today's diverse Muslim fundamentalists, from Algeria or Iran to America's urban ghettos, are ever ready for any atrocity or self-sacrifice in the name of 'the cause' and constitute a worrying trend. The threat may not lie specifically in the above movements but more generally in the disaffected 'lonely crowd's' propensity for totalitarian mobilization that was earlier witnessed in the 1930s (Gardner, 1997). Yet, in a strange way, these quasi-communities, at the same time, represent the strongest approximation to communal association that presently exist. For the first time in more than 100 years, the left's associative counterparts have disappeared from the public scene.

Radical left proponents of civic society appear in two distinct guises: on the one hand, there is the much more numerous socialist/communist movement, and on the other the anarchist wing. Dialectical materialism designates capitalism with the supreme historic function of bequeathing the perfection of 'machine intelligence'. Capitalist internal contradictions imply that 'there is a compulsory law by which every capitalist must perfect this machinery more and more, under penalty of ruin. But the perfection of machinery is making human labor superfluous' (Tucker, 1978: 707). Thus success impels self-destruction. Not only does the capitalist class, due to mass unemployment, undermine consumption as the source of its profit, the redundant masses will ultimately mobilize to take the potential riches as their own and capitalism will fall. Civic control will then come into its own. Machine intelligence will be harnessed towards the common interest, with allocation based not on profit but need. Work will cease to be alienated, becoming instead both socially useful and self-expressive. Furthermore, with scarcity overcome class conflict will become redundant. Marx's universalistic projection of 'from each according to his ability, to each according to his needs' will be realized (Tucker, 1978: 531). Under the logic of mankind as 'social animals' whose individual capacities are fashioned by social conditions, political and social commitment is there to be learned. As Seligman argues, practice makes perfect: hands-on participation will buttress the substance of coordination (Seligman, 1992).

At this point the two versions part company. The socialist/communist thesis, while committed to its faith in social justice and impelling the state to 'wither away', yet accepts that 'administration' remains in the interest of rational management. Coercion will no longer be active while accountable officeholders, liable to recall by popular will and no longer able to profit from their office, will nevertheless be invested with executive power. Anti-statist anarchism dismisses all such social distinction. 'Every state', they declare, whether bourgeois or socialist, is but a gendarme of the capitalist order' (Berman, 1992). The autonomous determination of the quality and direction of personal life is imperative. Essentially, humans are moral associational beings, electing to act altruistically when social conditions are totally free. Only the constraints of authority, vested privilege and social class have historically inhibited selfless action. Remove the barriers and under conditions of 'bottom-up collectivism' the path is clear. The critical institution for anarchist civil society will be the local assembly – the 'free association of individuals for mutual aid and collective action' (Berman, 1992: 9). Free associations are self-governing, democratic, cooperative and set up to resolve conflict by peaceful means. To provide a wider horizon, the local assemblies are horizontally as well as vertically linked to other like-minded communes, similarly cooperating in terms of free association. The local collectives determine the targets for production and distribution, and having abolished all traces of the wage system together with property rights, allocate consumption according to need. The unconditional right of secession warrants freedom of choice. Based on respect for persons that secures civil society against the threat of collectivism, communist anarchism promotes individualism, tolerance, pluralism and the politics of difference thereby replacing the system of oppression, exploitation and faceless conformity ruling today.

Needless to say, none of the four versions has hitherto even come close to implementation. We will, in the following sections, consider first the social currents that might indicate a move towards civic society, and then having turned to the obstacles that stand in the way, will finally examine the means by which such obstacles can be overcome.

3. CIVIC SOCIETY IN ACTION

As a model for civic society, Britain in the future could turn into a living experiment. Prime Minister Blair's long-standing commitment to the principles of 'community' and 'responsibility', as well as the 'stakeholding society' could be the test for a social democratic advanced industrial version that, culturally modified, other nations might emulate. Protected by his overwhelming parliamentary majority and supported by a record level of popularity, the way to a legislative program of change is wide open. Preparatory to winning power, he discarded outdated, ideological party commitments. The hotly contested Clause Four, committing the Labor movement since its inception to the pursuit of the common ownership of the means of production has been jettisoned. In the grim confrontations of the 1980s, Mrs Thatcher had brought the once-militant powerful unions to heel. And finally, the imperative of 'electability' had excised sufficient traces of socialism from the manifesto for all sectors of society to confidently embrace the document. Like the US Democratic party, Labour has moved towards the depoliticized middle ground so that its electoral victory in May 1997 was viewed with equanimity among the banking community. Indeed, the chancellor voluntarily ceded control of monetary policy to a more independent Bank of England. Pragmatism now overrides ideological dogma.

So far, the indications of a move in the direction of civic society are still largely rhetorical. Yet, the economic preconditions are overwhelmingly favorable. As the century moves to its end, Britain has turned itself into the prime western outpost of American technological excellence and informatics know-how. By European standards, its unemployment rate is low. Trade unions have learned compliance. The once-virulent class war, widely branded as the principal cause of the nation's precipitate postwar decline, is in abeyance. The USA and China apart, Britain attracts more foreign investment than any other nation. And in regard to the labor force profile of low-wage service sector employment, absence of job security, and the tolerance of inequality, Britain stands well primed for the advent of future change. Having finally reconciled the endemic differences with its European Union partners, nothing prevents movement in a new direction.

Blair's four principles of modernization, defined as 'a flexible economy, a modern welfare state, constitutional reform, and a clear identity and role for ourselves in the outside world' (*The Econ-*

omist, 1996b: 18), chime in well with the moderate version of civil society that could be underway. Constitutional reform in the shape of devolution for both Scotland and Wales has been one of the earliest political acts of the new administration. Designed to bring power closer to the people by giving them a voice in directing their own affairs, it is hailed as a step in the right direction. The background towards the 'flexible economy' has already been refered to. Slimmed down by deregulation, detached from union-championed worker solidarity, inured to discretionary work patterns of every description, gender integrated, as well as mobile, the workforce stands ready for future challenges. The intricacies of 'the modern welfare state' are, as in America, still highly elusive. Workfare, occupational retraining, plus firm attacks against the welter of self-perpetuating dependencies have proved a double-edged sword. Expanding the public sector by recruitment of the newly trained swells budgetary deficits. Subsidizing private re-employment is likely to bring newcomers into employment at the expense of incumbents. And limiting welfare provision in the absence of an expansion of skill-matched job opportunities, will only shift the burden of maintenance into different, often more costly directions. However, a start has been made.

Blair's passionate Christian advocacy linking responsibility and duty to wider opportunity is applauded with education being the key. Britain's role in the outside world, however, offers wider potentialities. As a mentor for a new concept of civil society, the possibilities are virtually endless. Social discontent, even in countries that have passed from near-subsistence to consumer affluence, is widespread and chronic. The 'optimism index', designed to reflect the level of contentment over a range of socio-economic indices, has in Germany moved into the negative field by a margin of 19 percent, while in France it has descended to a record low of minus 34 percent (*Los Angeles Times*, 9 October 1997: 14). Conversely in America, 74 percent of the public are recorded as dissatisfied with the way the country is shaping up, and more than one in two people questioned expect their children to have a life less good than their own (Bok, 1996: 1). Within the context of the status quo, prospects are gloomy. The gradualist evolution towards a middle-of-the-road civic society, implicit in the Blair administration's capacities, could offer a way out of the diverse dilemmas, and is epitomized by his call for a 'Third Way.'

4. FUTURE PROSPECTS

In this final section, three possible models of civic society – stakeholding, connexity and deliberative democracy – will be explored before we define a new positive agenda for a future post-scarcity society.

There is nothing in the above scenario to offend American political susceptibilities. Indeed, in many ways, the United States appears better equipped for the challenge even than Britain. The basis of bipartisan common ground is unique. We have already referred to the fact that both President Clinton and Vice-President Gore publicly embrace civic society values. It is less well known that Bob Dole as the Republican presidential candidate in the course of his 1996 campaign, in turn, expressed his conviction that 'Americans feel nostalgia for the fading values of small towns which is why politicians on all sides have embraced the language of "responsibility" and "community"... Americans enjoy the grandeur of federal power, the knowledge that Washington is the world's capital again. Again, Americans like to recall stable communities, the fellowship of the boy-scout troops and village clubs, the civic virtues of the Founders' (*The Economist*, 13 July 1996: 30). The personal involvement in the form of active participation inherent in implementing the ideals of civic society are becoming apparent. Community voluntarism, as Drucker documents, is more extensive than often realized, and gaining strength. An astonishing one million non-profit organizations, accounting for as much as one-tenth of GNP and constituting the largest single employer, are active within the community, comprising some 90 million adults (every other American) who work at least three hours per week in institutions such as churches, hospitals, health care agencies and community services. He further projects that by 2010 as many as 120 million will devote at least five hours per week to the extension of community life (Drucker, 1993: 175 *et passim*).

Before that occurs, however, he warns that the existing intrusion of 'the megastate' will have to be overcome. Once accomplished, the knowledge revolution will be given free reign to reinforce the community spirit and usher in the growth of a civic society. We cannot endorse such a sanguine projection. Until the still expanding levels of inequality, the growing problem of the underclass and not least the pervasiveness of avaricious materialism are addressed, expectations of social harmonization appear unrealistic. Even the new thinking implicit in the concepts of the stakeholder economy, connexity and deliberative democracy, for all the added dimension they bring to the debate, cannot be effective in the absence of social change.

At this stage, the stakeholder concept is still relatively inchoate. Within Europe, it anticipates taking the German-type *Mitbestimmung* status, designed to give workers a voice within companies, a step further. Apart from the manager-cum-worker arrangement, the additional dimensions of suppliers and customers, together with representatives of the wider community affected by companies' activities, are also included. Business, while remaining dominant within the market economy, is not only the concern of management plus shareholders, but belongs to us all. Some take the innovation further, claiming that empowerment cannot be confined to token representation, but must extend to office rotation plus actual co-ownership. Only then, the argument continues, can there be safeguards against the hegemony of vested interests and the increasing penetration of transnationals disruptive of civic life (Rustin, 1985).

Historically within the United States any measures threatening to introduce collectivism through the back door are taboo (Keane, 1988). The stakeholder concept has thus undergone a startling conversion. Republican representatives reinterpret the concept as affirming the intensification of civic empowerment by pointing to the increasingly widespread investment by individuals and families in bonds and in stocks. The growth of portfolios, i.e. 'stakeholding', that has taken place is taken as evidence of democratization to a point where not only wealth but equally power are presumed to be shared.

Neither version, the USA's less than the European, is truly convincing. Equating the petty shareholding of the average investor with civic empowerment borders on absurdity. Conversely, worker participation more often than not results in co-optation rather than a firm countervailing voice. Furthermore, cooperatives, wherever implemented, have failed to achieve their desired goals of consensus and harmonization. Thus longevity is rare, even in Spain where the experiment has been further advanced than elsewhere.

Connexity is a more subtle concept, linking the local and national context to the wider global community through the development of Internet-linked cooperation. The new universe of 'intimate citizenship', with its 'life-world' of expanding personal, social and sexual diversity, sets up a structure in which a new form of citizenship accustomed to mutual discourse over a wide range of topics is obtainable (Waites, 1996). Superimposed are the new networks of a cosmopolitan society, interlinked by free dialogue where differentiation of status, income or nationality has been surpassed. Already issues of environmental and moral concern are transcending conventional boundaries. The proudest example is the anti-landmine movement. The original initiative of one single committed person, Jodi Williams (now Nobel Laureate), in the span of a mere six years proved effective enough in leading to a worldwide treaty banning the weapons. Novel techniques such as intensive long-range lobbying, the directing of global campaigns towards specific trouble spots, mobilizing media exposure through world celebrities such as Princess Diana, demonstrate ways of linking prime policy-makers to the grassroots. Beyond that lies the impending technological capacity for electronic worldwide voting, capable of inducing new forms of citizenship where a revitalized civic order could thrive (Mulgan, 1997). However, the ever-present possibility that such new developments will lead to intolerance and unreason cannot be ignored. As history amply reminds us, it is far from certain that technological advance and social progress necessarily go hand-in-hand.

Deliberative democracy, the strongest contender, in contrast to connexity's global dimension, remains firmly anchored within the nation state. Most prominently associated with the writings of Jürgen Habermas, one of Europe's leading intellectuals, deliberative democracy decisively rejects the technological rationality implied by the connexity perspective. Instead, the 'constitutional patriotism' paradigm recognizes that concepts of the 'global community' are still premature. Habermas perceives the greatest hope as resting on the diffusion of issue politics with citizens' involvement in public affairs finding their best voice and outlet. Party democracy has turned into a sham. The spectacle of unceasing wrangling, overt partisanship, bogus debate, crass self-seeking and not least the various scandals of campaign finance, denial and graft have brought government into disrepute. Citizens realize that adequate redress must lie with focused interest groups where their participation brings results. There, the field is wide open and not merely to the ritual of voting. Routinely arguing one's position in public forums will foster the habit of weighing the flow of argument, inducing mutual comprehension of differing views, and achieving a workable compromise. Most vitally perhaps, in providing a background of consciousness movement towards civic society might emerge as the next logical step (Habermas, 1989, 1995).

However, as Hobbes warned long ago (and arguably this applies equally to Rousseau's 'general will'), deliberative assemblies have the unhappy tendency of being turned into arenas where self-interested orators habitually rise to the top (Berkowitz, 1996; Guttman and Thompson 1996). Etzioni joins those who take issue with 'deliberation' as an idealized process of fair procedure where political actors engage in reasoned argument for the purpose of finding the best objective solution for all (Etzioni, 1996: 98). His objections are threefold. Firstly, not all participants have the same knowledge and available time. Were this the case, then debate would go on for ever. Secondly, it is not individuals but sub-groups with their sectarian agendas that are the characteristic context of interest groups. Hence, caucus formation instead of 'reasoned argument' typically carries the day. Thirdly, and most importantly, issues that communities face are predominantly neither empirical nor logical, but normative to the extent that harmonization might be unachievable. Where values diverge, differences are likely to reward skillful orators, who are nowadays likely to be members of 'the knowledge elite', with in-built advantages that their protagonists cannot match.

Yet for all that, one would be unwise to dismiss the more recent perspectives as inappropriate to widening the context of the debate. Critiques operate under assumptions of unchanged conditions while evidently this will not be the case. Capitalism's prime strength, as Schumpeter reminded us some while ago, lies in its in-built capacity to renew itself in advance of crises reaching their breaking point (Schumpeter, 1951). Advanced capitalism has nearly reached such a stage once again. While conditions of a 'two-thirds' society, with a larger sector of haves confronting a sizeable growing minority of have-nots, persist, notions of civic society must be a chimera. Two issues, to us, appear to be uppermost. They are the widening levels of inequality, together with the pressures of downsizing that cannot be ignored for long.

As noted earlier in Chapter 4, earning inequalities have doubled in the past two decades, moving Thurow to declare that in the 'winner take all' society of today, the 'compensation' of the average *Fortune* magazine executive, as against that of the average employee, has escalated from a multiple of 35 in the 1980s, to as much as 157 times some fifteen years later, exceeding comparable countries' average differential many times over (Thurow, 1996: 21). Even more dramatically, the arch-conservative political commentator Arianne Huffington, levels the charge that 'the divisions between the inner cities and the suburbs are daily growing starker – gated communities and housing projects are separated by walls of resentment and indifference... Every day 2660 American children are born into poverty and 8493 are abused and neglected, while 15 million are growing up in homes that are breeding grounds for criminal behavior' (Huffington, 1996: B6). At the end of some two centuries of momentous achievement, capitalism may have reached the decisive internal contradiction which Marx posed as its grim apogee: a surplus redundant sub-proletariat requiring sustenance, yet who cannot find work commensurate to their needs. Within Europe the prime bane is the crisis of unemployment, while in the United States the threat lies in the growth of 'discretionary employment' linked to the chronic condition of the largely black underclass.

Though it is true that 'since the 1980s, the American economy has lost 42m jobs and created 67m jobs, a net gain of 25m jobs, compared to only 4m for continental Europe in the same period' (Hale, 1997: 56), it is equally the case that concurrently some 45 million were located within the nether end of the solidifying dual economy where vastly inferior conditions prevail. Dahrendorf's earlier reference to the redundant and unwanted is gloomily apt. With automation, computerization and now the informatics network, millions of jobs historically performed by human labor have become the preserve of the modern machine. Inanimate labor is infinitely more productive, precise, dependable and compliant than the men and women they have replaced. Indeed, according to authoritative observers, were it not for the inhibitions put in the way by business, labor as well as government to halt 'the march of progress' for their own sectional ends, the pace of replacement would already have gone much further than it has already (Rifkin, 1995; Newman and de Zoysa 1995).

It may well be premature to endorse Jeremy Rifkin's presumption of 'The End of Work', but Judith Schor's analysis (noted earlier in Chapter 4) of halving the working year indicates what might have been accomplished. The implications are startling. For the first time in history, the problems of scarcity and toil can be consigned to the past. For the advanced industrial nations the problem of production has been virtually resolved. When the remaining problem of distribution is brought into line, a good quality of life, hitherto the monopoly of a tiny elite, can be made available to the masses. For the first time ever, there is now the prospect of the proverbial free lunch. While men and women, under conditions of a modicum work commitment, cultivate lifestyles that optimize their various talents, our 'mechanical slaves' will produce the goods needed. Stonier was clearly over-optimistic in his 1983 prediction that in twenty years' time, one-tenth of the workforce will be adequate to fulfill all of society's material needs (Stonier, 1983), but in any event, André Gorz seems closer to the mark. Gorz projects that in the foreseeable future, a lifetime total work commitment of some 20 000 hours – fairly close to one-half the current average working span – will be sufficient to provide ample for everyone, subject to fair shares for all (Gorz, 1985).

Were this to happen, conceivably within the next two to three generations, the prospects for civic society would be utterly transformed. The impediments of disparate status and income, of incapacity to partake in civic affairs, and of access to social capital would be removed. The advent of post-scarcity conditions and of civic society are, in fact, symbiotically interrelated in three different ways. First, advocates of civic society are exceptionally in a position to accelerate the advent of post-scarcity conditions. Secondly, post-scarcity society will uniquely provide a framework where civic participation can flourish more effectively than ever before. And thirdly, once established the two will interact in concert in many ways. Initially civic society adherents will need to give recognition to the potentialities lying ahead. Relief from the problem of scarcity will lessen the impulse of fear and greed, will equalize the quality of life together with access to knowledge and education, while dispersing the potential enjoyment of lifestyles to an extent where all can equally be involved in the conduct of public affairs. The issues that matter will not be resolved by exhortation to self-regeneration, but need to be focused on the realistic priorities impending today. With work no longer secure and turning into a scarce commodity, the untrammeled free market can no longer be allowed to rule the roost. Systematically monitored by grassroots activism, issues such as the reduction of statutory working hours, schemes of work-sharing and office rotation, plus a comprehensive extension of educational access are vital. Most importantly an extension of the 'work' definition into such spheres as voluntary labor, community service, ecological protection, child and disabled care, preventive medicine and not least all forms of person-enhancing and socially useful self-expression will advance both causes simultaneously. If work defines status and dignity then this component is crucial.

Once operative, post-scarcity society will unquestionably function best by integrating the aims of civic society. Participation, empowerment, communal networking and deliberation – all under conditions of unceasing scrutiny guarding against differentiation – will provide a framework where universalization, in the sense of affording each and every individual their optimal life chance, can at last be approached. As we have argued, civic society will not come about until current structural impediments have been removed. Similarly, the potentialities for universalization that post-scarcity conditions offer are bound to be thwarted unless civic participation, in the sense of an authentic public commitment, arises.

If this scenario seems unduly utopian, so be it. This does not imply unawareness of the many constraints that will need to be overcome. Gloomy prognosis centering on apocalyptic potentialities such as the endemic clash of civilizations, the decline of the west, nuclear proliferation, ecological destruction or internal chaos, are all too abundant. What we project may well not materialize in the face of countervailing forces gaining the upper hand, yet that does not imply that the aspirations should not be pursued. Civic society looks back on a past checkered career (Newman and de Zoysa, 1998). Prospects ahead could qualitatively turn out much better.

REFERENCES

Atkinson, D., *The Common Sense of Community* (London: Demos, 1995).
Bell, D., 'American Exceptionalism Revisited: the Role of Civic Society', *Public Interest*, No. 95 (1996), 38–56.
Berkowitz, P., 'The Debating Society', *New Republic* (25 November 1996), 36–42.
Berman, P. (ed.), *Quotations from the Anarchists* (New York: Praeger, 1992).
Bok, D., *The State of the Nation: Government and the Quest for a Better Society* (Cambridge, Mass.: Harvard University Press, 1996).
Bork, R., *Slouching Towards Gomorrah: Modern Liberalism and American Decline* (New York: Regan Books, 1996).
Cohen, J. L. and Arato, A., *Civic Society and Political Theory* (Cambridge, Mass.: MIT Press, 1992).
Cranston, M., *The Solitary Self: Jean-Jacques Rousseau in Exile and Adversity* (Chicago: Chicago University Press, 1996).
Derber, C., *What's Left: Radical Politics in the Post Communist Era* (Amherst: University of Massachusetts Press, 1995).
Drucker, P. F., *Post Capitalist Society* (New York: Harper Business, 1993).
Durkheim, E., *The Division of Labor in Society*, trans. George Simpson (New York: Free Press, 1964, orig. French 1893).

Elshtain, J. B., *Democracy on Trial* (New York: Basic Books, 1995).
Etzioni, A., *The Spirit of Community: the Reinvention of American Society* (New York: Touchstone, 1994).
—— (ed.) *New Communitarian Thinking: Persons, Virtues, Institutions and Communities* (Charlottesville, VA: University Press of Virginia, 1995).
—— *The New Golden Rule: Community and Morality in a Democratic Society* (New York: Basic Books, 1996).
Fukuyama, F., *Trust: Social Virtues and the Creation of Prosperity* (New York: Free Press, 1995).
—— *The End of Order* (New York: Social Market Foundation, 1997).
Gardner, J., *The Age of Extremism* (Toronto, CA: Birch Lane, 1997).
Gellner, E., *Conditions of Liberty, Civil Society and its Rivals* (London: Penguin, 1994).
Gorz, A., *Paths to Paradise: the Liberation from Work* (New York: Norton, 1985).
Guttman, A., and Thompson, D., *Democracy and Disagreement* (Cambridge, Mass: Harvard University Press, 1996).
Habermas, J., 'Citizenship and National Identity', in Ronald Benier (ed.), *Theorizing Citizenship* (Albany: Suny Press, 1995).
—— *The New Conservatism* (Cambridge, Mass.: MIT Press, 1989).
Hale, D., 'America's Amazing Strength', *The Economist* (20 September 1997).
Havel, V., *The Art of the Impossible* (New York: Knopf, 1997).
Hirsch, H. N., 'The Threnody of Liberalism: Constitutional Liberty and the Renewal of Community', *Political Theory*, 14(3), (August 1986), 423–49.
Hodgson, G., *The World Turned Right Side Up: a History of the Conservative Ascendancy in America* (New York: Houghton Mifflin, 1996).
Howard, R. D., *Human Rights and the Search for Community* (Boulder, Co: Westview Press, 1995).
Huffington, A., 'What Kemp Should Say in San Diego', *San Diego Union Tribune* (13 August 1996).
Ignatieff, M., 'After the Revolution', *New Republic* (19 & 26 August 1996).
Keane, J., *Democracy and Civil Society* (London: Verso, 1988).
Krammick, I., 'Civilization and its Malcontents', *New Republic* (17 March 1997), 40–5.
Lind, M., *Up from Conservatism: Why the Right is Wrong for America* (New York: Houghton Mifflin, 1996).
Mulgan, G., *Connexity* (London: Chatto and Windus, 1997).
Newman, O. and de Zoysa, R., 'The Underclass, Welfare, and Joblessness', *CSA Topics* (San Diego State University: October 1995), 1–29.
—— 'Perspectives on Civic Society: the prospect ahead', *DMI Rapport*, No. 2 (Sundsvall, Sweden, 1998).
Nisbet, R. A., *The Quest for Community* (New York: Oxford University Press, 1953).
Rifkin, J., *The End of Work* (New York: Putnam, 1995).
Rustin, M., *For a Pluralist Socialism* (London: Verso, 1985).
Schumpeter, J. A., *The Theory of Economic Development* (Cambridge, Mass.: Harvard University Press, 1951).
Schweickart, D., *Against Capitalism* (Boulder, Co: Westview, 1996).

Selbourne, D., *The Principle of Duty: an Essay on the Foundations of Civic Order* (London: Sinclair-Stevenson, 1994).
Seligman, A. B., *The Idea of Civil Society* (New York: Free Press, 1992).
Sklar, H., *The Dying American Dream* (Boston, Mass.: South End Press, 1995).
Spragens, T. Jr., 'Communitarian Liberalism', in Amitai Etzioni (ed.), *New Communitarian Thinking* (Charlottesville, VA: University Press of Virginia, 1995), 37–51.
Stonier, T., *The Wealth of Information* (London: Thames Methuen, 1983).
The Economist, 'Bob Dole, Neighbour and Statesman' ((a) London, 13 July 1996), and 'Blair's Vision Thing' ((b) 17 September 1996).
Thurow, L. C., *The Future of Capitalism* (New York: William Morrow, 1996).
Tonnies, F., *Community and Association*, trans and supplemented by Charles P. Loomis (London: Routledge, 1995; orig. German ed. 1887).
Tucker, R. C., *The Marx-Engels Reader* (New York: Norton, 1978).
Wainwright, H., *Arguments for a New Left: Answering the Free-Market Right* (Oxford: Blackwell, 1996).
Waites, M., 'Lesbian and Gay Theory, Sexuality and Citizenship', *Contemporary Politics*, 2(3) (Autumn 1996), 139–50.
Walzer, M., 'The Communitarian Critique of Liberalism', *Political Theory*, 18(1) (January 1990), 6–23.
Wilcox, C., *Onward Christian Soldiers: the Religious Right in America* (Boulder, Co: Westview, 1996).
Willetts, D., 'Conservatism Now', *Prospect*, Issue 23 (London, October 1997), 16–17.

7 Learning Curves

1. EXCEPTIONALISM REVISITED

Early this century the German sociologist Werner Sombart visited the United States in his quest for the secret of American classlessness. Socialist aspirations, he tersely concluded, had run aground on a universal enjoyment of 'roast beef and apple pie' (Sombart, 1976: 126). At a time when class schism was rife throughout Europe, widespread social contentment had averted a similar fate befalling the United States.

America has always prided itself on its unique status of classlessness. While other industrial societies had generated a distinctive proletariat with militant socialist parties promoting workers' solidaristic consciousness and exacerbating endemic class tension, in America the pathway to ascent and the good life stood open to all. Individual freedom and equal opportunity, plus a mobility ladder that, given effort and talent, could lead even to the White House, had averted the social divisions that others displayed.

Paradoxically, at a time throughout the advanced world when class consolidation has dramatically abated, within the United States the evil is distinctly rearing its head. Not, it needs to be added, in the historic form of capitalist versus proletariat bifurcation, but instead in a manner quite new. America is in the process of creating a four-fold division with two firmly entrenched classes at each polar end, plus two fluid amorphous class-based formations lying in between. At the apex there is the novel phenomenon of a concentrated ruling plutocracy made up primarily of very rich people with vested wealth and power positions, supplemented by a sprinkling of the emergent 'knowledge elite'. Next in line comes the broad mass of the well-to-do middle class – well established, well paid, qualified and for the first time in history deriving a sizeable part of their lifestyle from investments in stocks and bonds. The third tier comprises the exceedingly fast-growing component of the contingent labor force, scratching a meager insecure living from part-time, casual, seasonal and increasingly 'independent contractor'-type work. At the bottom of the social scale resides the other novel phenomenon of the underclass. Though not quite as homogeneous as is widely assumed, it is nevertheless composed of a largely jobless ethnic minority, detached from the productive economy, stigmatized and increasingly imbued with a 'subversive subculture' that has severed itself from the mainstream.

The new ruling class is an unprecedented phenomenon. Characterized as 'the haute bourgeoisie' (Sherman, 1996: 133–4), it is a compact elite amounting to a mere 2 percent. Its sociological role model more closely resembles the South American plutocracies than the western-type ruling class. Made up of diverse multimillionaires, corporate chief executives, entrenched politicians, military leaders, national and regional king makers, together with the media and the entrepreneurial elite, they are more crucially in control of the commanding heights of the state than ever before. They are prototypically the first and only global elite. Overwhelmingly metropolitan-based, reciprocally interlinked with other societies' governing elites, possessed of immense holdings of wealth, and with access to the best global brains and other resources, their power is immense. For them, constraining laws or morals have been abolished. Refracted via the ubiquitous media as 'the great and the good', their Olympian glamour is made to dazzle uncounted millions throughout the world. Moreover, amidst all their wealth and privilege they have learned one vital lesson that ruling groups often forget: in order to retain power, it is essential for elites constantly to revitalize their membership. The new American plutocracy uniquely has an ideal influx at its disposal. The equally recent 'knowledge elite' supplies the ideal pipeline for revitalization. Technologically adept at the very latest advances, flexible and imbued with a matching entrepreneurial ideology, it is ever ready to step into the footsteps of those who drop out.

The rewards are dramatic. The average major corporation executive officer (whose 'compensation' incidentally has risen five-fold in the past fifteen years) now lays claim to an annual paycheck of $4.5 million alone, quite apart from the stock options, deferred emoluments, extensive fringe benefits, etc. at his command (Sweeney, 1997: 14–15). Compared to the average production worker, in today's 'winner take all society', their pay has risen from a multiple of 35 to an astonishing 157 in the past twenty years (Thurow, 1996). The wealthiest 1 percent now control one-third of national wealth (and as much as 56.2 percent of private business assets), fully equaling the holding of the lesser-endowed 90 percent of the American population (Steel, 1997: 27). During the same period the top executive's salary has ballooned by 951 percent – at five times the rate of inflation (Barlett and Steele, 1996: 8). In one single year, the Disney corporation chief executive received the staggering sum of $203 million in salary and other awards, while thanks to the corporation chiefs' growing practice of awarding each other huge benefits, the Coca-Cola chairman now has amassed $672 million of his company's stock (Hacker, 1997: 25). Contrast this with the fact that in 1995 as many as 20 million American families, some 28.4 percent of the national population, were making do with earnings of less than $25 000 (ibid.: 225) – barely enough to secure sufficiency – and Schwarz's terse comment that inequality trends could lead America to 'become a class society like those in Latin America' (Schwarz, 1996: B5), ceases to sound extreme. While in virtually all other western societies class schisms remain largely reconciled while the postwar Social Compact continues to hold, exceptionally the United States seems set on a course where, for the first time in its history, class conflict has emerged as a distinct possibility.

What has saved that exigency is the presence of the two intermediate classes – the bulk of the American population who remain settled and pacified. Thanks to the never-ending boom of the stock market the broad middle class, increasingly enjoying the luxury of private investment benefit, more than ever embraces the strict market nexus ideology that offers employment and keeps them secure. Similarly, the discretionary labor force, now approximating one-quarter of Americans, while objectively sharing much of their social destiny with the lower class, due to the entrepreneurial character of their existence remains anchored to the American dream. The middle class itself, roughly one-half of the US population, is an amorphous heterogeneous group. At the top stands the knowledge elite, distinguished by their command of the latest information technology, adept at transnational skills, while significantly providing the creators, operators and purveyors of the emergent post-industrial post-service economy. In their lifestyle and prospects some of their echelons supremely straddle the classes. An orthopedic surgeon can now earn above $300 000 in one single year, while computer wizards, trading-floor operators or sports and media stars still in their twenties can, at one single swoop, parachute their way into the elite. Below the knowledge elite – already exceeding one-tenth of the labor force – come the broad base of professionals, managers, supervisors, moderate business owners plus a whole range of middle-class production and service workers who to a greater or lesser extent supplement their earnings with income-producing investment. These, together with the rising element of well-to-do retirees, outstandingly the beneficiaries of the stock market boom, remain firmly attached to the status quo.

The discretionary labor force could prove the decisive factor. With downsizing set to intensify for the foreseeable future, their ranks are destined to swell while their earning potential will decline. Altogether, the class process is in a condition of flux. The structure can be perceived in the form of a sliding scale. The momentum of downsizing, that started the process, is still in its prime. Downward mobility can thus be a common destiny for both the middle and the contingent class. When more and more of the latter join up with a truculent underclass, the entire social order could be faced with a nasty jolt. Even today's confident optimism that follows a buoyant economy might not withstand the tide of popular dissent. Meanwhile the middle class has resolutely set its face against intervention. Distributive government action or increased taxation remain strictly taboo. Indeed, welfare provision is being cut back further, while even the moderate role of the Internal Revenue Service is under attack. Not merely the wealthy but no less that broad band of the middle class remain wedded to the unfettered market ideology that equates welfare with penalizing effort and merit, while unearned largesse rewards the idle. They firmly demand to remain free, to enjoy the fruits of their labor (no less than the bounty of the market boom) and accusingly point to the crass covert inequalities that accompany even the milder planned economies. Sheltered within their gated communities they choose to turn a blind eye to rising surveillance costs and the prevalence of street crime, and experience nothing wrong with the ongoing workings of the American dream.

Reformers, on the other hand, reject the mood of equanimity that prevails today. They point to the fact that compared to its peers, hyper-affluent America has a higher proportion of its citizens in prison, on the streets or suffering poverty; that the constantly growing apparatus of police, private security and prison officials, together with the expense of special education, AIDS and drug addiction – all disproportionately directed towards the underclass – far exceed the costs of a tolerable safety net. Furthermore, government support for corporate welfare and subsidies (quite apart from violating the 'hands-off' code) is vastly expensive; and last but not least, the massive inequalities that characterize America today are fundamentally at odds with all notions of a moral democracy, or the aspirations for a civic society in which all play their part.

A few words regarding the role of the informatics highway appear apt. Generally, informatics is rated as a force for democratization and equalization. The Internet's capacities provide a unique 'window on the world', foster the growth of 'a global village' in which all can participate equally, and operate in a climate of social equality where income or status criteria no longer apply. Yet, privileged as America is in regard to ownership and access to the world of computers, constructive use remains confined to a minority who use the informatics revolution to buttress their wealth and their privilege. In regard to the rest, critics claim, the informatics highway is another vacuous palliative of confusing messages, mindless video games plus the violent fantasies of virtual reality projections that further aggravate their depressed condition. Within the current development, both options are equally evident. We will elaborate on the effects in the section below.

2. THE INFORMATICS HIGHWAY

Among the public at large, computerization is generally perceived as an unmixed blessing. It advances knowledge, speeds up production and diversifies communication throughout the world. Some critics, however, view it more ambiguously. The reasons are varied: it reinforces the pressure of standardization and commodification; it lends itself to manipulation and misinformation; and it puts ever more power and wealth into the hands of the mighty and rich. It further divides the rich from the poor domestically as well as internationally; creates a false consciousness where material wants push moral and social considerations aside; and replaces intensive face-to-face cultures with an alienated mechanical surrogate where people no longer talk to each other, but become mere adjuncts of lifeless machines. There are equally serious reservations regarding surveillance. Informatics has put immense power into the hands of controllers in regard to the invasion of privacy, dossier formation and discrimination plus misinformation of many kinds, thus seriously limiting the dissemination of non-conformist opinion. Access to data is widespread, not merely confined to political leaders and administrators, but no less to business interests using the information for their own ends. The rights of privacy are seriously undermined. Even the presumed educational benefits are open to question. The bland standardization of study and research, the access to esoteric sources for plagiarization, together with the loss of the literary tradition are widely deplored (Comor, 1994; Schiller, 1996).

Yet for all that, the expectation remains that technological advance will lead to progress and modernization. Computerization affords such comprehensive access to knowledge and information that the sum total of human achievement as well as happiness will uniformly advance. Broadly based civic participation is bound to promote democratization, while opening up the entire universe to commerce and exploration. Further, the habits of freely flowing exchange will establish a parallel giving-based culture to balance the profit calculus pertaining elsewhere. Not least, the expanding network of diversified ground level electronic communication will offer a strong safeguard against conflict and war (Howard, 1997). In the words of noted researchers: 'With the power of telecomputing, it is possible to expand dialogue, to show people that individuals can be effective, and organize groups of strangers into communities. There are few more important tasks at every level from neighborhood to the planet in the days ahead' (Dewart and Rheingold 1988: 2–8).

The facts speak for themselves. During the 1980s, the aggregate value of the world communication services increased by 800 percent. By 1986, the output of the international information economy – comprising mass media, electronic services, communication equipment plus processes – amounting to $1.185 trillion, was by far the fastest growing component of the world's recorded output. If anything, during the 1990s the pace has accelerated. The United States, outstandingly the largest producer of informatics hardware and software, now has more than two-thirds of the workforce directly employed in the production, promotion and distribution of informatics services (Fredrick, 1993: 58–9). Computers are commonplace in classrooms, retailing outlets, home offices, churches, clubs and voluntary associations. Universally, each and every commercial undertaking, bank, insurance office or supermarket carries its battery of interconnected computers. Holes in the wall dispense bundles of cash, while airline, theater or sporting event tickets are bought and sold by means of the Internet. The global village has entered millions of homes via access to libraries, art displays, archaeological sights, historic research, vicarious visits to beauty spots or virtual reality games. Commodity shopping, meals at home delivery, or global networking with contacts all over the world are spreading daily, while millions transact all their affairs from insurance and banking to portfolio investment via the worldwide web. By pressing a few buttons, virtually every schoolchild in the near future should have gained entry into the entire universe of human knowledge while (as needs to be added) conversely the computer non-literate will have become even more sidelined than they are now.

Yet amidst all that traffic there is an altogether deafening noise when it comes to dissent. Popular movements for social change which in the past had provided correctives to excess exploitation or public abuse have been downsized, degraded and, as 'cost non-effective', consigned to oblivion within a market economy in which the profit nexus reigns supreme. It is both the strength and no less the weakness of the US model that it cultivates the belief that there can be no alternative to the course that now prevails. Denying alternative options in part makes the model odious and in a different manifestation makes it supreme. Its power, greatly reinforced by the logistics of information technology, is virtually total. The social alternatives of collective control, made synonymous with communist tyranny, have been consigned to the dustbin of history. The liberal model concerned with the quality of civic life for the entire community is dismissed as utopian impracticability, unable to meet the calculus of profitability. Now that the 'Asian model' for all the world to see has been exposed as an ineffective and corrupt paper tiger, the 'there is no alternative' message rules all it surveys. Domestically, with the profit calculus outranking all else, dissent has been stilled, while globally the self-same American message is echoed by international bodies such as the World Bank and the IMF.

Yet, while its force is compelling, the momentum is not quite as categorical as it may seem. Corporate power in the form of the transnationals increasingly appears to be gaining pre-eminence over the nation state. Thus the very absolutism that is anathema to the pluralist philosophy on which democratic capitalism rests, is steadily gaining more ground. 'Increasingly', as Schiller observes, 'the voices that reach national audiences are those that secure the support and the financing of the moneyed crowd' (Schiller, 1996: xiv). Paradoxically, under conditions where the means of communication are hugely advanced, 'at the top of the ivory tower, the watchword is silence'. No one wants to stand guilty of rocking the boat. Academic inquiry, ever eager for 'cost effective' grants, is railroading itself into safe channels so as not to offend corporate donors. The media need to maximize advertising revenue to stay in business, while, with political caucuses filtering scarce news releases to favorite outlets, reporters and journalists need to guard against biting the hand that feeds them. Finally, with communication moguls, on the basis of market returns, firmly convinced that the public will only pay for good news, the charmed circle of the silent conspiracy finds itself closed. Nothing can better illustrate Gramsci's 1920s identification of cultural hegemony, that thanks to willing compliance serves the ruling class as the supreme instrument of hermetic control. With ideology masquerading as objective truth, to all intents and purposes dissent is practically stilled (Gramsci, 1971; Gill, 1993).

On the world stage, America's role is similarly ambivalent. On the one hand, it is the benevolent superpower dispensing benefits in every direction, and on the other, a predatory self-seeking hegemon. America's unquestioned pre-eminence in all the various channels of the informatics age – from hardware to software, products to processes, digitalization to miniaturization, as well as in the fields of banking, finance, communication, fashion and pragmatic know-how, and above all its long lead in the news and entertainment media field – makes its cooperation virtually indispensable to all who wish to be part of the post-industrial age. What America cultivates and uses today, the entire world covets without delay. Notably, Pax America now hinges much less on the nation's economic or military might than on America's dominance of the informatics highway. At the same time, America's penetration of the tastes, habits, culture and increasingly fantasies of the whole world is in many quarters perceived as insidious control and colonization. Be it depicted as the 'Great Satan', 'the ugly American' or indeed ever-smiling Uncle Sam with his wide-open purse, what America stands for and represents in the informatics age lends itself ideally to vilification and demonization. The almighty dollar may no longer outrank the yen or the deutschmark but Hollywood, the Big Mac and now Windows 98 symbolize in the minds of millions the world over the true face of US hegemony that obliterates other cultures without a second thought. Mind control, product addiction or universal internalization of the dictum that 'there is no alternative' are construed as devices that, aiding American imperialism, bind without chains. Moreover, that the market nexus, as the instant efficiency of the southeast Asian bailout to preserve investment demonstrates, will always stop short of hurting one's own, does little to help. Hypocrisy, real or perceived, destroys the facade. Western pursuit of naked power and wealth finds itself juxtaposed to the putative indigenous cultures of accord and harmonization allegedly devoured by American greed.

Informatics, in such a context, can be seen as a double-edged sword. Making a fetish of cost-control and deregulation undermines the substance on which civic society depends. It threatens the fabric of social existence no less than the integrity of the nation state. Not all will accord with the view that what is good for the Disney corporation or Microsoft is essentially good for the United States. Transnationals, whose reach is greatly enhanced by the informatics revolution, are notoriously fickle in their allegiance and accustomed to want their own way. Internally capitalism functions best within a context of pluralistic democracy, while externally competition is an imperative. Under current contingencies both presumptions are threatened. We will next consider the status of the nation state – an essential element in the debate – and will then turn to the options that the informatics revolution offers the future ahead.

3. THE NATION STATE

It is widely argued that the logic of the information revolution, with its momentum towards globalization, inevitably spells the end of the nation state (Hirst and Thompson, 1996; Featherstone, 1990; Ohmae, 1995). Increasingly world trade, the rise of the transnationals, the burgeoning volume of speculative capital, together with the accelerating speed and cheapening of communication have rendered the nation state obsolete. The historic functions of protecting the security and trade of national communities have fallen away. Thanks to computerization, production costs have been reduced, while the world over, producers with regular incomes are turned into ready consumers. Transcending parochial ideology, international corporations in concert with regional associations such the European Union, NAFTA, ASEAN and MERCOSUR as well as with global formations such as the United Nations, the IMF, OECD and the World Bank, are superseding the role of the nation state. Post-industrial society, in short, has left behind the era of the nation state that marked the age of industrialization, leading first to regional associations and ultimately to globalization where territorial boundaries will have virtually disappeared. Susan Strange takes the analysis a stage further. In her contention, the nation state is already an anachronism in any event: no longer able to protect its own borders or currency; incapable of imposing a stable policy in regard to taxation or labor laws; environmentally dependent upon the goodwill of other communities; and finally, in today's world of global mafias devoid of the means to enforce legislation on drugs, terror or crime (Strange, 1996).

Characteristically there are two models of the future ahead. On the one hand, it is considered that: 'The nation state is now obsolete, as a result of the telecommunications development and the development of transnational corporations, which have produced a genuinely global market that transcends national boundaries, and renders the nation state currently irrelevant.' Conversely, the argument is put forward that: 'The nation state is not yet obsolete, and.... efforts to control foreign, political, military, economic and cultural domination are an essential component of strategies of transition, both domestically and to promote a more firmly grounded political economy' (Parker, 1994: 55; both quotations).

Defenders of the nation state deny the assumptions of 'the halfway house', namely the thesis that the nation state in the global age has sunk to the level of the previous municipal administration: responsible mainly for the nuts and bolts of daily household affairs such as lighting, transportation, sewers plus the minutiae of local government (Ohmae, 1995). It is true that the Weberian imperative of the monopoly of the means of violence within a distinctive territory no longer strictly applies (Weber, 1968: 56). National security, exchange fluctuations, communications, environmental considerations and military contingencies typically are no longer exclusively national concerns. But, as happens under conditions of flux, as some functions expire others move into place. Primarily, boundaries are now more critically defined demographically than ever before. Frontier societies such as the wide open spaces of the Americas or the Antipodes no longer exist. For the millions of the less well-off and lower-skilled the past secure safety valve of emigration has been closed off. Now that demand for that type of labor is significantly lower than the available supply, states guard their borders with protective walls and militarized patrols. The very working classes who in the past were said to 'have no fatherland', are the very social groups who, in defense of their interests, have developed a consciousness in which the cosmopolitanism of the knowledge elite plays no part. The fervor of nationalistic partisanship apparent in all kinds of contexts, above all the growing rituals of sporting events, speaks volumes for the currents of change.

Moreover, the presumption of transnationals as utterly stateless is claimed as mistaken. In common with the general run of the business community, transnationals draw a wide range of benefits from their home base. Especially, 'US firms have very real benefits in remaining distinctly American that stem from the power and functions of the national state.' It is evident that 'the dollar remains the medium of international trade, that regulatory and standard-setting bodies like the FAA and FDA are world leaders and work closely with US industry, that the US courts are major means of defense of commercial and property rights throughout the world, that the federal government is a massive subsidizer of R&D and also a strong protector of the interests of US firms abroad' (Hirst and Thompson, 1996: 187).

As far as the ordinary citizen is concerned, ultimately it can only be the national state which is able to act as a counterweight to the mythical presumption that 'there is no alternative' to the relentless logic of the market nexus. That henceforth there is no defense to the impending ravages of globalization – the dynamics of the growing schism between the world's rich and poor; the vast despoliation of the environment; the exhaustion of vital resources, together with the momentum of predatory unrestrained materialism – in the end could prove the undoing of capitalism itself (Kapstein, 1994; Reich, 1991).

The informatics dynamic and the complexities of globalization are critically connected. Neither sovereignty nor globalization possess one single face. In the interest of balance we will therefore briefly review the pro and con arguments, particularly as they affect America's prospects.

'America', as the Tofflers proclaim, 'is where the future normally happens first' (Toffler and Toffler, 1994: 87). In 1995, the US had 40 computers per 100 households, twice as many as Germany or France and four times as many as Japan. Increasingly connection extends to e-mail plus the very latest appliances, five times as frequently as Europe and twelve times more than Japan (*The Economist*, 21 September 1996: 45). 'The best jobs created in the Innovation Age', projects the Workforce 2020 report, 'will be filled by Americans' (Judy and D'Amico, 1997: 3). The potentialities this offers for social equalization are profound. The means of production, hitherto a closely guarded monopoly of the financial elite, are being democratized. Within the millions of 'electronic cottages' production is being relocated within the home. The hollowed-out virtual corporations, slimmed down to a core of essential direct employees, have as an unintended by-product of their downsizing restored family life and made possible the resurgence of civic communities who are learning to manage their own affairs. Additionally, thanks to informatics technology, the closed network of secret files and classified information has become public property. The 'daily referendum' that Ross Perot held out as a means of popular control during his presidential campaigns could reappear in a new guise, no longer in the form of unending national polls exploited for political ends, but a way of allowing the community direct intervention within their collective affairs. That the informatics network also is classless, inasmuch as modes of speech, dress or demeanor are not made overt, is a further factor in support of the 'trans-spatial network nation' that may well arise (Howard, 1997: 111).

These optimistic assumptions are not universally shared. 'Cybernetic capitalism', as Hewson terms it, seizing upon the convergence of computer and telecommunications technology, has brought about an informatics revolution where 'capital invades the very cracks and pores of social life ... the reach of capital extends throughout society' (Hewson, 1994: 69). In the first instance, the state's capacity penetrates the very nooks of civic society by means of its monopoly over access to income, rule enforcement, economic and manpower control and increasingly the masterminding of information (Mann, 1988). Eventually however, manipulating the economy plus the media in the guise of 'objective and neutral' management, the transnationals will emerge supreme. Once integrated within the national economy, their voracious appetite for ever more subsidy plus their ever-present threat of deserting their home base for greener fields leaves behind a scorched earth of joblessness plus decayed plant and pollution. This leads to a role reversal in which the nation state ultimately becomes the subsidiary partner in the relationship (Melody, 1994).

More poignant still is the Council of Foreign Affairs' projection that within the 'winner take all societies' 'rapid technological change and increased international competition are fraying the job markets of major industrial countries ... The global economy is leaving millions of disaffected workers in its train. Inequality, unemployment and endemic poverty have become its handmaidens' (*The Economist*, 21 September 1996: 4). The dissolution of the carefully assembled twentieth-century social contract with social justice as its principal aim, is in all likelihood the principal threat. That it simultaneously opens the door towards the outstanding promise for social advance, where scarcity could become a thing of the past, is less often taken into account. We will turn to this issue in the section below.

4. THE JOBLESS REVOLUTION

The most explicit statement (noted earlier in Chapter 4) derives from Ralf Dahrendorf, who admits that 'some people are – awful as it is even to put this on paper – simply not needed... they are a cost to the rest, not a benefit' (Dahrendorf, 1995: 25). Directing his analysis to the 'precarious balance' that exists between the ever more pressing competitive imperative and the need for social cohesion, his analysis points to the growing millions whom, as a consequence of the informatics revolution, society apparently no longer needs: they are surplus to the economy, a negative factor in the national balance, and thus a burden without which their fellow citizens would be better off. The phenomenon, common to all advanced industrial societies, is being dealt with in three different ways. In the least advanced societies such as Russia and in South America, the typical mode of response is one of non-intervention, leaving the unwanted to fend for themselves, being challenged to either sink or swim. The European democracies stand at the opposite end of the pole. There, the effects of market forces are mitigated by social legislation that at various levels and by various means provides the jobless with benefits that, if short of the normative income, nevertheless affords an existence above subsistence, sufficient for many to have become reconciled to their fate. The US model is the most intricate and also the most efficient (at least in the short run). The unwanted contingent is dealt with in two ways. One part, the larger predominantly white and above the minimally skilled, constitutes the contingent labor force who subtly, by the nature of their quasi-entrepreneurial identity, are integrated into the American dream. The other part, the underclass consisting of 'the largely non-white hard-core of people caught up in a vicious circle of poverty and social collapse' (Krugman, 1994: 26), segregated as they are, barely impinge upon the more fortunate mainstream national community.

Effective as these devices may have proved for the moment, none of the methods can for any length of time be expected to endure. The numbers of those who will fall into the unwanted category will inevitably rise over time, while societies based on the precept of democracy cannot for ever sustain a system of wholesale exclusion. The force of bayonets, the time-honored tool of authoritarian oppression, inappropriate even in its own day, is in the long run destined to fail. In western democracies, not least the United States, the traditions of participation and empowerment are too strongly embedded. The social contract that, for all its disruptive potentialities, gave us progress as well as stability has grown deep roots. Even minorities have the means of having their protest heard. And above all, the threat of over-spill enrolls ever widening circles for reform with the cause of the deprived. Even the current levels of crime, family breakdown, drug-dealing and norm rejection among the underclass have aroused echoes of social contagion among the youth of the privileged classes on whose social compliance the system critically depends.

The logic of technological progress itself is an even greater obstacle to the permanence of the status quo. A recent juxtaposition of what might lie ahead has implications not immediately apparent. The pace of the computer revolution has been stupendous, while in other branches of the economic system productive advance has lagged badly behind. Computer costs, over the entire range of their capacity, have fallen by 99 percent and are now a mere 1 percent of their 1970 costs. 'If the price of automobiles had dropped at a corresponding rate', records the Workforce 2020 report, '1975's Rolls Royce would have cost $4.50 in 1995' (Judy and D'Amico, 1997: 14). 'If cars had developed at the same pace as microprocessors over the past two decades', echoes *The Economist*, 'a typical car would cost less than $5 and do 500 000 miles to the gallon' (*The Economist*, 21 September 1996: 8). The imbalance is less of a mystery than it may seem. Information technology has been an unexplored virgin field where restrictions on progress have been largely absent. Vast amounts of resources have been made available, a high proportion of top-level qualified manpower – the pick of the knowledge elite – have been attracted to this breakthrough field, while inhibitions to innovative advance, formal as well as informal, have been few and far between. Similar to the nineteenth-century goldrush, the era of railway construction, the early days of electronic discovery led by Bell and Edison, and above all the Fordist conveyor belt revolution in the mechanical field earlier this century, or the apogee of the space program, there has seemed no end to human ingenuity, when everything became possible for a period of time. Except that now, the pace of change thanks to computer science, miniaturization, digitalization plus the informatics breakthroughs, has accelerated to an extent undreamed of earlier. Elsewhere, however, if not actually standing still, the dynamics of progress have already been set. Massive capital investment, proven methods of service as well as production, the natural inertia of established practice, and not least the vested interest of millions of workers in defense of their jobs have stood in the way of parallel progress. The pace of advance is always uneven. This time, with the momentum of change hugely enhanced, the disproportion between the traditional arenas as against the pioneer field has been hugely expanded.

However, the critical point is not the hypothetical question of what might have been, but the unique insights into the future. Were it not for prevailing inhibitions – most significantly, we suggest, the natural defense of self-interest – the relationship between informatics progression and advances in other areas, though not close to actual parity, could have been more closely aligned. Restricted resources, the weight of committed investment plus the fear of the unknown have all played their part. Yet for all that, the major constraint has been the natural concern of millions of people to hang on to their jobs – not to be downsized, turned into contingent insecure workers, and above all not to join the surplus army of the unwanted – all of which has held back the pace of parallel advance. To speculate on what might have been is clearly unrewarding. It is far more important to think ahead. If we take advantage of the technological capacities that now are available, it appears manifest that in the near future – at least as far as the advanced industrial societies are concerned – the problem of scarcity might at last be overcome. What this potentially entails stretches one's imagination. Hunger, poverty, exploitation and deprivation – the immanent accompaniment to human existence since time immemorial – could become a dim memory of the past. Naturally it would be idle to put forward the view that even then the entire range of social problems would, at one stroke, be resolved. There does not exist a once and for all panacea for the resolution of human self-interest, irreconcilable wants, or the inadequacy or lack of prevision. Yet these might be significantly mitigated when scarcity lessens and the impact of predatory greed offers lesser reward. Come what may, the sum total of human self-fulfillment would be immeasurably advanced were the pressures on the struggle for subsistence curtailed once and for all. We will, in the current section, first review the problem of joblessness, then consider the prospects for the overcoming of scarcity, and finally reflect on the types of social arrangements that thanks to the transformation might be lying ahead.

We have chosen to stay clear of the numbers game. Jobless figures are notoriously contentious, especially so in the United States where within a short period registration brings little reward. Authoritative sources consider that, even in Europe where welfare provision is generalized, official data underestimate the true incidence by possibly as much as one-half, due to the fact that a considerable proportion are discouraged by prospects and cease to register for work. French and German totals (not to speak of the unemployed leaders such as Spain) would not be far off an alarming one-sixth of the labor force, though this would hold the American rate to something slightly over 8 percent, still some 12 million people nevertheless (Thurow, 1996: 165). At a safe guess, at least one-quarter of these – at a very low estimate of 3 million people – belong to the underclass where the pressure of an inherent counter-culture and not least a decisive withdrawal from the productive economy have become a way of life. Guessing the extent of the contingent labor force is even more hazardous. The very definition of the term – do billionaire lawyers and media stars not equally count as contingent? – is so fraught with its own contingencies that any firm figure would be open to dispute. Betty Friedan, whose long career in the field of social policy must lend her authority, considers that 'twenty-five percent of all Americans are now temp workers, and 35 percent will be by the end of the century' (Friedan, 1997: 42). For our purposes we are obviously unconcerned with the elite self-employed fringe. Our discussion will center upon those whose way of life and life chances are problematic as well as precarious – downsized, laid-off reluctant entrepreneurs and 'independent contractors' whose foothold is so erratic that they catapult in and out of so-called careers. Above all, the massive army of casuals and part-timers whose pattern of moonlighting and multiple jobs destine them to a checkered existence where uncertainty, instability and insufficiency are built-in contingencies, are all part of the same group. The fact that the Manpower Services Commission has become the largest single employer in the United States speaks for itself. If challenged to guess on the basis of lay-offs, individual bankruptcies and casual work registration, we would be inclined to put forward a figure at least equal to that of the real unemployed, namely some 12 million people as a component part of the inherently at-risk labor force.

When it comes down to brass tacks, this is a proportion not far off the 'point of no return' level of the major European continental democracies.

Wherever the guesstimate falls, the numbers are likely to change with economic fluctuations and not least the mounting incidence of computerization. Whether the grand total is around 20 million more or less, hardly matters except to those directly affected. For the sake of secure authenticity we will notionally cut back the estimate by as much as one-half. Even then, it leaves at least 10 million or more Americans who have ended up on the wrong side. More telling data disclose that in today's affluent boom-time America, a majority of full-time workers stand in fear of impending job loss. The message of the volatile nature of the labor market with its dramatic reconstruction currently underway is obviously not lost amongst those engaged in earning their living.

That the implications of this transformation have impacted far less upon the scholarly community is clearly surprising. A mere handful of serious researchers have in any consistent way directed their focal concern upon this revolution. The 'jobs, jobs, jobs' refrain that, despite all the evidence pointing towards a different direction, still looks to workfare or retraining as a solution stands in the way. Reliance is still placed upon obsolete remedies while the vision of what could point to a much more rewarding future is overlooked. We have already referred to Judith Schor's research, reminding us that were we to take advantage of the productive advances of recent decades, the work week now standing at an average close to forty hours, could have been cut by one-half (Schor, 1991). Other researchers take an even more positive view. Toffler, in one of his rare downbeat moods, warns us of 'some dystopian fantasy in which two percent of the population use robots and perform all the work, while 98 percent do none' (Toffler, 1983: 29), projecting a future in which, with inanimate labor predominant, work as we know it will have become the monopoly of a tiny elite. Stonier, though somewhat more moderate, belongs to the over-sanguine camp. His 1983 forecast that in twenty years' time one-tenth of the workforce would be sufficient to fulfill all society's needs', has obviously been unfulfilled (Stonier, 1983: 122). The more workable analyses, particularly those of Jones, Handy and Gorz offer a more plausible approximation of the inanimate-to-human relationship, as well as projections of the type of society potentially lying ahead.

Before turning to these, a few words need to be said regarding the topic of the 'free lunch'. Especially in today's climate of the stringent exchange calculus, the view prevails that there can be no free lunch. All that individuals and groups wish to possess or consume has to be paid for 'by the sweat of their brow': you get what you pay for, no more and no less, as nothing comes free. Thus, if desiring eight hours' pay, you had better do eight hours' work. Any more is not needed, while any less falls on your neighbor. However, computerization – our acquisition of armies of 'mechanical slaves' – dramatically transforms the equation. Once installed and operating on a general basis, while we eat, sleep, idle or follow 'non-work' pursuits, they busily turn out the things that we need, without pause, distraction or signs of fatigue.

The hypothetical $4.50 Rolls Royce poignantly illustrates the perspective. A computerized, digitalized, robotized artificial intelligence workforce could with a modicum of human interaction produce the whole range of products that we need in diverse profusion, leaving us free to cultivate a whole host of free-time pursuits. According to Jones, the advent of the post-service telematics society, integrating the breakthroughs of computerization plus telecommunication and embodying the 'convivial economy', will make possible all manner of publicly funded provision for education, entertainment, sport and the arts together with generous levels of municipal health and welfare services, capable of bringing about communal well-being on a generous scale. Having solved the economic subsistence problem, *homo ludens* succeeding *homo labores* will be able to direct her/his energies to activities where the commodity culture no longer dictates (Jones, 1984). Handy envisages a transition where the typical lifespan job commitment will have been reduced by one-half. In such circumstances, lifetime portfolios will rank above lifelong jobs, and flexibility will outrank patterns of programmed careers. Work, when no longer perceived as labor and transformed to expressive type work, paid or unpaid, will acquire dimensions beyond those familiar today (Handy, 1984). The most coherent exposition is owed to André Gorz. He speaks of a coming era of auto-production plus auto-surveillance where the old verities of the industrial age will have fallen away – a generalized lifetime job commitment of 20 000 hours (approximately one-half of today's), utilized at personal will, and sufficient to provide all of society's needs. Work activity will be focused on macro-social work providing functional and normal needs; a micro level comprising local, self and voluntary activities; and autonomous individual, family or small group activities. 'Monetary relations', he argues, 'are thus abolished; exchange assumes a non-market form.' And the old Marxist maxim becomes everyday reality: 'From each according to his abilities, to each according to his needs' (Gorz, 1985: 62–3).

One might be inclined to dismiss the Gorz-type analysis as merely utopian pie in the sky. But if not an actual blueprint for a future social existence, it is nevertheless more than a straw in the wind. The trends are inherent, the signpost too evident to be brushed aside. Just the same, a caveat needs to be entered, both for the sake of dialectical balance as well as showing awareness that even in societies where the latest miracle of technology has been best utilized, problems will still need to be faced. We can group the reservations under four different headings: 1. the end of scarcity; 2. positional goods; 3. collective intelligence; and 4. Trojan horse.

In social terms, scarcity is a relative concept. Over the past century living standards have risen immeasurably. Even the richest families a mere hundred years ago would have looked at the consumer wealth now taken for granted by so many with skeptical awe. Productive capacity, gross domestic income or personal wealth have multiplied several times over in western societies. Each generation has more or less started where the previous one has left off. In terms of physical well-being, health, diet, living conditions, longevity, occupational toil – not to mention mobility or disposable time – what we have attained are riches that would have appeared beyond the human aspirations even of the elite. The point is that, in the light of experience, demands appear to rise in parallel with expanded supply and however more abundant the range of supplies, there are still unfulfilled wants. Even under the utmost conditions of artificial intelligence, the problem of scarcity will never be entirely resolved.

The problem of inherent scarcity is uniquely highlighted in the 'positional goods' perspective that Hirsch presents (Hirsch, 1977). Not all commodities, Hirsch reminds us, are capable of infinite supply expansion. In fact, in many instances, it is the very scarcity factor that determines the attraction. Not everyone can occupy a front seat at a sporting or cultural event; just as honor or fame if too widely bestowed can become swiftly devalued. Hirsch vividly recounts how England's widely voted 'most unspoiled village', overnight came to be overrun by masses of tourists plus coach parties, advertising agents, eager new settlers together with diverse sellers of tawdry souvenirs to an extent that settled residents considered moving elsewhere. In the US, mindful of how the Yosemite's natural beauty stands in danger of being despoiled by the very attraction it offers to tourists, one could extrapolate the application of positional constraint inhibitions to countless areas of communal life: from the unfulfilled demand for performance admission, to homes with unique characteristics or to the ubiquity of congested highways, where even within conditions of 'post-scarcity society', some will continue to have while others will not.

Equally critical is the concern for the character of 'the global village' that Marshall McLuhan had foreshadowed in the mid-1960s. An intense debate, hitherto principally confined to European intellectual circles, is arising around what Pierre Lévy terms 'the knowledge tree' (Lévy, 1997: 17). As he views it, knowledge historically has been fragmented and competitively retained for personal use, thus alienating the broad masses from social, cultural or political participation. The cybernetic revolution changes all that. Universal computerization will 'promote the construction of intelligent communities in which our social and cognitive potential can be mutually developed and sustained' (ibid.: 17), to a point where the expansion of 'knowledge trees' of global cybernetic interaction 'incorporates and enlarges the scope of self knowledge into a form of group knowledge and collective thought' (ibid.: 23) – a most alluring projection where knowledge is free, mutual and cumulatively reciprocal to a point where all are enlightened and none compelled to stay on the outside. How far this image reflects reality – impending no less than current – is problematic, however. Already universally available pornography has grown into the primary Internet source. Hate messages, exploitation of fear and prejudice abound, and on the evidence of what exists now, expresses far less a universe of edification than a spectacle of gruesome titillating preoccupation. 'If video games are any guide', concludes *The Economist* survey, 'tomorrow is going to be a bleak day... The overwhelming theme: one way or another... Each person is out for himself. One must shoot or be shot, consume or be consumed' (*The Economist*, 3 January 1998: 81–3). We have previously made reference to the expected restoration of family life that thanks to work, interests and leisure is apparently being relocated within the home. The cosy interactive electric cottage of Toffler's projection, however, fits ill with the far gloomier (and no less prevalent) actuality that the above survey projects. Even were the excesses to be constrained, one still faces the possibility that instead of being liberated, isolated and enraptured by trivial pursuits we could potentially end up as enslaved to our mechanical slaves.

Last, the fear must remain that the despised and discredited command economy might stage a come-back as fearsome as that of the ex-Soviet states. The universalizing 20 000-hour lifetime work commitment might turn into a Trojan horse of supervisory absolutism where depersonalized remotely controlled life could come closer to Orwell's *1984* than to the liberalization that Gorz projects. However advanced our conquest of scarcity, not all would be able to follow their primary choice. Sewers would still need to be maintained and garbage collected; some might take their work aversion to the point of unyielding refusal while other puritan ethic devotees would seize more than their share. With market criteria diminished or set aside, bureaucracies or, conceivably, knowledge elites could impose a regime that, were the option put to the vote, one guesses a large majority would firmly reject.

Yet for all that, the reformers' projection does not hold out the promise of heaven on earth. Persuaded as we are that social conditions largely determine individual consciousness, we would cling to the view that material progress will find a positive echo in other directions. One could reasonably anticipate that a resolution of scarcity as we know it would significantly diminish the stringency of competitiveness, the urge for accumulation or the rewards of avid greed. Removal of toil and of the fear of impoverishment, together with a dramatic expansion of disposable time, should hopefully advance a general inclination towards cooperation, participation and mutual identification. Even were it for the sake of its own ends alone, relief from the pressures that scarcity exerts should be pursued. If there then emerges a set of social conditions that allow enhanced self-fulfillment and harmonization, then the pursuit of the promise that advanced technology offers will prove doubly worthwhile.

REFERENCES

Bartlett, D. L. and Steele, J. B., *America, Who Stole the Dream?* (Kansas City, MO: Harvard University Press, 1996).

Comor, E. A., 'Communication Technology and International Capitalism: the Case of the DBS', in E. A. Comor (ed.), *The Global Political Economy of Communication* (London: Macmillan, 1994), 83–102.

Dahrendorf, R., 'A Precarious Balance: Economic Opportunity, Civil Society, and Political Liberty', *The Responsive Community*, 5(3) (Summer 1995), 13–39.

Dewart, R. and Rheingold, H. (eds.), *Electronic Citizenship* (San Francisco, CA: Pacific Bell 1988).

Drucker, P. F., *Post-Capitalist Society* (New York: Harper Business, 1993).

Featherstone, M. (ed.), *Global Culture: Nationalism Globalization and Modernity* (London: Sage, 1990).

Fredrick, H. H., *Global Communication and International Relations* (Belmont, CA: Wadsworth, 1993).

Friedan, B., *Beyond Gender* (Baltimore, MD: Johns Hopkins University Press, 1997).

Gans, H. J., *The War Against the Poor: the Underclass and Anti Poverty Policy* (New York: Basic Books, 1995).

Gill, S. (ed.), *Gramsci, Historical Materialism and International Relations* (Cambridge: Cambridge University Press, 1993).

Gorz, A., *Paths to Paradise: On the Liberation from Work* (London: Pluto Press, 1985).

Gramsci, A., *Selections from the Prison Notebooks of Antonio Gramsci* (London: Lawrence and Wishart, 1971).

Hacker, J., *Money: Who Has How Much and Why* (New York: Scribner, 1997).

Handy, C., *The Future of Work* (Oxford: Basil Blackwell, 1984).

Hewson, A., 'Surveillance and the Global Political Economy', in E. A. Comor (ed.), *The Global Political Economy of Communication* (London: Macmillan, 1994), 61–80.

Hirsch, F., *The Social Limits to Growth* (London: Routledge, 1977).

Hirst, P. and Thompson, G., *Globalisation in Question* (London: Routledge, 1996).

Howard, T. W., *The Rhetoric of Electronic Communities* (London: Ablex Publishing Company, 1997).

Huffington, A., 'What Kemp Should Say in San Diego', *San Diego Union Tribune*, 13 August 1996.

Jones, B., *Sleepers Wake! Technology and the Future of Work* (New York: Oxford University Press, 1984).

Judy, R. W. and D'Amico, C., *Workforce 2020: Work and Workers in the Next Century* (Indianapolis, IN: Hudson Institute 1997).

Kapstein, E. B., *Governing the Global Economy: International Finance and the State* (Cambridge, Mass.: Harvard University Press 1994).

Krugman, P. R., *The Age of Diminished Expectations* (Cambridge, Mass.: MIT Press, 1994).

Lévy, P., *Collective Intelligence* (New York: Plenum Press, 1997).

Lind, M., *The Next American Nation* (New York: Free Press, 1995).

Mann, M., *States, War and Capitalism* (Oxford: Blackwell, 1988).

Melody, W. H., 'The Information Society: Implications for Economic Institutions and Market Theory', in E. A. Comor (ed.), *The Global Political Economy of Communication* (London: Macmillan, 1994), 21–36.

Ohmae, K., *The End of the Nation State* (New York: Free Press, 1995).
Pakulski J. and Waters, M., *The End of Class* (London: Sage, 1996).
Parker, I. C., 'Myth, Telecommunication and the Emerging Informational Order: the Political Economy of Transitions', in E. A. Comor (ed.), *The Global Political Economy of Communication* (New York: St. Martin's Press, 1994), 37–60.
Reich, R. B., *The Work of Nations: Preparing Ourselves for the Twenty-First Century* (New York: Knopf, 1991).
Schiller, H. I., *Information Inequality: the Deepening Social Crisis in America* (New York: Routledge, 1996).
Schor, J., *The Overworked American* (New York: Basic Books, 1991).
Schwartz, J. T., 'America's Economic-Technological Agenda for the 1990s', *Daedalus* (Winter 1992), 139–65.
Schwarz, B., 'The American Dream vs. the American System', *Los Angeles Times* (15 April 1996), B5.
Seligman, H. J., *The Problem of Trust* (Princeton, NJ: Princeton University Press, 1997).
Sherman, H. J., 'An Approach to Class Analysis', in Victor E. Lippit (ed.), *Radical Political Economy* (Armonk, NJ: M. E. Sharpe, 1996), 117–39.
Sombart, W., *Why is There No Socialism in the United States?* (White Plains, NY: International Arts and Sciences Press, 1976; orig. German ed. 1906).
Steel, R., 'The Bad News', *New Republic* (2 October 1997), 27.
Stonier, T., *The Wealth of Information: a Profile of the Post-Industrial Economy* (London: Methuen, 1983).
Strange, S., *The Retreat of the State* (Cambridge: Cambridge University Press, 1996).
Sweeney, J. J., 'America Needs a Raise', in Steven Fraser and Joshua B. Freeman (eds.), *Audacious Democracy* (New York: Houghton Mifflin, 1997).
The Economist, 'The Hitchhiker's Guide to Cybernomics,' *The Economist, Special Survey* (21 September 1996), 1–46.
—— 'Dip into the Future, Far as Cyborg Can See and Wince' (3 January 1998), 81–3.
Thurow, L. C., *The Future of Capitalism: How Today's Economic Forces Shape Tomorrow's World* (New York: William Morrow, 1996).
Toffler, A., *The Third Wave* (New York: Morrow, 1980).
—— *Previews & Premises* (New York: Morrow 1983).
Toffler, A. and Toffler, H., *Creating a New Civilization* (Atlanta, GA: Thoner Publishing, 1994).
Wattenberg, B., 'Go it Alone, Go Global, or Both?', *San Diego Union Tribune* (30 December 1997).
Weber, M., *Economy and Society, Vol. 1* (New York: Bedminster Press, 1968).
Wood, G. S., 'Doing the Continental', *New York Review* (20 November 1997), 51–4.

8 New Visions

1. MODELS OF POST-SCARCITY SOCIETY

Researchers have been remarkably slow in paying attention to the mapping out of the future ahead. Overall, futurologists' characteristic excesses have given the topic a bad name. Faced with a subject where disproof is highly unlikely, they have tended to allow their imagination to run wild. Even renowned academics have been unable to resist the temptation to pontificate, proclaim grand theories and dismiss inconvenient evidence in attempts to construct a singular line for the future. The latest Asian crisis débâcle is a good case in point. Even while internally the economic structure had already started collapsing, recognized scholars were still proclaiming the 'Asian century' and praising the superior qualities of 'the Asian way' (Huntington 1996). Instead, while the trumpets still sound, *The Economist*'s 'Asia's Coming Explosion' exposes the fallacy conclusively (*The Economist*, 21 February 1998). A similar lack of prevision occurred over the fall of the Soviet Empire, the Middle East confrontations and not least the oft-preached imminence of America's present decline (Kennedy, 1993; Fallows, 1994; Naisbitt, 1995).

Our objective is a great deal more modest. Guided by the maxim that 'to work, democracy needs a vision of utopia – a route to a better society' (Thurow, 1996: 255), we consider it proper to elaborate the previous chapter's contention that machine intelligence will increasingly impact on social life and that, in consequence, the end of scarcity seems a feasible prospect for the century ahead. Attempting to desist from dogmatic assertion as well as pre-judgment we will initially reflect on the evidence of the downsizing trend. We will next turn to considering the changing nature of work and its impact on joblessness. Then we will explore how a post-scarcity society might manage to operate. And finally we will turn to the question of whether and how the ending of material scarcity will result in the emergence of what used to be termed 'a new man' – a social being freed from the negative characteristics of 'industrial man' and capable of reaching towards self-fulfillment and universalization – before giving attention to countervailing inhibitions as well as constraints.

Block (in his recent oddly titled *The Vampire State*) sets out a scenario of developments that have already occurred. According to official data, he reminds us, a mere 1.8 percent of American agricultural workers are able to produce quantities of food abundant enough to satisfy domestic plus foreign consumption. The productive manufacturing component in the labor force has already declined to below 10 percent. Allow a further 2–3 percent for emergency health care, garbage collection or other contingencies and in his presentation, some '15% of the current labor force working an average work year of 1,900 or 2,000 hours provides our society with an absolutely unprecedented degree of freedom in shaping work arrangements... As long as the relatively small percentage of employees who produce and distribute the really necessary goods and services attend to their tasks, the rest of us can be preparing gourmet meals in restaurants, selling greeting cards, writing novels, providing social services, producing movies, staffing theme parks, and invent new types of services' (Block, 1996: 233). For all its overt flippancy, this states the position well. It shows where we already stand and where appropriate action towards taking advantage of available change could lead us shortly. We are brought back to Judith Schor's eye-opening message dating back to the start of the present decade to the effect that even then productive advance should have enabled us to cut back the work commitment by fully one-half. Manifestly, Block's boldly stated 15 percent labor force work requirement needs upward revision. His figures do not allow for a host of other requirements such as administrators, educators, security personnel or banking, insurance, transport or construction workers – a potential further 10 percent. Allow furthermore a like figure for those engaged in the various pursuits that are needed to pay for the import of goods and services, and we are left with a labor force total of 35 percent. Add to that, for the sake of staying clear of underestimation, an additional 15 percent for intangibles, and we have arrived back at the Schor as well as the Gorz prior equation, namely the evident fact that in today's United States potentially one-half of the labor force could comfortably provide all of society's normal material needs (Schor, 1991; Gorz, 1985). This is a potent reminder of the benefits that the machine revolution is able to bring.

However, the visions of what lie ahead are distinctly divergent. Block describes the present, indicating some points of prevision. Gorz's understanding, in contrast, looks to the future ahead and depicts conditions that await implementation. Further, Block's tongue-in-cheek account rests on the premise of the maintenance of unfettered free-market conditions. Gorz's model, on the other hand, presupposes intervention and regulation. Quite manifestly, the 20 000-hour lifetime work voucher scheme cannot operate without some measure of planning as well as control. It rests its case first on the equitable share-out of available work and then on the presumption that all tasks, unpleasant as well as attractive, are willingly done. Block's scenario, however, reflects America today with a minority of the intensively occupied technologically advanced labor force accounting for the nation's production and creation of wealth, counterposed to an overwhelmingly larger sector involved both in the provision of post-industrial refinements no less than the fripperies that make up affluent everyday life.

In the context of much of quotidian reality, there is not a great deal awry with that projection. It constitutes, after all, substantially what billions the world over heartily wish to attain: comfort, choice, diversity plus a rich panoply of all kinds of desirable consumer goods. Yet not all view this image through the same rosy spectacles. Miller's 'Egotopia' deprecates what it presents from beginning to end. His satirically dubbed 'dark satanic malls' scathingly analyzes what he finds at fault. For all its abundant glitter and gulch, he argues that as epitomized in the reality of ever-burgeoning shopping malls, Americans have fashioned for themselves a way of life that is barren, mindless, deculturated and privatized in the extreme. Consumerism means commodification, standardization and alienation brought to a level where all sense of essential self as well as of community has been foregone. Choice and authentic identity have turned into a chimera. Base self-interest and acquisitive greed have emerged as supreme (Miller, 1997).

Bleak dystopias have rarely turned out as bad as projected. There is much that the world rightly envies in the American way of life. Yet the gross inequalities in income, life chances and living conditions must raise the question of whether the option of the unfetttered market nexus is the sole path. With machine intelligence capable of consigning material scarcity to the dim, primitive past there must surely be more sociable options. There must be matching social arrangements that, while maintaining liberty, more equitably fulfill individual interest as well as collective needs. For that to arise, a modicum of planning and intervention appears imperative. Above all else, the mantra that 'the government is the problem and not the solution' needs to be set aside. Adherence in no way inhibits business leaders' appetite for massive subsidies, for government contracts, tax concessions or the underwriting of financial ventures abroad. Nor does it stop others who in the economic sphere equally extol the virtues of the invisible hand, from demanding government intercession in regulating moral and social affairs. Equally, workers and professional associations do all they can to induce the government to block innovation that threatens their members' jobs. Anathema to central involvement, in other words, is a markedly selective preoccupation. One ought not to forget that it was government action that gave the United States its prevalent transport system, the highways, technological head-start or the training of scientists who are leading the world in a great many fields.

In the light of what it can do for humankind, few would dissent from the view that the overcoming of scarcity is a highly desirable aim. Yet existing conditions put serious obstacles in its way, while ultimately social accord is inconceivable under circumstances when a tiny elite has laid claim to all the work that remains while the great majority has to make do with what the margins provide. Gorz's model of an attainable future where work is available to all on an equal basis and where all can enjoy a workload reduced by one-half, appears not only a feasible project but one that in the United States, with a moderate degree of regulation, could benefit all. Attempts to resolve the dilemma by palliatives of job-sharing or part-time and casual work cannot be enough. Until all are assured of an adequate income in return for fulfilling the norm, advance will be blocked. The issue of lifetime work vouchers needs to be accompanied by sanctions against shirkers as well as workaholics who usurp others' share. There also needs to be a grading process that ensures that menial, dirty or non-social character tasks will be accomplished, as well as a system that guards against excess fluctuations in voucher performance. All that could be done consensually in a broadly based participatory manner free of coercion. Friction as well as dissent are a part of the human condition and will not, even were cornucopia ever to come, disappear overnight. Yet the repression and compulsion that we have witnessed in command economies need no longer inhibit social arrangements that ensure a fair share for all. We need to elaborate further on potential options.

2. IMPLEMENTATION

Whichever the circumstances, the coming of post-scarcity society must be some way off. Even were one to make a start here and now, realization will take a while. In the first place, for it to happen a variety of obstacles will need to be overcome: one can readily think of vested interests' manifold opposition; the blockage exerted by trade unions, professional associations and similar interest groups; the natural inertia on the part of those fully employed, earning good incomes and enjoying progressive careers; the natural reluctance to pin one's hopes on vague utopias; the incapacity to perceive the attainment of 'the free lunch'; and last but not least, the understandable fear of excessive regulation plus pervasive control. Other questions include who is to decide what is to be done by whom, when and where; what is to be done about norm-breakers as well as shirkers; or how, in the absence of sanctions as well as incentive, the spirit of innovation and enterprise will be maintained. Will prices and compensation still be determined by market forces or will there be a return to the medieval notion of the just price? How will those in positions of authority come to be vested or divested of power? Will there be recourse against unfair decisions, citizens' tribunals or a court of appeal? And not least, who is to guard the guardians against personal enrichment, excess accretion of power, or indeed overt corruption? All of these are fair, proper questions which, however appropriate, will for the most part have to be taken on trust. We can never know in advance the future or in a precise manner chart its trends. Yet, having sketched out the prospect of the post-scarcity option, we owe it to ourselves as well as readers to do our best to elaborate on what it might look like and how it might work. Three points seem essential: first, economic redistribution; second, empowerment and participation; and third, the emphasis on the convivial complementary society over inordinate differentiation and acquisitive greed.

It stands to reason that were they assured of a reasonable livelihood, most people would welcome the advent of machine intelligence. Thanks to technological progress, the twentieth century has seen an immense relief from sickening drudgery and back-breaking toil. Machine intelligence is capable of bringing even greater qualitative advance. Were we to open the doors to all it is able to offer, the burden of work – and this is what their daily job implies for most people – could assuredly within the next two generations be effectively cut by one-half. A 20 000-hour lifetime commitment would then provide all the goods and services that we have now. Block's sardonic option is one possible way, neither the one and only one nor, as it seems the most optimal. It follows that with one-half of existing collective effort, we could halve the work time all round, and still have the entire range of material benefits that accrue to us now. By the mere logic of current exigencies this state of affairs will come about in any event. It is within our power to advance it by foresight and communal partnership or to see it retarded by inertia, denial or the power of vested interest. We can equally well make use of this once and for all opportunity to move towards social equity by assuring all their due share, or we can leave it to the vagaries of unfettered laissez-faire provisions to lead to conditions where a small minority will take possession of greatly more than their proportionate share while the remainder is left with little or nothing at all.

Current inequalities imply a distribution that in any long-term perspective is incompatible with stable pluralistic conditions. In general terms, in an era where substantial productive gains have been regular and recurrent, the average earnings of the 80 percent of 'productive and non-supervisory' Americans whose jobs fall below the higher executive, managerial and technical levels, fell by 18 percent in the past twenty years. In contrast, the post-tax pay of corporate chief executives has risen by 66 percent. Even Alan Greenspan, the conservative head of the Federal Reserve, has warned Congress that the growing inequality of income in the United States is becoming 'a major threat to our society'. Robert Solow of MIT, a Nobel Prize winner for economics, has similarly warned that the pattern of inequality 'might turn mean and crabbed, limited in what it can do, worried about the future' (Head, 1996: 47). These are the very conditions that could seriously impede further advance on the road to the conquest of scarcity. It is all too tempting to perceive this as an issue of capitalism versus socialism, a struggle between right and left. This view is mistaken. As time passes, such formulations are becoming transcended. The record of the socialist command economies is even more dismal than the most dire free-market excess. We have noted in Chapter 4 how Michael Parenti, a self-declared sympathizer in terms of 'rewarding inefficiency' castigates the Soviet performance not only for its coercive constraints but equally for its glaring disparity between declared performance in its abject reality. The legacy of cynical apathy, rampant corruption, lack of pride in achievement and workmanship, chronic pilfering and not least the irreparable destruction of the natural environment speak volumes for the system's lack of efficiency. Once the curtain came down, the tragic reality of mismanagement, neglect and corruption surfaced for all to see (Parenti, 1997: 59–65). Though far less extreme, the milder western democracies' collapse under the weight of heavy-handed bureaucracy, wage inflation plus chronic industrial strife and budget deficits, has canceled these options from the progressive agendas of western societies.

At the same time, Heilbroner's curt aphorism that 'less than 75 years after the contest between capitalism and socialism officially began, it is over: capitalism has won', is only partly correct (quoted in Albert 1994: 104). As we approach the twenty-first century, the time-worn fixation with 'isms' is becoming redundant. For all the formal denial, there is a third way. The market unquestionably has been triumphant, but unless it is muted and pointed towards a progressive direction it could well frustrate all hopes for the future. Unless decisively redirected it will certainly, in all shapes and forms, substantially impede the coming of post-scarcity society that, under optimal conditions, seems well on the cards. While professing the principles on which the free market rests, we have dramatically departed from the underlying Adam Smith model claimed as its guiding light. Unjustly cited as the apostle of the unfettered free market, Smith never envisaged his 'invisible hand' permitting the disparities that now exist. His three 'great importance' principles that the government owed to society are clearly set out. They are, firstly, 'the duty of protecting the society from violence and invasion'; secondly, 'the duty of protecting, as far as possible, every member of society from the injustice or oppression of every other member of it'; and thirdly, 'the duty of erecting and maintaining certain public works and certain public institutions, which it can never be in the interest of any individual, or group of individuals, to erect and maintain because the profit would never repay the expense ... though it may frequently do much more than repay it to a great society' (Smith, 1937: 651). Under the impact of supply-side economics, the latter two maxims have visibly been pushed aside.

Smith's message unambiguously points to a third way. However odious the command system may be, undiluted free market economies are only a jot better. The government just cannot wash its hands of what goes on in its name. Intervention is essential, not only in the interest of social justice, but even more so for the system to work. If true in Smith's day, this is even more true in the era of transnational capital, globalization and above all the promise of machine intelligence and the conquest of scarcity. There are various ways forward, from the mildest, most moderate form of intervention, to prescriptions that are so regulative and severe that advanced western societies will surely reject them. In the interest of comprehensive coverage we will briefly review the major contenders.

3. MODELS

Havel's school of thought offers the mildest prescription. He relies primarily on a respect for rules, a spirit of justice and decency, a clean administration, public accountability plus the conservation of energy (Havel, 1998). The culture of equable human relationships, reciprocity and dedication to work that he advocates relies too closely on resembling the failed social democratic systems that have proved abortive. Relying primarily on exhortation and moral persuasion, it represents a soft communitarian option that, attractive as it may be in principle, has failed to make the public impact it may well deserve.

Thurow's model offers a more likely prospect. There is no doubt in his mind that the capitalist system based on market realities is the way forward. This is where man-made brainpower harnessed to modern technology will always flourish best of all. Yet, as matters now stand, critical considerations are being neglected. The balance between democracy's egalitarian foundations, best expressed in the 'one person, one vote' principle, are being submerged by the inequality of the market nexus that is disrupting community and driving people apart. Government, for two decades in retreat, has abrogated its functions and gross inequalities are rupturing social relations while the basic infrastructure, the lifeline of future progress, is suffering decay. 'Without a compelling vision of a better future', Thurow declares, 'social and economic paralysis sets in ... To hold together there has to be a utopian vision that underlies some common goals that members of society can work together to achieve' (Thurow, 1996: 257, 256). Good physical infrastructure (roads, airports, water, sewerage, electricity, etc.) and good social infrastructure, implying public safety, educational opportunities, plus research and development, are necessary if economic advance is to occur. The essence in attaining the vision is the fostering of manmade brainpower in all social spheres. Public technology strategies that exclude no one are central for this to be realizable.

Hacker's analysis proceeds in a similar vein. American inequalities, where a higher proportion of the population are in prison, on the streets, or are neglected children than in any other comparable nation, are not only the cause of serious socio-economic problems, but are threatening to undermine the moral culture on which progress and social cohesion depend. In the past twenty years, while average household income in real terms has grown by 20.3 percent, the top one-fifth did twenty-four times better than the bottom one-fifth (Hacker (1997: 11), producing an inequality index of 5.9, twice as skewed as in other advanced nations such as Germany or the Netherlands (ibid.: 54). While under such conditions an elite plutocracy confronts an increasingly marginalized underclass, the fostering of the future cadres of 'knowledge workers' who are the essential creators and standard-bearers of the coming post-industrial, post-service global economy has suffered decay. The restoration of a moral community requires firm action that can only derive from a democratically based central source.

Block puts 'qualitative growth' well above material progress that has set aside the prime qualities on which advance depends. His 'practical utopia' eschews the unachievable irreconcilable goals of the messianic versions (of which communism has been the latest) and focuses instead on what can and ought to be done (Block, 1990; 1996). Cooperative arrangements between employers and employees, democratization of decision-making at all levels, plus the establishment of a system of stakeholding in which all members of society acquire a tangible stake in their community are the primary aims. 'Popular entrepreneurism' that utilizes the talents that hitherto have been unexplored and emphasizes participatory initiative and teamwork at all grades of the productive process will be more effective than the elitist model that currently reigns. However, technological progress that has brought the United States to the point where a mere 15 percent of the labor force alone is sufficient to provide all material needs, has opened up new vistas, as yet mostly covert. One needs to rely far less on the predatory large corporations but should instead promote small business, employer cooperatives plus a host of non-profit organizations, capable of mobilizing the energy of the entire community.

The problem has ceased to be one of production, now taken care of by a mere fraction of the labor force, but centers essentially on distribution instead. The priorities have shifted in a big way. Societies need to ensure both adequate buying power to make use of the goods that machine power bestows, as well as restored social cohesion to optimize progress as well as accord. The main instrument, in Block's estimation, is the introduction of a universal income grant that sustains an adequate standard of living for all, irrespective of working performance or 'merit' as currently rated. This represents a dramatic step in an untried direction. The general assumption that income grants of any order, especially those ample enough to provide decent living standards free of the nexus of 'work', will lead to the loss of incentive plus a state of affairs where the menial unsociable jobs will no longer be done, no longer pertains. Block advances the very opposite view. Incentive, as countless inventions prove, has its own intrinsic rewards. Where material criteria matter far less, social recognition plus self-fulfillment will be sufficient incentives to ensure that progress will not become stalled. Moreover, were it to become necessary, he argues, to give superior reward for the performance of the lower grade tasks, that can only help further progress. Employers will then be motivated to automate more effectively – the very best recipe for attaining the post-scarcity goal even faster than now. Manifestly, the process is stalled when the rich seize huge profits while cheap labor, at the same time, vies for the lower grade jobs. Automation is the *sine qua non* for the fulfillment of the post-scarcity goal. The more effectively social arrangements promote its arrival, the more expeditiously the aim can be attained.

Productive disposable time in a climate of flexible lifestyles and individual choice now counts for more than the generalized 'work ethic' that for the majority, in the past, meant privation and drudgery. Ample scope towards self-enhancement, the acquisition of multiple skills, creativity in all possible spheres together with revived conditions of community life and voluntary work can only come when universal subsistence has been ensured. Then democratic planning habits and the mechanics of spontaneous participation can be brought down to the grassroots. Decentralization of political and economic decision-making will devolve to alliances of private and public legislative bodies who, mindful of communal interest, will administer resources in the interest of all. Block is insistent that the funding of income grants will not be a dilemma. The combined sources of progressive taxation, together with a transit tax on the many billions that now circle the globe, added to the benefits of enhanced machine intelligence will more than cover the cost while simultaneously working time will be drastically further reduced (Block, 1996: 267 et passim).

This brings us right back to Gorz's seminal contribution which first presented the mechanics of post-scarcity society in a practical way. Yet, predating the dismal fall of the Soviet system, Gorz continues to pin his faith in a socialist type of solution. In his 20 000-hour lifetime work commitment scenario all will be free to direct their personal working patterns and all will be able to develop their talents free of encumbrance while, at the same time, all will be equal and free. This critically hinges upon an emphatic rejection of the capitalist model where, as he argues, the dichotomies between the haves and the have-nots are destined to become more and more extreme. 'The way out of capitalism' must lie in the direction of terminating market relations, in abolishing wage labor, and in equalizing the life chances of all individuals and all social groups. Only collective control will ensure social conditions where all will be able to flourish and each and all will be able to obtain their fair share (Gorz, 1985: 40 et passim).

One would find it difficult to quarrel with his fundamental presupposition of 'the end of the society of work' and the consequences this should entail. Under circumstances where 'the quantity of labour needed for most material production and organizational activities rapidly becomes marginal' (Gorz, 1985: 33), the reappraisal of the principles of social existence that he posits appears highly credible. Gorz envisages social existence to take place within three different interrelated spheres. First stands publicly owed macro-social work, organized across society as a whole, and enabling it to function and provide general needs. Second comes micro-social activity that is self-organized and broadly based on the principle of voluntary participation. And finally there is autonomous activity that corresponds to the particular desires and projects of individuals, families and small groups that rounds off a pattern of social existence where all buttress the social weal while none is endowed with privileged power or wealth (Gorz, 1985: 63). For all the surface attractiveness, one is left doubting whether this model could function without substantial control and coercion. The performance of the 'socialist commonwealths' hardly encourages sanguine projections. How would one deal with miscreants, shirkers or others abusing the norm? Who would allocate the work to be done, and on what criteria? Who would oversee the discharge of vouchers, or ensure that the entire range of tasks that needed to be done was performed? In conditions when all can elect their own pattern of work, there will either be chaos or a greater necessity of regulation than Gorz will admit. There is, last but not least, the major problem of who, when market conditions have been abolished, will be there to oversee the custodians so that they do not use their office for self-enrichment, cronyism or the abuse of power.

To reach a more balanced viewpoint, it may be time to put the 'isms' firmly to bed. Evidence clearly exists that the dichotomy between capitalism and socialism that has riven this century may be over. Heilbroner, whose introductory comment to the effect that 'I would not be that foolhardy as to risk a grand prediction about the future... That does not mean that I have condemned myself to silence with regard to the prospects for the society in which our children and our children's children will live' (Heilbroner, 1993: 121) merits attention and makes the argument well. He is well aware of the pitfalls of twentieth-century capitalism: demand saturation, labor force degradation, cultural erosion, infrastructural decay, and last but not least, the impending threat of ecological shut-down. Yet, modified in the light of the next century's exigencies, it can still lead us to a new mixed system that is clear of its faults. Right and left divisions have ceased to apply. When the static view of technological potentialities has been abandoned, it is now a choice between continuing progress or regressing back. Through willingly embracing and institutionalizing the vistas that machine intelligence is able to offer, the fixation upon economism, accumulation and divisive acquisitiveness can be transcended once and for all. Heilbroner sets primary store upon centrally sponsored public investment, regular accounting and especially the establishment of a firm social contract in which business, labor and the government participate as equal partners. Labor is to be awarded seats on company boards with the power of co-determination. It will, in exchange, undertake to moderate wage demands that threaten inflation. Management will open its books and not attack unions, while, in its turn, the government will provide comprehensive programs of unemployment insurance as well as retraining, together with effective investment and export support (Heilbroner, 1993: 153–5).

'Participatory democracy' equally is a theme that Albert espouses (Albert, 1994). With scarcity no longer the ruling constraint, the old tensions between right and left have been superseded. The former represents the 'winner take all society' where destructive individualism sets people apart, while, for the latter, central planning imperatives lead to authoritarianism, public apathy plus a stifling bureaucracy within which chaos prevails. The wholesale transition from human labor to machine intelligence opens the way to a non-hierarchical, egalitarian, participatory and socially just democracy of freely entered contracts, where the axiom of 'from each according to ability, and to each according to effort' can soon lead to new vistas and where the precept of 'from each according to ability, and to each according to needs' can take its place. Citizens' councils in concert with federations of workers as well as consumers can negotiate terms of production with long-term plans. Thanks to the wonders of modern technology, all members of society can regularly vote in the form of 'the daily plebiscite' that, in his presidential bid, Ross Perot espoused. Encouraging all to perform some socially useful work outside their principal tasks will not only enrich social capital, but bring about a climate of solidarity where antagonistic social relationships will be consigned to the past.

Finally, Anthony Giddens, one of Europe's leading intellectuals, in a brief United Nations Research Institute survey, elaborates on 'affluence and post-scarcity society' lying ahead (Giddens, 1995). As he argues, in circumstances of manufactured uncertainty (i.e. man- and machine-made risk vagaries) plus de-traditionalization, 'everyone must confront and deal with multiple sources of information and knowledge, including fragmented and contested knowledge claims' (ibid.: 4). Productionism passes its peak and 'people are turning away from the overriding goals of economic growth and orienting their lives towards different values' (ibid.: 8). Even the value and impact of technology can no longer be determined solely in technological terms. 'Time pioneers' for some time already have opted for early retirement, flexible work schedules or mid-term changes in their careers. Such preferences can now be generalized. Social reflexivity and 'emotional lifestyle bargaining' will transform social relations to a point where the emancipatory values of self-fulfillment and enriched community life will outrank prevailing blind acquisitiveness and social strife.

4. SOCIAL PROGRESS

The dominant priorities appear to be:

- rapid progression towards machine intelligence leading to the overcoming of scarcity;
- a form of work voucher system reducing working hours and awarding all labor force members a share of available work;
- and/or a universal income grant to provide buying power and to alleviate poverty;
- economic redistribution and social equalization for the sake of community;
- the transition towards a 'Convivial Society' where material pursuit is matched by an emphasis on self-fulfillment and the enhancement of disposable time.

Enough has already been said on the first item not to demand further elaboration. Without specifying a time limit, we are convinced that, given public support and a change in official attitude, the advent is near. Once a stage has been reached where human input is equal or less than that of machines and where access to work – now a scarce commodity – has been equalized, for the United States at least (and soon for other advanced economies) the constraints of material scarcity can substantively be overcome. Ecological resource constraint is anyhow set to impose limits on endless consumption expansion (Weisskopf, 1996). Appetites may well find themselves muted once the struggle for existence has abated and accumulation accrues fewer rewards. Few would reasonably oppose a concerted effort to expand machine intelligence were profits secured, with work available to all those able and willing to do it, and with spending power at the same time enhanced. Already machine intelligence has reached a point where satellites beam pictures from Mars, smart bombs home in on targets with pinpoint accuracy, factories can virtually run by themselves, while a 'dumb machine' has developed the brainpower to beat the famed world champion at chess. One further 'small step', scientifically near completion, could lead us into an era of artificial intelligence where computers do their own thinking, make long-term plans and ultimately learn to reproduce themselves. Well before that, machine intelligence ('mechanical slaves') will have become capable of shouldering at least one-half of advanced societies' available work (Rifkin, 1995: 16).

Concomitantly, unfettered market conditions will further aggravate social imbalances. We favor a policy of sharing out the available work over income grants. Earned income is always a better stimulus, likely to promote the voluntarism crucial for moving things forward. We are fully aware that, however justly enacted, a voucher system can never be free of a modicum of regulative control. There will always be problems of abuse of authority, favoritism or allocation of duties that some will consider unfair. The closer the point of decision-taking is brought down to the grassroots, the greater the level of participation and the less onerous control will be felt.

Taxation policies that demand greater contributions from the well-off are vital. The current pattern in which the rich pay a far lesser share of their income than do the lower paid, and where corporations' creative accounting can make them virtually tax exempt – far more prevalent in the United States than elsewhere (Hacker, 1997) – are not only grossly unfair but dysfunctional in regard to solidarity and harmonization. We have in various parts referred to the growing polarization and marginalization that deprive the community of social capital in many directions. The immense costs of security, surveillance, health neglect, illiteracy and social inadequacy alone are an onerous burden. Such immeasurables as child neglect, substance abuse or proneness to violence, all disproportionately distributed, are incompatible with any aspiration of optimal social performance. Some economists favor indirect taxes as being less overt. We consider otherwise, both in the interest of effectiveness as well as equity. Graduated taxes, especially when post-scarcity makes workaholicism redundant, appears fairer and more efficient.

Social justice, not merely in rhetoric but in actual performance, is a must for the type of 'Convivial Society' that Jones holds out as the apogee of transforming social relations. In his view, the transition from *homo laboraces* to *homo ludens* is essential for both self-fulfillment and social accord. Once mankind has freed itself from privation and oppressive work, the promotion of voluntaristic contribution to such matters as municipal health, community services, education and care for the less fortunate can become normative. Creativity, self-enhancement, entertainment, sports and the arts can be made to flourish at the same time (Jones, 1984: 94–9).

Finally, a few words need to be said regarding what used to be called the 'New Man'. Will a better society produce individuals more effective or sociable, or will 'the Old Adam' assert itself to an extent that social behavior is no better than now? Marx had no doubts on that subject. Socialism would entail 'the free development of individuals where nobody has one exclusive sphere of activity, but each can become accomplished in any branch he wishes, society regulates the general production and thus makes it possible for me to do one thing today and another tomorrow, to hunt in the morning, fish in the afternoon, rear cattle in the evening, criticize after dinner, just as I have in mind, without ever becoming hunter, fisherman, shepherd or critic' (Marx and Engels, 1867: 618). *Homo socialis*, however, gave the lie to that vision. Especially in the USSR, China and Cambodia terror reigned, with massive atrocities, while social behavior overtly was unregenerate. Yet, the point can be made that in these societies – as is true to a lesser extent of the other socialist experiments – scarcity had by no means been overcome. The struggle for existence, if anything, had been greatly intensified. At the most modest level, once sufficiency were to be guaranteed one could anticipate individuals exhibiting fewer feelings of fear, anger and insecurity than they do now. This should lead to a lessening of self-destructive manifestations, a reduction in violence and, most importantly, an enhanced sense of self where personal development and self-realization count for more than at present. Or put somewhat differently, societies where the positive ego identification that now reinforces success among the privileged would find itself universalized. It would be naïve to assume that all will be high-minded, altruistic, compassionate or willing to put others' interests above their own. One might nevertheless be justified in hoping for a stronger spirit of civic awareness than exists now, for a more intensive level of social participation, a firmer requirement for accountability, together with a resolve to make optimal use of one's much expanded disposable time. Even were this to be all, we would rest content.

5. CONSTRAINTS

We identify four major constraints. They are:

(i) vested interests;
(ii) compulsion;
(iii) rich versus poor;
(iv) positional goods and egotopia.

(i) Vested Interests

There are two levels of opposition, one fairly self-evident, and the other a bit more opaque. Understandably, people threatened in their livelihood will do all they can to obstruct the advance of machine intelligence. At the less obvious level, old habits and embedded traditions, often obscured, stand equally in the way. Employers have steadily shifted the onus of delayed modernization on to the increasingly generic effect of 'globalization'. Millions of jobs have been exported to low-wage economies which have shouldered the task of computerization while supplying a docile and low-paid labor force at the same time. As long as globalization is seen as an irresistible force that cannot be contained, and as long as there remain parts of the third world that can be colonized, the process could well go on. American consumers are advantaged by the import of cheap goods and services, while corporations are free to roam the world in search of labor cheaper and more compliant than found at home.

Government, at the same time, benefits by boasting of the achievements of growth and prosperity without inflation as long as the downsized can be diverted into the contingent labor force, and transmuted into 'entrepreneurs' striving for the goal of individual success. Labor has been equally complicit. The downsized contingents are barely missed, while for the remaining millions – be they organized, professionalized or acting in personal self-interest – the motto is 'each man on his own'. Workers know only too well that the introduction of computers – let alone the coming of machine intelligence – comes at the cost of their own jobs. The shrinking of job opportunities could well leave them stranded; retraining for jobs that have been foregone is mainly a myth; and, until access to jobs is equalized, their best hope will be served by slowing down the coming of machine intelligence.

The second level of resistance will be tough to dispel. The culture of Fordism has been ingrained so deeply into the civic conscience of industrial societies that it will take a great effort of identification to desist from blocking the transition to a post-industrial normative structure in the decades ahead. Fordism dictates a hierarchical, vertical and firmly differentiated mode of production where bosses are bosses and the operatives mere 'hands' who have learned to keep their place. New times 'use much less energy, both physical and human, than they replace' (Mulgan, 1994: 116). Communication is no longer between superiors and subordinates and bound by a rigid division of labor, but horizontal, decentralized and no longer dependent upon leadership, but on cooperation and 'the use of creative chaos' instead. Face-to-face meetings, informal decision-taking and spontaneity now embrace all. The transition is truly dramatic – not merely learning new skills, but saying farewell to cherished habits once and for all. The unexplored universe of human ingenuity and talent is as yet beyond ken. How much better economic and social structures will work when vested interests no longer impinge and all will voluntarily partake in the workings of the community cannot be precisely specified. There is little doubt that, at least for some time, the groups used to power and privilege will feel a loss of their status. Yet, were it to come, relief from frustration and conflict will ostensibly benefit all. The weak power structures already apparent in such developments as the women's and environmental movements, the loose network of think-tanks, as well as the rise of 'virtual' chains of cooperation existing in electronic space (Mulgan, 1994: 125), all give hope that better times could be lying ahead. On a more cautionary note Castells, in the conclusion to his magisterial three-volume *The Age of Information*, remains pessimistic that 'the unleashing of unprecedented productive capacity by the power of the mind' will bridge the gap between 'our technological over development and our social under-development', as so much of our energy is self-destructive and limited by the prevailing values and interests that created them (Castells, 1998: 359).

(ii) Compulsion

We have at various stages already made reference to the oppressive effects of command economies. We will, in this section, point to other dis-benefits that could accompany interference with market imperatives.

They are:

(i) tyranny of the majority;
(ii) new demagogues;
(iii) loss of incentive.

(i) Liberals like John Stuart Mill in the last century warned how majority rule can be prone to turn into suppression of minority views. The principle of 'one man, one vote' awards virtually absolute power to elected majorities. These are not merely powers of delegation but are equally reinforced by a cluster of moral qualities. Once voted into office, opposition can easily be construed as sabotaging the will of the people, to undermining the general will, as unpatriotic or as inimical to what ought to be done. The hostile reaction that typically confronts dissenters – be they republicans within monarchies, conscientious objectors in times of 'national emergency', or merely idealists who defy public opinion – has often led to the stifling of free debate in western democracies (Taylor, 1957). Doing away with inherited privilege, challenging the aura of 'superior birth', or laying bare the welter of benefits that monopolization of social capital tends to bestow (Block, 1996), may well have served the cause of social justice, yet it undermines the sense of charisma that the ruled expect to find in their rulers. Enshrining 'the will of the people' as the primary arbiter in public affairs can well introduce a new absolutism in which minority views are considered subversive, and where minority groups find themselves barred from equal access.

(ii) Oscar Wilde's caustic aphorism that socialism can never be made to work as it consumes too much free time possesses more than a grain of truth. The welter of unending debate, the paper mountains that accompany open discussion, plus the lobbying and incessant committee work that it implies soon tires all but the fanatics, power seekers or socially desolate few who then, in charge of their exclusive domain, come to bestride their empires with dominant sway. Political commissars who trample on any sign of dissension, notorious shop stewards or back-room lawyers who steeped in the smallest minutiae of print terrorize their environment, or block wardens who in their partiality or ill-applied zeal sort out 'deviants' for punitive action have been all too prominent in recent decades. After a while the bulk of the people who wish to lead their own lives become disenchanted with the strain of unending circular debate, or will shrink from the opprobrium that becomes the lot of dissenters. They will have fallen away, with the field now left clear to demagogues who brook no dissent or obscurantists to whom bureaucracy represents utter bliss. As Gellner points out, the pursuit of 'liberty, equality and fraternity' has often given way to 'bureaucracy, nationality and excessive intolerance' (Gellner, 1991). The excesses of public tribunals, people's courts and 'spontaneous', on the spot retribution are of too recent memory not to stand as a warning. Weak political alignments, however, rather than the familiar omnipotent nation states, are ostensibly more appropriate structures for the post-industrial societies already incipient. One is left to hope that these will convert the above obstructions to positive use.

(iii) The proposition is simple. If humans are primarily motivated by power and wealth, then the removal of these rewards will equally abolish the types of incentives needed for continuing communal success. We have already indicated how in Soviet society the practice of 'rewarding inefficiency' became the prevailing norm. Where 'management was not motivated to succeed or produce' (Parenti, 1997: 61), sloth, inefficiency, corruption and 'the big lie' of public deceit ruled supreme. Fixed wages induced all workers to emulate the habits of shirkers. There was wholesale pilfering, gross neglect in the areas of maintenance, rent collection, storage or transportation; double accounting where the intricacies of management were withheld from public inspection; wholesale hoarding of labor and materials; plus devastating despoliation of the environment, all of which conspired to bring the system down to its knees.

That similar breakdowns may occur in advanced industrial society must be a legitimate fear. Even the western social democracies, subjected to inordinate pay demands and chronic industrial disputes, have fared only a bit better. As many consider, it needed the 1980s' Reagan/Thatcher revolution of privatization and market criteria as the primary nexus to bring societies back to an even keel. Hence, the axiom that it is – and can only be – the rule of the market that assures progress and prosperity, carries understandable conviction. There are accordingly only two options: on the one hand, the ineffective command economy; and on the other, the market system rewarding merit and universally providing fair shares. Alas, the unfettered market system, as we have learned only too well, has its own pattern of drawbacks. In its prevailing manifestation, it displays crass inequalities, social discord plus the degradation of public morality that, bad as it is, is set to get worse. We reject the presumption that there is no third way. Already the 'collective intelligence' informatics revolution has the potential to 'promote the construction of intelligent communities in which our social and cognitive potential can be mutually developed and enhanced' (Lévy, 1997: 17). Were it to come, post-scarcity society would offer a climate where the race for self-enrichment had become far less intense. When material appetites have become integrated with the values of social esteem plus self-fulfillment, even the evolution of 'knowledge trees' of global cybernetic interaction that 'enlarge the scope of self knowledge into a form of group knowledge and collective thought' (ibid.: 23) may not be beyond realization. A distant vision perhaps, but worth striving for nevertheless.

(iii) Rich versus Poor

To more than one-half of mankind the very framework of our discussion could appear almost perverse. Millions the world over spend their lives in conditions of poverty, malnutrition, privation and chronic ill-health. The pressing concern for daily subsistence must make projections of post-scarcity a mere futile pipe-dream. To the historic evils of daily hunger (more than one-half of the population in India, Bangladesh or Indonesia still exists in absolute poverty) have been added the industrial scourges of deforestation, polluted air, contaminated water, together with the miseries of urban squatter encampments that stunt personal growth and consume scarce resources on a huge scale. An estimated one-tenth of budgets need to be allocated to maintenance costs alone. Yet for all that, 'almost a billion people in the developing world currently lack access to safe drinking water; probably twice as many live in cities without adequate water sanitation' (Easterbrook, 1998: 25). Bad as they currently are, under Malthusian conditions of population expansion, they are destined to turn even more dire (*The Economist* 21 March 1988).

The graphic '7: 84' equation of the 1960s, indicating that at that time 7 percent of the world's population were laying claim to 84 percent of global wealth, no longer quite holds. Its very displacement by a global scenario where, thanks to the informatics revolution, major undeveloped communities have in record time parachuted into near post-industrial circumstances, gives some ground for hope. In southeast Asia, China, parts of South America and increasingly now the African continent, technological progress in manufacturing and services has leapt centuries in less than decades. The rising tide of momentum may not lift all nations alike, but what has occurred in these regions may not stay unique for long. With the informatics revolution set to move up a notch, the benefits (and problems no less) of artificial intelligence may well, in years ahead, become equally shared. The projection we have advanced may, sooner than expected, become valid for all.

(iv) Positional Goods and Egotopia

'Positional goods' refers to an insight which we are well advised to remember. As Hirsch posits, even in an ideal society not all demands can be satisfied. There will always be objects whose scarcity no amount of prosperity can make available to all, at will. He cites in particular such desirable assets as country houses, exclusive locations or views, great works of art, or indeed externalities such as honor or fame (Hirsch, 1977). No matter how advanced the technology, how universalized globalization, how abundant is production or even equalized distribution among all possible groups, there never can be enough to satisfy all possible wants. There are never enough Rembrandts to greet each and everyone as they enter their homes, sufficient highways to enable all to swiftly reach their destinations, an adequate supply of beauty spots or national parks to provide quietude to all potential admirers, or enough avenues of distinction to cover all with acclaim. In short, not even the near-miracle of overcoming the scourge of scarcity will supply eternal happiness, perfect accord or the removal of 'want'. However beneficial the social arrangements, the residues of envy, jealousy, superstition or occasions of conflict will always remain.

It will hardly come as a surprise to our readers that social existence is not unalloyed bliss. None of the above reservations need imply that progress cannot be made. Already the advances made in this century in the areas of diet, medical services, living conditions, life expectancy, purchasing power, and conditions of work, plus many more, are truly immense. The center point in recent years has notably shifted to personal comforts as well as disposable time. A recent survey points out how in the past 100 years, American budgets have moved from necessities to a far greater emphasis on spending for leisure. The three-fold relative increase in recreational spending is owed to the fact that a far higher proportion can now afford the luxury of money and time to participate in recreational pursuits and that, as a result, the scope for all kinds of leisure activities has greatly expanded (Costa, 1997). Costa argues that limits are far from having been realized. As demand has grown, so there has come a corresponding expansion of all kinds of supply. Traditional recreational activities have mushroomed in every direction, while new ones find themselves added on year after year. One can readily think of opportunities such as physical fitness, recreational travel, a whole welter of new sports, the habits of reading, and particularly the entirely novel electronic facilities from movies and television, to personal computers plus the Internet in more and more homes. Affluence exacts its own price. Yet, at the same time, opportunities for innovation are by no means exhausted. 'Fun for the masses' undoubtedly brings us right up against the constraint of positional goods. It does, however, at the same time, describe a universe where access to the good things in life is increasingly set to become universalized.

Miller contends that we are caught up in a lifestyle that we all desire, but few of us want. The 'Egotopia' he depicts is the outcome of an imposed technological myth that promises riches but instead involves a Faustian bargain that leaves us frustrated and spiritually poorer than ever before (Miller, 1997). That not all is gold that glitters is an adage more apt than ever before. 'The dark satanic malls' that entice us into mistaking appearance for substance, are but a one part of his concern. Equally insidious is the non-stop onslaught of advertising that feeds the acquisitive appetite that deep down finds consumption a form of vanity. Disenchantment can only be assuaged by narcissistic psychotherapeutic validation that by means of either intensive counseling or through prescribed drugs, keeps the acquisitive spirit alive.

We take a less apocalyptic view of even the ongoing laissez-faire free market conditions. The 'dark satanic malls', in their dual role as both social centers as well as marketing educators, have their positive side, while even the proliferation of counseling therapy has its restorative benefits. The 'New Man' axiom that 'bigger is better' and that 'more is better than less' (Miller, 1997: 75), is no more than mildly apparent in United States' private or public life. One would not dissent from the conclusion that commercialism should be reined in and that the buck ought to rule less supremely, but the vibrancy, joy in life, civility and sense of fellowship one encounters in all manner of exchanges in American life give reassurance. Much can be changed or improved, yet essentially when it comes to a challenge, as ever the substance is there.

REFERENCES

Albert, M., *Stop the Killing Train: Radical Visions for Radical Change* (Boston, Mass.: South End Press, 1994).
Block, F., *Postindustrial Possibilities: a Critique of Economic Discourse* (Berkeley, CA: University of California Press, 1990).
—— *The Vampire State* (New York: New Press, 1996).
Cairncross, F., *The Death of Distance: How the Communications Revolution will Change our Lives* (Boston, Mass.: Harvard Business School, 1997).
Castells, M., *End of Millennium* (Oxford: Blackwell, 1998).
Costa, D., 'Less of a Luxury: the Rise of Recreation since 1888'; NBER Working Paper No. 6054 (June 1997).
Easterbrook, G., 'Hot and Not Bothered', *New Republic* (4 May 1998).
Fallows, J., *Looking at the Sun: the Rise of the New Asian Economic and Political System* (New York: Pantheon, 1994)
Gellner, E., *Plough, Sword and Book* (London: Palladin, 1991).
Giddens, A., 'Affluence, Poverty and the Idea of a Post-Scarcity Society' (Geneva: United Nations Research Institute for Social Development, 1995).
Gorz, A., *Paths to Paradise: On the Liberation from Work* (London: Pluto Press, 1985).
Greenberg, S. B., 'Popularizing Progressive Politics', in S. B. Greenberg and T. Skopol (eds.), *The New Majority: Toward a Popular Progressive Politics* (New Haven: Yale University Press, 1997).
Hacker, A., *Money: Who Has How Much and Why* (New York: Scribner, 1997).
Havel, V., 'The State of the Republic'; *New York Review*, 45(4) (5 March 1998), 42–6.
Head, S., 'The New Ruthless Economy', *New York Review* (29 February 1996), 47–52.
Heilbroner, R., *21st Century Capitalism* (New York: W. W. Norton, 1993).
Hirsch, F., *The Social Limits to Growth* (London: Routledge, 1977).
Huntington, S., *The Clash of Civilizations and the Remaking of the World Order* (New York: Simon & Schuster, 1996).
Jones, B., *Sleepers Wake! Technology and the Future of Work* (New York: Oxford University Press, 1984).
Kennedy, P., *Preparing for the Twenty-First Century* (New York: Random House, 1993).
Lévy, P., *Collective Intelligence* (New York: Plenum Press, 1997).
Marx, K. and Engels, F., *The German Ideology* (1867) as quoted in Robert C. Tucker, *The Marx-Engels Reader* (New York: Norton, 1978), 160.
Miller, J., *Egotopia, Narcissism and the New American Landscape* (Tuscaloosa, AL: University of Alabama Press, 1997).
Mulgan, G. J., *Politics in an Antipolitical Age* (Cambridge: Polity Press, 1994).
Naisbitt, J., *Megatrends Asia* (Deltran, NJ: Newbridge Communications, 1995).
Parenti, M., *Blackshirts & Reds* (San Francisco: City Light Books, 1997).

Rifkin, J., *The End of Work: the Decline of the Global Labor Force and the Dawn of the Post-Market* (New York, G. P. Putnam's Sons, 1995).
Schor, J., *The Overworked American* (New York: Basic Books, 1991).
Smith, A., *The Wealth of Nations* (New York: Modern Library, 1937).
Taylor, A. J. P., *The Trouble Makers* (London: Hamish Hamilton, 1957).
The Economist, 'Development and Environment' (21 March 1998) 1–14.
Thurow, L., *The Future of Capitalism* (New York: William Morrow, 1996).
Weisskopf, T. G., 'Marxian Crisis Theory and the Contradiction of Late Twentieth-Century Capitalism', in V. D. Lippit (ed.), *Radical Political Economy* (Armonk, NY: M. E. Sharpe, 1996).

Conclusion

'We are, after all, the world's only superpower. We do have to lead the world.' (President Clinton, April 1995)

As the Millennium comes within sight, the United States has never been as prosperous. The stock market index regularly breaks record highs, unemployment stands at a twenty-eight year low, exports are booming, while the fears of everlasting budget deficits have effectively been stilled. Yet for all that, almost two-thirds of Americans express the view that, compared to ten years ago, they are further away from the American dream. The fault, we contend, is inherent in structural exigencies rather than lying in the eyes of the beholder. For all their immense ingenuity and their capacity to surmount setbacks, Americans remain wedded to a value system parts of which, cherished as they may be, inhibit them from getting the best out of ongoing trends. While the Internet traffic is doubling every hundred days, and while 62 million Americans are now using the worldwide network, the axiom of the 'wide open spaces' and the 'melting pot' still prevails. The impending next step in the informatics revolution, foreshadowed by Vice-President Gore in his April 1998 address, will be a giant leap forward, bringing the entire contents of the thirty-volume *Encyclopedia Britannica* on to one single hairbreadth part of a disc.

Our focus lies more strongly in the direction of machine intelligence which we perceive as lying ahead. Were we to make best use of this unique opportunity, its endpoint could lead to the conquest of scarcity that in its full complexity opens more vistas than could fit into one single text. The virtual replacement (no longer 'displacement') of human labor by that of machines might conceivably even come about were we to leave matters just as they are. But left to the vagaries of pure chance, the process would doubtless take a lot longer, and moreover would bypass desired ends. The optimal, most rapid and painless progression lies, we consider, in the direction of a moderate central intervention by public authority. A measure of redistribution comes first and foremost. Both access to work, already increasingly a scarce commodity, plus the distribution of income and wealth need to be more equalized than they are now; the former by means of equitable work distribution (the voucher system may, in the final analysis turn out to be the best option) once the time is ready, and the latter through progressive taxation together with 'demogrants' – i.e. a social wage as of right – at least within the foreseeable future while scarcity still impinges. Beyond that lies a universe of possibilities, which we have referred to in various parts of the text. None, singly or combined, would lead to a heaven on earth, but if they could ever be achieved – a greater measure of social equality, a system of participatory democracy, less emphasis on acquisition and adversarial relationships, plus individual lifestyle portfolios that gave scope to self-realization – would be enough.

America stands in the vanguard and, in a number of leading fields, is capable of offering inspiration in the future ahead. The point is frequently made that the rich and powerful will not idly stand by while their wealth and privileges are taken away. One of capitalism's great saving graces has been throughout its capacity to adapt to crises ahead. This has been true in the past and is, we believe, valid again. As the Asian crises vividly spotlight, at the very pinnacle of success and prosperity there is a tendency for disaster to lurk. We by no means put the United States in the same category, yet similar setbacks could arise were the challenge of the new revolution to be met by narrow complacency. If either the diffusion of labor-saving devices were blocked for self-seeking reasons, or the ruling elites were to monopolize the fruits of progress all for themselves, social peace would be seriously compromised. Far wiser to maximize technological power, equalize benefits, stay close to the helm, and rely on the fact that even after a relative share-out, the knowledge elite will not be far away from the forefront.

Would it not be more effective and prudent to set an example rather than fall by the wayside in an encounter that, however resolute the resistance, can only be lost in the end? A bright future awaits those who are prepared to be flexible and are smart enough to seize the day when it arrives. One is confident that when it comes to the crunch the American ruling class, in concert with other western equivalent groups, will not be found wanting. Indeed, as of now, in the words of the old proverb, 'a stitch in time saves nine'. There are enough warning signs in over-full prisons, disaffected minorities, the decaying fabric of the inner cities, burgeoning inequalities, the growth of political apathy, plus scandalous conduct in leading quarters to suggest that much is amiss. Self-interest alone, once eyes are unveiled, should promote changes that provide greater openness to the dramatic benefits that machine intelligence can bring. Once underway, progress can be swift as well as self-evident and enough to gain ever wider depths of support. At the end of the line there may not stand utter utopia as such, but at least a generalized way of life in which toil has been eased, rifts have been mended, talents more widely explored, and democratic foundations firmly buttressed by cooperative participation. Were we to have been fortunate enough to have made a modest contribution to this achievement, we would count it as more than ample reward.

Select Bibliography

Alba, R., *Ethnic Identity: the Transformation of White America* (New Haven: Yale University Press, 1990).
Albert, M., *Stop the Killing Train: Radical Visions for Radical Change* (Boston, Mass.: South End Press, 1994).
Alterman, E., *Sound and Fury: the Washington Punditocracy and the Collapse of American Politics* (New York: Harper Perennial, 1993).
Arnold, G., *World Government by Stealth: the Future of the United Nations* (London: Macmillan, 1997).
Aronowitz, S. and DiFazio, W., *The Jobless Future and the Dogma of Work* (Minneapolis: University of Minnesota Press, 1994).
Bailyn, B., *The Ideological Origins of the American Revolution* (Cambridge, Mass.: Harvard University Press, 1967).
Bartlett, D. L. and Steele, J. B., *America, Who Stole the Dream?* (Kansas City, MO: Harvard University Press, 1996).
Bass Warner, S., *The Private City: Philadelphia in Three Periods of its Growth* (Philadelphia: University of Pennsylvania Press, 1979).
Beard, C. A., *An Economic Interpretation of the Constitution of the United States* (New York: Macmillan, 1935)
Benier, R. (ed.), *Theorizing Citizenship* (Albany: Suny Press, 1995).
Berman, P. (ed.), *Quotations from the Anarchists* (New York: Praeger 1992).
Bialer, S. and Sluzar, S. (eds.), *Sources of Contemporary Radicalism* (Boulder, Co: Westview Press, 1977).
Block, F., *Postindustrial Possibilities: a Critique of Economic Discourse* (Berkeley, CA: University of California Press, 1990).
—— *The Vampire State* (New York: New Press, 1996).
Bloom, A. and Breines, W., *'Takin' it to the Streets': A Sixties Reader* (New York: Oxford University Press, 1995).
Bok, D., *The State of the Nation: Government and the Quest for a Better Society* (Cambridge, Mass.: Harvard University Press, 1996).
Boorstin, D. J., *The Genius of American Politics* (Chicago: University of Chicago Press, 1953).
Bork, R., *Slouching Towards Gomorrah: Modern Liberalism and American Decline* (New York: Regan Books, 1996).
Boyer, P., *Urban Masses and Moral Order in America 1820–1920* (Cambridge, Mass.: Harvard University Press, 1978).
Brimelow, P., *Alien Nation: Common Sense About America's Immigration Disaster* (New York: Random House, 1995).
Brown, D., *Bury my Heart at Wounded Knee: an Indian History of the American West* (London: Vintage, 1991).
Brown, R. E., *Charles Beard and the Constitution* (Princeton: Princeton University Press, 1956).
Brzezinski, Z., *The Grand Chessboard* (New York: Basic Books, 1998).

Select Bibliography

Cairncross, F., *The Death of Distance: How the Communications Revolution will Change our Lives* (Boston, Mass.: Harvard Business School, 1997).
Castells, M., *End of Millennium* (Oxford: Blackwell, 1998).
Chomsky, N., *Class Warfare: Interview with D. Barsamian* (London: Pluto Press, 1996).
—— *New World Orders Old and New* (New York: Columbia University Press, 1994).
Cohen, J. L. and Arato, A., *Civic Society and Political Theory* (Cambridge, Mass.: MIT Press, 1992).
Comor, E. A. (ed.), *The Global Political Economy of Communication* (London: Macmillan, 1994).
Coyle, K., *The Weightless World: Strategies for Managing the Digital Economy* (Oxford: Capstone Books, 1997).
Craig, S. C., *Broken Contract? Changing Relationships between Americans and their Government* (Boulder, Co.: Westview Press, 1996).
Cranston, M., *The Solitary Self: Jean-Jacques Rousseau in Exile and Adversity* (Chicago: Chicago University Press, 1996).
Danziger, S. and Gottschalk, P., *America Unequal* (Cambridge, Mass.: Harvard University Press, 1995).
Davies, P. J., *An American Quarter Century: US Politics from Vietnam to Nixon* (Manchester: Manchester University Press: 1995).
Degler, C. N., *Out of our Past: the Forces that Shaped Modern America*, 3rd ed. (New York: Harper Torchbooks, 1985).
Dewart, R. and Rheingold, H. (eds.), *Electronic Citizenship* (San Francisco, CA: Pacific Bell 1988).
Docherty, T. D. (ed.), *Postmodernism: a Reader* (New York: Basic Books, 1993).
Drucker, P. F., *Post-Capitalist Society* (New York: Harper Business, 1993).
D'Souza, D., *The End of Racism: Principles for a Multicultural Society* (New York: Free Press, 1995).
Dunn, R. S. and Yeandle, L. (eds.), *The Journal of John Winthrop: 1630–1649*, abridged edition (Cambridge, Mass.: Belknap Press/Harvard University Press 1997).
Durkheim, E., *The Division of Labor in Society*, trans. George Simpson (New York: Free Press, 1964, orig. French 1893).
Ehrlich, P. and Ehrlich, A. H., *The Population Explosion* (New York: Simon and Schuster, 1990).
Engbersten, G., Schuyt, K., Timms, J. and van Warden, F., *Cultures of Unemployment* (Boulder, Co: Westview Press, 1993).
Elshtain, J. B., *Democracy on Trial* (New York: Basic Books, 1995).
Etzioni, A., *The Spirit of Community: the Reinvention of American Society* (New York: Touchstone, 1994).
—— (ed.), *New Communitarian Thinking: Persons, Virtues, Institutions and Communities* (Charlottesville, VA: University Press of Virginia, 1995).
—— *The New Golden Rule: Community and Morality in a Democratic Society* (New York: Basic Books, 1996).
Ewen, S. and Ewen, E., *Channels of Desire: Mass Images and the Shaping of American Consciousness* (Minneapolis: University of Minnesota Press, 1992).

FAIR, *Why Americans Should Support a Moratorium on Immigration* (Washington DC: The Federation of American Immigration Reform, 1994).
Fairfield, R. P. and Brown, A. T. (eds.), *The Federalist Papers* (New York: Doubleday Anchor, 1961).
Fallows, J., *Looking at the Sun: the Rise of the New Asian Economic and Political System* (New York: Pantheon, 1994).
Featherstone, M. (ed.), *Global Culture: Nationalism Globalization and Modernity* (London: Sage 1990).
Fraser, S. and Freeman, J. B. (eds.), *Audacious Democracy* (New York: Houghton Mifflin, 1997).
Fredrick, H. H., *Global Communication and International Relations* (Belmont, CA: Wadsworth, 1993).
Freedman, S. G., *The Inheritance: How Three Families and America Moved from Roosevelt to Reagan and Beyond* (New York: Simon and Schuster, 1996).
Friedan, B., *Beyond Gender* (Baltimore, MD: Johns Hopkins University Press, 1997).
Fukuyama, F., *Trust: Social Virtues and the Creation of Prosperity* (New York: Free Press, 1995).
—— *The End of Order* (New York: Social Market Foundation, 1997).
Gaddis, J. L., *We Now Know: Rethinking Cold War History* (New York: Oxford University Press, 1997).
Galbraith, J. K., *A History of Economics* (London: Penguin Books, 1989).
—— *The Culture of Containment* (London: Penguin Books, 1993).
Gans, H. J., *The War Against the Poor: the Underclass and Anti Poverty Policy* (New York: Basic Books, 1995).
Gardner, J., *The Age of Extremism* (Toronto, CA: Birch Lane, 1997).
Geary, M. G. H. and Lynn, L. (eds.), *Urban Change and Poverty* (Washington, DC: National Academic Press, 1988).
Gellner, E., *Conditions of Liberty, Civil Society and its Rivals* (London: Penguin, 1994).
—— *Plough, Sword and Book* (London: Palladin, 1991).
Giddens, A., 'Affluence, Poverty and the Idea of a Post-Scarcity Society' (Geneva: United Nations Research Institute for Social Development, 1995).
Gidley, M. (ed.), *Modern American Culture: an Introduction* (London: Longman, 1993).
Gill, S. (ed.), *Gramsci, Historical Materialism and International Relations* (Cambridge: Cambridge University Press, 1993).
Gitlin, T., *The Twilight of Common Dreams: Why America is Wracked by Culture Wars* (New York: Metropolitan Books, 1995).
Glazer, N., *We are all Multiculturalists Now* (Cambridge, Mass.: Harvard University Press, 1997).
Glazer, N. and Moynihan, D., *Beyond the Melting Pot* (Cambridge, Mass.: MIT Press, 1963).
Gleason, P., *American Identity and Americanization* (Cambridge, Mass.: Harvard University Press, 1980).
Gorz, A., *Paths to Paradise: on the Liberation from Work* (London: Pluto Press, 1985).

Gramsci, A., *Selections from the Prison Notebooks* (New York: Columbia University Press, 1992).
—— *Selections from the Prison Notebooks of Antonio Gramsci* (London: Lawrence and Wishart, 1971).
Grant, L., *A Beleaguered President, a Fizzled Economic Stimulus Package, and a NAFTA Time Bomb* (Teaneck, NJ: Negative Population Growth, 1993).
Gray, J., *False Dawn: the Delusions of Global Capitalism* (London: Granta Books, 1998).
Greenberg, S. B. and Skopol, T. (eds.), *The New Majority: Toward a Popular Progressive Politics* (New Haven: Yale University Press, 1997).
Greenfeld, L., *Nationalism. Five Roads to Modernity* (Cambridge, Mass.: Harvard University Press, 1992).
Greider, W., *One World Ready or Not: the Manic Logic of Global Capitalism* (London: Allen Lane, Penguin Press, 1997).
Griffin, S., *American Constitutionalism* (Princeton, NJ: Princeton University Press, 1997).
Guttman, A. and Thompson, D., *Democracy and Disagreement* (Cambridge, Mass.: Harvard University Press, 1996).
Habermas, J., *The New Conservatism* (Cambridge, Mass.: MIT Press, 1989).
—— *The Past as Future* (Nebraska: University of Nebraska Press, 1994).
Hacker, A., *Two Nations: Black and White: Separate, Hostile, Unequal* (New York: Scribner, 1992).
—— *Money: Who Has How Much and Why* (New York: Scribner, 1997).
Handler, J. T. and Hasenfeld, Y., *We the Poor People: Work, Poverty and Welfare* (New Haven and London: Yale University Press, 1997).
Handy, C., *The Future of Work* (Oxford: Basil Blackwell, 1984).
Havel, V., *The Art of the Impossible* (New York: Knopf, 1997).
Hays, S. P., *The Response to Industrialism 1885–1914*, 2nd ed. (Chicago: University of Chicago Press, 1995).
Heilbroner, R., *Visions of the Future* (New York: Oxford University Press, 1995).
—— *21st Century Capitalism* (New York: W. W. Norton, 1993).
Herman, E. S. and Chomsky, N., *Manufacturing Consent: the Political Economy of the Mass Media* (London: Vintage, 1994).
Himmelfarb, G., *The De-Moralization of Society* (New York: Knopf, 1995).
Hirsch, F., *The Social Limits to Growth* (London: Routledge, 1977).
Hirst, P. and Thompson, G., *Globalisation in Question* (Cambridge: Polity Press, 1996).
Hodgson, G., *The World Turned Rightside Up: a History of the Conservative Ascendancy in America* (Mariner Books: Houghton Mifflin, 1996).
Hofstadter, R., *The American Political Tradition* (New York: Vintage Books, 1961).
Hohm, C., *Population: Opposing Viewpoints* (San Diego, CA: Greenhaven Press, 1995).
Howard, R. D., *Human Rights and the Search for Community* (Boulder, Co.: Westview Press, 1995).
Howard, T. W., *The Rhetoric of Electronic Communities* (London: Ablex Publishing Company, 1997).

Hughes, R., *American Visions: the Epic History of Art in America* (London: Harvill, 1997).
—— *The Culture of Complaint: the Fraying of America* (London: Harvill, 1994).
Huntington, S., *The Clash of Civilizations and the Remaking of the World Order* (New York: Simon & Schuster, 1996).
Jones, B., *Sleepers Wake! Technology and the Future of Work* (New York: Oxford University Press, 1984).
Jencks, C. and Peterson, P. E. (eds.), *The Urban Underclass and the Poverty Paradox* (Washington, DC: The Brookings Institution, 1991).
Jones, M., *American Immigration*, 2nd ed. (Chicago: Chicago University Press, 1992).
Judy, R. W. and D'Amico, C., *Workforce 2020: Work and Workers in the Next Century* (Indianapolis: Hudson Institute 1997).
Kapstein, E. B., *Governing the Global Economy: International Finance and the State* (Cambridge, Mass.: Harvard University Press 1994).
Katz, M. (ed.), *The Underclass Debate: Views from History* (Princeton: Princeton University Press, 1993).
Keane, J., *Democracy and Civil Society* (London: Verso, 1988).
Kellner, D., *Media Culture: Cultural Studies, Identity and Politics between the Modern and Postmodern* (London: Routledge, 1995).
Kemp, T., *The Climax of Capitalism: the US Economy in the Twentieth Century* (Harlow: Longman, 1992).
Kennedy, P., *Preparing for the Twenty-First Century* (New York: Random House, 1993).
—— *The Rise and Fall of the Great Powers: Economic Change and Military Conflict from 1500 to 2000* (London: Fontana, 1989).
Kim, Y. J., *The New Pacific Community in the 1990s* (Armonk, NY: M. E. Sharpe, 1996).
Kolchin, P., *American Slavery 1619–1877* (London: Penguin Books, 1995).
Krugman, P. R., *Peddling Prosperity* (New York: Norton, 1994).
—— *The Age of Diminished Expectations* (Cambridge, Mass.: MIT Press, 1994).
—— *Pop Internationalism* (Cambridge, Mass.: MIT Press, 1996).
Kuttner, R., *Everything for Sale: the Virtues and Limits of Markets* (New York: Knopf, 1997).
Landes, D. S., *The Wealth and Poverty of Nations: Why Some are so Rich and Some so Poor* (New York: Norton, 1997).
Lazere, D. (ed.), *American Media and Mass Culture: Left Perspectives* (Berkeley: University of California Press, 1987).
Lévy, P., *Collective Intelligence* (New York: Plenum Press, 1997).
Lind, M., *Up from Conservatism: Why the Right is Wrong for America* (New York: Free Press, 1996).
—— *The Next American Nation: the New Nationalism and the Fourth American Revolution* (New York: Free Press, 1995).
Lippit, V. D. (ed.), *Radical Political Economy* (Armonk, NJ: M. E. Sharpe, 1996).
Lipset, S. M., *The First New Nation* (expanded ed. orig. 1963, New York: W. W. Norton, 1979).

—— *American Exceptionalism: a Double-Edged Sword* (New York: W. W. Norton, 1996).
Luttwark, E. H., *The Endangered American Dream* (New York; Simon and Schuster, 1993).
Mackenzie, G. C. and Thornton, S., *Bucking the Deficit: Economic Policy Making in America* (Boulder Co.: Westview Press, 1996).
Magee, B., *Popper* (London: Fontana Modern Masters, 1973).
Magnet, M., *The Dream and the Nightmare: the Sixties' Legacy to the Underclass* (New York: William Morrow, 1993).
Maier, T., *American Scripture: Making the Declaration of Independence* (New York: Knopf, 1997).
Mann, M., *States, War and Capitalism* (Oxford: Blackwell, 1988).
Marx, K. and Engels, F., *The German Ideology* (New York: International Publishers, orig. German ed. 1845).
Massey, D. S. and Denton, N. A., *American Apartheid: Segregation and the Making of the Underclass* (Cambridge, Mass: Harvard University Press, 1993).
McQuaid, K., *The Anxious Years: America in the Vietnam-Watergate Era* (New York: Basic Books, 1989).
McRae, H., *The World in 2020. Power, Culture and Prosperity: A Vision of the Future* (London: Harper Collins, 1995).
Medved, M., *Hollywood vs America: Popular Culture and the War on Traditional Values* (New York: Harper Collins, 1992).
Miller, J., *Egotopia: Narcissism and the New American Landscape* (Tuscaloosa, AL: University of Alabama Press, 1997).
Mishel, L. and Bernstein, J. (eds.), *The State of Working America, 1992–93* (Armonk, NY: M. E. Sharpe, 1993).
Mosley, A. G. and Capaldi, N., *Affirmative Action: Social Justice or Unfair Preference?* (London: Rowan and Littlefield, 1996)
Mulgan, G. J., *Connexity* (London: Chatto and Windus, 1997).
—— *Politics in an Antipolitical Age* (Cambridge: Polity Press, 1994).
Murray, C., *Losing Ground: American Social Policy, 1950–1980* (New York: Basic Books, 1984).
Myrdal, G., *An American Dilemma* (New York: Pantheon, 1975).
Naisbitt, J., *The Global Paradox: the Bigger the World Economy, the More Powerful its Smallest Players* (London: Nicholas Brealey Publishers, 1994).
—— *Megatrends Asia* (Deltran, NJ: Newbridge Communications, 1995).
Newman, K. S., *The Withering Away of the American Dream* (New York: Basic Books, 1993).
Newman, O. and de Zoysa, R., *The Underclass, Welfare, and Joblessness* (San Diego: San Diego State University, CSA Topics, October 1995).
—— *Perspectives on Civic Society: the prospect ahead, DMI Rapport, No. 2* (Sundsvall, Sweden: Demokratiinstitutet, 1998).
Nisbet, R. A., *The Quest for Community* (New York: Oxford University Press, 1953).
O'Hare, W. P., *African Americans in the 1990s* (Washington, DC: Population Reference Bureau Books, 1991).
Ohmae, K., *End of the Nation State: the Rise of Regional Economies* (London: Harper Collins, 1996; New York: Free Press, 1995).

Organization for Economic Co-Operation and Development, *The OECD Jobless Study: Facts, Analysis, Strategies* (Paris: OECD, 1994).
Paine, T., *Common Sense* (New York: Penguin Books, 1986).
Pakulski, J. and Waters, M., *The End of Class* (London: Sage, 1996).
Parenti, M., *Blackshirts and Reds* (San Francisco: City Light Books, 1997).
Patterson, J. T., *Grand Expectations: the United States, 1945– 1974*, The Oxford History of the United States, Vol. 10 (Oxford: Oxford University Press, 1996).
Pessen, E., *Jacksonian America: Society, Personality and Politics* (Chicago: University of Chicago Press, 1985).
Peter-Martin, H. and Schumann, H., *The Global Trap: Globalization and the Assault on Democracy and Prosperity* (London: Zed Books, 1997).
Peterson, W. C., *Silent Depression: the Fate of the American Dream* (New York: W. W. Norton, 1994).
Petras, J. and Morley, M., *Empire or Republic? American Global Power and Domestic Decay* (London: Routledge, 1995).
Phillips, K., *Arrogant Capital: Washington, Wall Street and the Frustration of American Politics* (New York: Little Brown, 1994).
Piore, M. J., *Beyond Individualism* (Cambridge, Mass.: Harvard University Press, 1995).
Portes, A. and Rumbaut, R., *Immigrant America* (Berkeley, CA: California University Press, 1990).
Powers, S., Rothman, D. J. and Rothman, S., *Hollywood's America: Social and Political Themes in Motion Pictures* (Boulder, Co. and Oxford: Westview Press, 1996).
Real, M., *Exploring Media Culture: a Guide* (Thousand Oaks, CA: Sage, 1996).
Redclift, N. and Minione, E. (eds.), *Beyond Employment* (Oxford: Blackwell, 1985).
Reich, R. B., *The Work of Nations: Preparing Ourselves for the Twenty-First Century* (New York, Knopf, 1991).
Rifkin, J., *The End of Work: the Decline of the Global Labor Force and the Dawn of the Post-Market Era* (New York: G. P. Putnam's Sons, 1995).
Rodrik, D., *Has Globalization Gone Too Far?* (Washington DC: Institute for International Economics, March 1997).
Rustin, M., *For a Pluralist Socialism* (London: Verso, 1985).
Saul, J. R., *The Unconscious Civilization* (London: Penguin, 1998).
Schiller, H. I., *Information Inequality: the Deepening Social Crisis in America* (New York: Routledge, 1996).
Schlesinger, A. M. Jr., *The Disuniting of America: Reflections on a Multicultural Society* (Knoxville, TN: Whittle Direct Books, 1991).
—— *The Cycles of American History* (New York: Houghton Mifflin, 1986).
Schor, J., *The Overworked American* (New York: Basic Books, 1991).
Schumpeter, J. A., *The Theory of Economic Development* (Cambridge, Mass.: Harvard University Press, 1951).
Schweickart, D., *Against Capitalism* (Boulder, Co: Westview, 1996).
Selbourne, D., *The Principle of Duty: an Essay on the Foundations of Civic Order* (London: Sinclair-Stevenson, 1994).
Seligman, A. B., *The Idea of Civil Society* (New York: Free Press, 1992).

Seligman, H. J., *The Problem of Trust* (Princeton: Princeton University Press, 1997).
Sen, G. and Germani, A., *Population Policies Reconsidered: Health, Empowerments and Rights* (Cambridge, Mass.: Harvard University Press, 1994).
Simon, J., *The Economic Consequences of Immigration* (Oxford: Blackwell, 1989).
Skidelsky, R., *The World After Communism: a Polemic for our Times* (London: Macmillan, Papermac, 1995).
Sklar, H., *The Dying American Dream* (Boston, Mass.: South End Press, 1995).
—— *Eyes Right* (Boston, Mass.: South End Press, 1995).
Smith, A., *The Wealth of Nations* (New York: Modern Library, 1937).
Sombart, W., *Why is There No Socialism in the United States?* (White Plains, NY: International Arts and Sciences Press, 1976; orig. German ed. 1906).
Steigerwald, D., *The Sixties and the End of Modern America* (New York: St. Martin's Press, 1995).
Stonier, T., *The Wealth of Information: a Profile of the Post-Industrial Economy* (London: Methuen, 1983).
Strange, S., *The Retreat of the State: the Diffusion of Power in the World Economy* (Cambridge: Cambridge University Press, 1996).
Sutherland, P. and Sewell, J. W., *The Challenges of Globalization* (Washington, DC: Overseas Development Council, 1998).
Tagaki, R., *A Different Mirror: a History of Multicultural America* (New York: Little Brown, 1993).
Taylor, A. J. P., *The Trouble Makers* (London: Hamish Hamilton, 1957).
Thurow, L. C., *The Future of Capitalism: How Today's Economic Forces Shape Tomorrow's World* (New York: William Morrow, 1996).
Toffler, A., *The Third Wave* (New York: Morrow, 1980).
—— *Previews and Premises* (New York: Morrow, 1983).
Toffler, A. and Toffler, H., *Creating a New Civilization* (Atlanta, GA: Thoner Publishing, 1994).
Tolchin, S. J., *The Angry American: How Voter Rage is Changing the Nation* (Boulder, Co: Westview Press, 1996).
Tonnies, F., *Community and Association*, trans and supplemented by Charles P. Loomis (London: Routledge, 1995; orig. German ed. 1887).
Tucker, R. C. (ed.), *The Marx-Engels Reader* (New York: Norton, 1978).
Updike, J., *Rabbit at Rest* (London: Penguin Books, 1991).
Valladao, A. G., *The Twenty-First Century will be American* (London: Verso, 1996).
Vidal, G., *United States: Essays 1952–1992: 'The Second American Revolution'* (London: André Deutsch, 1993).
Wainwright, H., *Arguments for a New Left: Answering the Free-Market Right* (Oxford: Blackwell, 1996).
Waldinger, R., *Still the Promised City? African-Americans and New Immigrants in Postindustrial New York* (Cambridge, Mass.: Harvard University Press, 1996).
Walker, M., *The President they Deserve* (London: Vintage Books, 1997).
Walsh, L. E., *Firewall: the Iran-Contra Conspiracy and Cover-Up* (New York: Norton, 1997).

Walzer, M., *What it Means to be an American* (New York: Marsilio, 1992).
Waters, M., *Globalization* (London: Routledge, 1995).
Watkins, T. H., *The Great Depression: America in the 1930s* (Boston: Back Bay Books, Little Brown, 1993).
Weber, M., *Economy and Society, Vol. 1* (New York: Bedminster Press, 1968).
Weisberg, J., *In Defense of Government* (New York: Scribners, 1996).
Wilcox, C., *Onward Christian Soldiers: the Religious Right in America* (Boulder, Co: Westview Press, 1996).
Wilson, W. J., *When Work Disappears: the World of the New Urban Poor* (New York: Knopf, 1996).
—— *The Truly Disadvantaged: the Inner City, the Underclass, and Public Policy* (Chicago: University of Chicago Press, 1987).
Woirol, G. R., *The Technological Unemployment and Structural Unemployment Debates* (London: Greenwood Press, 1996).
Wolfe, A., *The Marginalized in the Middle* (Chicago: Chicago University Press, 1996).
—— *One Nation, After All* (New York, Viking, 1998).
Wood, G. S., *The Creation of the American Republic 1776–1787* (New York: Norton, 1972).
Woodiwiss, A., *Post Modernity USA: The Crisis of Social Modernism in Postwar America* (London: Sage, 1993)
Yates, M. D., *Longer Hours, Fewer Jobs* (New York: Monthly Review Press, 1994).
Zelnick, B., *Backfire* (Washington, DC: Regenery, 1996).
Zinn, H., *A People's History of the United States* (London: Longman, 1980).

Index

affirmative action, 52–6
Afro-centrism, 50–1
Aid to Families with Dependent Children, (AFDC), 78
American dream, 38, 47–9, 60, 92, 100, 114, 141, 215
American exceptionalism, 3, 32, 37, 91, 167–71
American expansionism (domestic), 11–12
  foreign, 19
American franchise, 11–12
  women, 19
American socialism, 18, 33–7
anarchism, 155
ASEAN bloc, 119

Beard, Charles, 9
Bergsten, Fred, 122
Blair, Tony, 77, 82, 106–7, 141, 156–7
Block, Fred, 191, 198
Bok, Derek, 64, 80
Bork, Robert, 25, 125–6, 143
Brimelow, Peter, 40
Buchanan, Pat, 70, 153
Buckley, William, 67

Carnegie, Andrew, 17–18
Castells, Manuel, 207
Chomsky, Noam, 83, 91, 129
Christian Coalition, 70, 153
civic society, 146–55
civil rights, 43, 66
Civil War, 14
Clinton, Bill, 25, 26, 42, 53, 65, 71, 72, 77, 90, 93, 97, 141, 158, 215
communitarianism, 141–6
connexity, 159–60, 207
Constitution, 8–11, 63
Contract with America, 69
Coyle, Diana, 123

culture, 75, 128
  counter-, 67, 126–8
  mass, 17
  sub-, 44–5
  wars, 125–6, 129–30, 174–5
cybernetic capitalism, 178

Dahrendorf, Ralf, 94, 162, 179
declinism, American, 22–8
deliberative democracy, 160–1
Democratic Leadership Council, 71
discretionary labor, 90–1, 106, 170, 182–3
Disney, 131, 169
downsizing, 101, 105, 170, 182
Drucker, Peter, 60, 77, 158
dual economy, 90–1
'dumbing down', 54, 131

economism, 124
egotopia, 212
entitlement programs, 22, 68, 72
Erie Canal, 15–16
Etzioni, Amitai, 141, 143, 145, 161
Eurocentrism, 50
European Union, 24, 26, 75, 76, 87, 103, 118, 121, 137, 175

Farrakhan, Louis, 48, 51, 96, 153–4
Fordism, 20, 206–7
Freedman, Samuel, 67
Fukuyama, Francis, 83, 149

Gaddis, John Lewis, 133
Galbraith, John, 20, 106
Giddens, Anthony, 202
Gingrich, Newt, 62, 69
Gitlin, Todd, 49, 131
Glazer, Nathan, 48, 49
globalization, 113–20
  and culture, 125–32
  and new world order, 132–7
  and USA, 120–5

Index

Gorz, André, 107, 163, 184–5, 187, 191–2, 200
Gramsci, Antonio, 34–5, 36, 174
Great Depression, 20, 39
Greider, William, 119–20
Gulf War (1991), 26, 74

Habermas, Jürgen, 160–1
Hacker, Andrew, 100, 101, 169, 198, 204
Havel, Vaclav, 114, 146, 197
Heilbroner, Robert, 100, 196, 201
Helms-Burton, 76
Himmelfarb, Gertrude, 49
Hirsch, Fred, 185–6, 211
Hirst, Paul, 116, 117, 177
Hollywood, 114, 130–2
Hughes, Robert, 6, 131
Huntington, John, 114, 136–7, 190

immigration, 16, 37–46, 53–4
 current, 40–6
 early, 14, 16, 18, 33
Independence, American, 8–11
industrialization, early, 15–19
inequality, 99–105, 117, 161–2, 168–9, 195, 198, 210
information age, 116, 120, 123, 171–5, 178
 highway, 171–5, 177–9
Internet, 116, 172
 encryption problem, 116
Iran-Contra scandal, 61

Jackson, Andrew, 14, 61
Jefferson, Thomas, 8, 11, 13
joblessness, 26, 87–92, 179–87
Johnson, Lyndon, 22, 62
Jones, Barry, 108, 184, 204

Keenan, George, 133, 134–5
Kennedy, John F., 66
Kennedy, Paul, 25–6
Keynes, John Maynard, 20, 23–4, 87
King, Martin Luther, 48, 51
knowledge elite, 167, 169–70
 sector, 77, 186
 tree, 186, 209 10
Kolchin, Peter, 14

Korean War, 22
Krugman, Paul, 101, 120, 179

laissez–faire, 16, 33
Lincoln, Abraham, 61
Lind, Michael, 33, 42, 50, 71
Lipset, Seymour, 13, 16, 32, 36, 60
Los Angeles, 84

MAI (Multilateral Agreement on Investment), 119
market
 free, 64–5, 113–14
 global, 72–7
 nexus, 124, 196
 social, 151–2, 159
Marx, Karl, 33, 104, 205
McCarthyism, 22
media concentration, 128–30
Medved, Michael, 130
Miller, John, 130, 192, 212
Morgan, J. P., 18
Morris, Dick, 71
multiculturalism, 46–51
Murray, Charles, 93

NAFTA, 25, 71, 75, 116, 122, 175
National Commission on Race (1997), 52, 79, 97
nation state, 72–7, 137–8, 175–9
Native Americans, 5
nativism, 16, 38, 106
Nato, 21, 24, 115, 134–5
New Deal, 20–1, 67, 80, 97, 99
new world order, 132–7
New York, 15, 84
Nisbet, Robert, 142–3
Nixon, Richard, 23, 61, 62
NOW (National Organization of Women), 70

OECD Job Study 1994, 87–90
Ohmae, Kenichi, 116, 176
OPEC (Organization of Petroleum Exporting Countries), 23
open frontier, 37–46

Paine, Tom, 12, 38
Parenti, Michael, 101, 195–6, 209

participatory democracy, 146, 150, 201–2
Perot, Ross, 65, 178
Philadelphia, 7, 16, 84
pluralism (cultural), 126–7
Political Action Committee, 62
political gridlock, 64
Popper, Karl, 54
population growth, 42
positional goods, 185, 211–12
post-scarcity society, 163–4, 190–3
  implementation, 194–202
Promise Keepers, 70, 154
Proposition 187 (California), 45
punditocracy, 63
puritanism, 5–7

Reagan, Ronald, 61, 65, 68, 99, 127, 131, 133, 153, 209
Reich, Robert, 72, 99, 105, 177
Rifkin, Jeremy, 91, 94, 101, 103, 105, 106, 162, 203
Robertson, Pat, 153
rogue state, 135
Roosevelt, Franklin, D., 20–1, 80

Schlesinger, Arthur, Jr., 5, 47, 49
Schor, Judith, 104, 107, 162, 191
Schumpeter, Joseph Alois, 161
SDS (Students for a Democratic Society), 22
Selbourne, David, 149
slavery, 6–7, 11, 14
Smith, Adam, 196
social conservatives, 19–20, 25, 67, 69–71, 130–1, 153
  in the UK, 148
social progress, 203–5
  constraints, 205–12
  market, 151
'soft money', 62–3
'soft power', 114, 120
Sombart, Werner, 33, 36, 167

Soros, George, 118
stakeholding, 156, 159
Strange, Susan, 74, 77, 175–6

Talbot, Margaret, 44
Thompson, Graeme, 116, 117, 177
Thurow, Lester, 26, 118, 161, 182, 190, 197–8
Tocqueville, Alexis de, 13
Toffler, Alvin, 107, 177
Tonnies, Ferdinand, 142
trade unions, 14, 18, 34, 62, 71, 75, 122, 156, 194
transnationals, 73–4, 117, 123, 124, 173

underclass, 51, 83, 92–9, 105–6, 162, 170, 198
unemployment, 87–92
United Nations, 22, 74, 175
US Steel, 18

Valladao, Alfredo, 75–6
values, American, 11–15, 31–2
Vietnam War, 22, 23, 66

Wagner Act (1935), 21
Wainwright, Hilary, 152
Waldinger, Roger, 98–9
Walzer, Michael, 32, 151
Washington, George, 13
Watergate, 23, 68
Weber, Max, 176
welfare, social, 64–5, 68, 77–9, 95, 157
  reform, 77–81
Wesleyanism, 17
Willetts, David, 148
Wilson, Julius, 79, 93, 106
Winthrop, John, 5
Wood, Gordon, 10

Zangwill, Israel, 46